AMERICA 1844

AMERICA 1844

RELIGIOUS FERVOR, WESTWARD EXPANSION,
AND THE PRESIDENTIAL ELECTION THAT
TRANSFORMED THE NATION

JOHN BICKNELL

Copyright © 2015 by John Bicknell
All rights reserved
Published by Chicago Review Press Incorporated
814 North Franklin Street
Chicago, Illinois 60610
ISBN 978-1-61373-010-2

Library of Congress Cataloging-in-Publication Data
Is available from the Library of Congress.

Interior design: PerfecType, Nashville, TN

Printed in the United States of America
5 4 3 2 1

For Arwen

Contents

1844 Chronology

January

28 William Miller begins his final East Coast tour in Boston.

29 The Quorum of the Twelve Apostles nominates Mormon prophet Joseph Smith for president of the United States.

February

19 John C. Frémont crosses the summit of the Sierra Nevada into California.

22 An article in the Adventist newspaper *Midnight Cry* questions the March 21 date for the second coming of Christ.

28 An explosion aboard the USS *Princeton* kills six people, including Secretary of State Abel P. Upshur.

March

6 President John Tyler nominates John C. Calhoun as secretary of state.

21 The first date on which Millerites expected the second coming of Christ passes and is dubbed the "spring disappointment."

APRIL

3 Samuel Snow's February article on the October date for the second coming is reprinted in the *Advent Herald*.

12 Annexation treaty between Texas and the United States is signed.

13 Samuel Colt's "submarine battery" sinks the *Styx* in a demonstration off the Washington Navy Yard.

22 Texas annexation treaty is submitted to the Senate.

23 James K. Polk's letter supporting annexation is published.

27 Anti-annexation letters from Henry Clay and Martin Van Buren are published, as is Calhoun's Pakenham Letter.

MAY

1 Whig Party convention nominates Henry Clay for president and Theodore Frelinghuysen for vice president. The news is sent to Washington via an uncompleted telegraph line.

6–8 Violence between nativists and Irish Catholics ravages Philadelphia's Kensington neighborhood and results in at least six deaths.

17 Joseph Smith is officially nominated for president by an Illinois state convention of his supporters in Nauvoo.

18 The Stevens-Townsend-Murphy party departs Council Bluffs, Iowa, for California.

24 Before an audience of congressmen, Samuel F. B. Morse taps out "What hath God wrought" on the first completed telegraph line, running between Washington and Baltimore.

25 The *Baltimore Patriot* publishes the first telegraphed news dispatch, concerning a House vote against debating the Oregon question.

27 A rump convention of supporters nominates President John Tyler as an independent candidate for reelection.

29 Democrats nominate James K. Polk for president, with George M. Dallas of Pennsylvania for vice president. The news is spread via the telegraph line between Baltimore and Washington.

JUNE

8 The Senate votes 16–35 against the Texas annexation treaty.

12 In accepting the Democratic nomination, Polk announces he will not seek a second term.

15 Charles Goodyear is granted a US patent for the vulcanization of rubber.

26 John Tyler marries Julia Gardiner, becoming the first president to wed while in office.

27 Joseph Smith is shot to death by a mob at the Carthage, Illinois, jail.

JULY

1 Clay's first "Alabama Letter" is published.

6–7 Riots rage in Philadelphia's Southwark neighborhood between nativists and militia acting to protect local Irish Catholics.

27 Clay's second "Alabama Letter" is published.

AUGUST

6 Frémont arrives back in St. Louis.

8 Brigham Young is chosen to succeed Joseph Smith as leader of the Church of Jesus Christ of Latter-Day Saints.

15 Fifty thousand Democrats gather in Nashville for a pro-Polk rally.

20 John Tyler withdraws from the presidential race.

SEPTEMBER

2 Clay publishes a letter distancing himself from antislavery remarks by his distant relative, Cassius M. Clay.

4 New York Democrats nominate Silas Wright for governor.

23 Another letter from Clay tries and fails to reconcile the Texas positions from his previous letters.

OCTOBER

22 The "Great Disappointment" leaves Millerites still waiting for Christ's
second coming.

NOVEMBER

4–12 Polk is elected president.
15 Stevens-Townsend-Murphy party reaches Donner Lake.

DECEMBER

4 House repeals the gag rule; presidential electors cast their votes in
state capitals.
21 Delia Webster is convicted of aiding the escape of a Kentucky slave
family and sentenced to two years in prison.

Prologue

New Year's Day at the White House

Continuing a tradition older than the White House itself, a buoyant President John Tyler opened the executive mansion to the public to celebrate the first day of 1844. Three thousand people from all walks of Washington life showed up on the unseasonably warm day to shake his hand and have a peek inside.

What they saw might have been something of a disappointment. While the elevation of the land on which the White House sat provided "a splendid view of the Potomac" and the "grounds are laid out very finely with shrubbery & forest trees & intersected with broad graveled walks," the interior was showing its age.

As the throngs paraded into the public reception room to spend a brief moment with the president, they saw marble tables that "were once no doubt very beautiful, but now they are rusty with age," and furniture "that generally is among the 'has beens.'" The carpeting was "in threads & tatters & patched in many places with other colors." The high-ceilinged room maintained some of its grandeur out of sheer size, and a facade of authority provided by Corinthian-styled pilasters on the wall. But, between the columns, "the papering . . . now looks in some places soiled."

The New Year's reception, begun by George Washington when the seat of government was in New York and continued by John Adams after he moved into the not-quite-finished White House in the new capital named after his predecessor, hosted both the general public and official Washington. Protocol dictated that the unwashed masses be paraded through in the afternoon—after members of congress, the diplomatic corps, the cabinet and lesser government officials, many of whom owed their positions to John Tyler, had paid their respects.

Tyler, on the other hand, owed his position to fate. Elected vice president on the Whig ticket in 1840, the understudy on the "Tippecanoe and Tyler Too" team, the aristocratic Virginian with the prominent aquiline nose had assumed the presidency when William Henry Harrison died a month and a day after taking office. At fifty-one, he was the youngest man ever to ascend to the position.

No other president had ever died in office, and no one seemed quite sure if Tyler was actually president. One former president, John Quincy Adams, now a member of congress and politically hostile to Tyler, insisted on referring to him as "acting president." Francis P. Blair, an intimate of former president Andrew Jackson and still a formidable powerbroker in the city, called Tyler "a poor weeping willow of a creature."

Adams and Blair were both astute observers of the political scene, but in this case they misjudged their man. Tyler quickly seized the reins and left no doubt in anyone's mind that he intended to lead the government. On the day of Harrison's funeral, the *National Intelligencer* newspaper in Washington praised Tyler as "a true Whig." But he wasn't, really; he abandoned the party soon after. The Whigs, a loose coalition bound together by their hatred of Andrew Jackson, believed in an activist government and a weak executive. Tyler believed in neither. He vetoed Whig legislation and installed loyalists from both parties in key positions. As if to impress upon the nation that he really was president, Tyler was often at his desk by 3 AM, tending to business. And he felt no compunction about challenging the leading lights of the government, as when he challenged Kentucky's Henry Clay. "Go you now then, Mr. Clay, to your end of the avenue where stands the Capitol," he had told the eminent leader of the Whigs, "and there perform your duty to the country as you shall think proper. So help me God I shall do mine at this end of it as I shall think proper." Clay had assumed, as had many others, that upon Harrison's death he would rule while Tyler reigned. When that proved not to be the case, Clay didn't take it very well. One of his colleagues noted that Clay was "much more imperious and arrogant with his friends than I have ever known him, and that you know, is saying a great deal." Like many assumptions Clay would make over the coming four years, the belief that Tyler would be his legislative lapdog proved wildly inaccurate.

Having made an enemy of Clay and most other Whigs, Tyler did little to endear himself to the Democrats, either, appointing Whigs to senior posts and doing nothing to build up the party. As 1844 rolled around, Tyler found himself a man without a party, the few loyalists he could claim owing their allegiance to him only through the virtue (or vice) of patronage. But still, he thought he might like to be reelected. Tyler demonstrated through his command of patronage that he was no shrinking violet, at least where his prospects for reelection were concerned. If he refused to lend assistance to the infrastructure of either national party, he certainly took steps to build one of his own. In one of the most audacious examples, he hired journalist Alexander G. Abell to write a campaign biography, then threatened postmasters with unemployment if they refused to buy and distribute copies.

JOHN TYLER. *Library of Congress*

With the election year upon him, Tyler was working along two tracks to make his reelection possible.

He believed that if he could welcome Texas, the breakaway Mexican republic that had won its independence in 1836, into the union, he would be hailed a hero for bringing closer to reality Thomas Jefferson's long-cherished dream of a continental nation. To that end, his secretary of state, Abel Upshur, was secretly negotiating with representatives of the Lone Star Republic to attach Texas to the United States. Texas was, in the words of the young woman who would soon become Tyler's wife, the "great object of his ambition."

Tyler's other tactic was a good deal simpler. As president, he hoped to use the appointment power to winnow the field of competitors. On New Year's Eve, he had started with former president Martin Van Buren, the leading candidate for the Democratic nomination.

Among the members of Congress who came to the White House on New Year's Day was Van Buren's closest Senate ally, fellow New York Democrat Silas Wright, who probably noticed the worn furniture and dirty walls. His penchant for worrying about such things would be sorely tested over the next several months, and he might have wondered whether the condition of the White House was a metaphor for the condition of the republic, which lately seemed to be fraying at the edges if not quite coming apart at the seams. "In my deliberate judgment," he would soon write, "our Union was never so much in danger as at this moment."

Wright's reasons for thinking so had been bolstered only the day before. John Thompson Mason, scion of a prominent Virginia family, onetime Texas adventurer, and a Jacksonian functionary, showed up unexpectedly at Wright's boarding house on New Year's Eve, interrupting Wright's pre-holiday relaxation to sell him on a preposterous idea.

Wright, ever the gentleman and one of the most respected members of Congress, invited Mason in, and the Virginian wasted no time on pleasantries. Supreme Court Justice Smith Thompson, a New Yorker and Van Buren ally, had died about three weeks earlier. The seat, Mason said, should remain in New York's hands. Van Buren, he believed, was the right man for the job. Would the former president, he asked Wright, be interested in joining the court?

Wright was renowned for his seriousness of purpose, not for his sense of humor. He knew that Van Buren and Thompson were so close that Van Buren had named one of his sons after the judge. So Wright fought hard to lend the occasion the dignity he thought it deserved.

He failed. "I can usually keep my face when I try hard to do so and have any warning that the effort will be required," he would soon report to Van Buren, "but this took me too much by surprise and I did not succeed at all."

Mason's inquiry was met with a "most immediate fit of laughter," through which the Virginian sat stone-faced. Wright, realizing Mason was serious, caught himself quickly and regained his composure. It dawned on him that this was not some speculative inquiry or idle chitchat. Mason was here to make a serious offer on behalf of President Tyler.

And so the two men got down to it. Mason stayed for two hours, pressing the issue. Van Buren, the leading Democratic candidate for president in 1844, could not be elected, Mason said (begging Wright's pardon, for he knew how intimate the two men were). Mason also rudely suggested that, were Van Buren elevated to the Supreme Court, Wright would be the next logical man in line for the Democratic presidential nomination.

This surely disgusted the honorable Wright, one of the few men in public life—and certainly one of the few senators—who did not wake up each morning and see a would-be president in the mirror, although many thought he would make a fine one. Mason then compounded his absurdity by claiming that Tyler knew nothing of his visit and that he had not even discussed the possibility of a Van Buren appointment with the president, while confessing that he knew others had. Wright didn't react, but he saw only two possibilities. Either Mason was a fool to be acting without Tyler's imprimatur, or he was lying. And Wright knew Mason was no fool.

As the harangue drew to a close, Mason asked Wright point-blank: Would the Van Buren men in the Senate support his nomination if it came before them?

Wright, ever the diplomat, said simply that he didn't know how he could vote no in such a circumstance.

Mason giddily took this as assent. "You are right, you are right, you can't vote against him," he chirped.

As he rose to take his leave, Mason asked Wright if he had a closing thought, which Wright assumed would be relayed directly back to Tyler, despite Mason's earlier assurance of the president's non-involvement.

"Tell Mr. Tyler for me that if he wants to give the whole country a broader, deeper, heartier laugh than it ever had, and at his own expense, he can effect it by making the nomination," Wright said as the two men stood by the door. Mason, without responding, turned on his heels and left. Wright listened as Mason's footsteps grew fainter and fainter and finally faded away, then "laughed myself almost sick."

Tyler's ploy to get Van Buren out of the race had failed, and similar efforts in the coming months to dispose of other potential rivals would yield the same result. But his other gambit—Texas—was still alive. It was a plan so outlandish that it would soon split both parties and, eventually, the nation.

The move to annex Texas revealed the wide gap between the two visions of America represented by the Democratic and Whig parties—one expansionist, one consolidationist. The Democrats wanted to spread across the continent. Whigs were content to build up the nation as it currently existed. As 1844 opened, Tyler felt a confidence that many, including Wright and Clay, believed was unwarranted. They feared for the future of the republic.

But the competing visions of the Democrats and Whigs were not the only possible futures that Americans considered in 1844, and the fate of the republic was not the only concern. A tumultuous year lay ahead. Political and religious violence would leave an indelible mark on the presidential election contest. Without taking sides in that race, hundreds of emigrants would give life to the vision of expansionist politicians by leaving their homes and heading for California, Oregon, and Texas. Miraculous advances in science would forever change the way people communicated, traveled, and interacted with the natural world.

And while politicians feared for the union, or claimed to, others believed the dire circumstances of the moment ran much deeper than mere politics. They feared for the world itself.

{ 1 }

"THIS GLORIOUS HOPE"

For a man absolutely certain he had less than two months left on Earth, William Miller was remarkably calm about his fate. He was a preacher, not a prophet, and a "plain farmer," as friends referred to him. Miller didn't even like people to call him "Reverend," although he spent much of his adult life spreading the Word of God. In February 1844, this self-described "stammering old man" and "poor feeble creature" had come to the nation's capital in a presidential election year to deliver a message that was anything but feeble: the world was about to come to an end, and the people of Washington—politicians included—had better get right with their Lord.

The Washington trip marked the final leg of a seven-week lecture tour for Miller, who tried very hard not to let his condition deter him, though it often had in the past. A wrinkly, stocky, broad-shouldered man of sixty-two, with a slight head shake that made him look even feebler than he actually was, "Father" Miller—one title his followers had adopted that he seemed to like—had begun this latest journey in Boston on January 28, where the crowds were so thick that people stood for hours to hear him speak, and "multitudes" were turned away. From Boston he moved on to New York on February 6, then to Philadelphia five days later. In both cities he was greeted by congregations numbering in the thousands.

At each stop the message was the same. Jesus is coming back. The reign of man on earth is coming to an end. Those who are with Christ will be saved. Those who are not will perish. And Miller wasn't pointing to some mythical judgment day sometime in the distant, indeterminate future. He meant in a couple of weeks.

Miller arrived in Washington on February 20. Millerite preachers—they preferred the term "Adventist"—had been there before, but his direct brand of end-of-the-worldism had not made much of an impact in a city where silver-tongued orators were as common as horse dung in the muddy streets.

However unpleasant getting from one place to another was in the capital, many found the city beautiful indeed. Others considered the sobriquet the "city of magnificent distances" just a nice way of saying there was a lot of empty space between the clumps of undistinguished government buildings, "a great village with houses scattered here and there." The population was about twenty-five thousand. Pennsylvania Avenue, the main thoroughfare running nearly a mile between the Capitol and the White House—the only macadamized stretch in town—was typically crowded with carriages. One visitor in 1844 judged the view down Pennsylvania Avenue "as good a one as I have ever seen . . . nowhere in the Union can a stranger spend a few days more agreeably than here." But the district also included its share of cow pastures, swamps, slaughterhouses, and pig pens.

This time, Miller himself made the trip, and he brought reinforcements. "Although we never visited a place where we saw so few Bibles, yet every Bible there is, seems to be in good demand," reported Miller's senior lieutenant, Joshua Himes. Before they were through on March 3, Miller, Himes, and another associate, Josiah Litch, would deliver thirty-four sermons and launch a localized version of the movement's newspaper, the *Southern Midnight Cry*. The first issue had a press run of ten thousand copies.

Miller was from the generation of charismatic preachers who had arrived on the scene in the wake of the dissolution of established state churches, the fruit of the Second Great Awakening, a Protestant revival movement that had blossomed in the early United States as a reaction against deism, the civil religion of Jeffersonian Republicanism. Men like Miller were not necessarily learned, but they understood the Bible and, more importantly, they understood their audience. Religious life and religious practice had become democratized by state disestablishment—the states' withdrawing of government support for churches—and new practitioners were flooding into the market, hawking new wares, selling a new brand of Christianity to a new nation. It was a very American idea: the individual, freed from the constraints of hierarchical tyranny, would discover and interpret the Word for himself. Along the way, Americans would learn that these independent churches were much better equipped to tend to the needs of their flock—and to the needs of society through the creation of moral reform groups—than the established churches, such as the Congregationalists in Massachusetts, ever were.

These new preachers disagreed with the theological and structural rigidity of the established denominations, but they didn't all agree with one another. Many were critical of Miller's vision of an impending premillennium in which Christ would be physically present on Earth for a thousand-year reign. Alexander Campbell, an early leader in the movement that would eventually develop into the Disciples of Christ, thought Miller's millennialism was misplaced. But he was just as critical of those who derided Miller

WILLIAM MILLER. *Jenks Collection*

personally. Some of that might have been simple Christian charity. Some of it was experience. Campbell and his father had both been treated roughly by the Presbyterian hierarchy when they began questioning that church's doctrine.

As a theological matter, Miller never strayed far from traditional Bible-focused teaching. Where he parted company with everyone from Anglicans to Anabaptists was in his insistence that the "soon coming" of Christ was a practical reality. He even had a date in mind.

The 1844 presidential election was not scheduled to come until November, although maneuverings had been going on for months. Miller was confident that Election Day would never take place. While among the politicians in Washington, he wrote that he planned to "show them that an important revolution will take place before long, which will supersede the necessity of choosing a president by ballot; for the King of Kings will soon be inaugurated into the Chair of State." March 21 was the anointed date, although Miller maintained enough ambiguity on that point to give himself some wiggle room if Christ did not return and incinerate his enemies at such time.

Unlike many of his contemporaries, Miller was more didactic than inspiring. Though he preached at revivals, a favorite venue for charismatic preachers in the Second Great Awakening, he was not in the tradition of the fiery camp meeting orator. In Washington, his first meeting was in the Baptist church near the Navy Yard, where the maritime service's gargantuan new ship, the *Princeton*, had recently tied up. That meeting house proved too small for the crowds wanting to hear Miller preach, so he switched venues to the larger Apollo Hall, not far from the White House.

One senator noted that he knew the Millerites were in town, "for I never heard so much singing and praying in Washington before." A typical evening of preaching like those he spent in the capital would include a dissertation from the book of Daniel, an explanation of the kingdom of God on Earth, and a plea for listeners to ready themselves for its arrival. Miller usually included his complicated exegesis of the Biblical timeline that proved the end was nigh. He rarely worked himself into a frenzy and never fell into paroxysms of hellfire and brimstone. He was more like a persistent prosecutor making his case before a skeptical but persuadable jury.

It might be harder to sway an urban audience in Washington, New York, or Philadelphia than small-town folk in upstate New York or rural New Jersey; as one Brooklynite asserted, "there are very few here who are weak enough to patronize the delusion of Miller and his followers." But that never deterred Miller.

The *New York Herald* described a Millerite camp meeting in a long story accompanied by a rendering of the movement's portable tent, with its fifty-five-foot center pole, and its campground:

> They seem to be making the most of the little time they have left 'em, to preach, sing, shout, and pray all the time. They begin at daylight in the small tents and are at it in some shape or other till nearly or quite midnight; and I doubt very much whether they are not at it also during the still watches of night. They are most vehemently and voraciously pious. I took a stroll down to the camp ground yesterday, and although the big tent was lowered, they were at it in one of the smaller tents, into which about 25 men and 15 women were crammed around a stove, till the air was reeking hot, and the stench was insupportable. They were all, men and women, down in the straw, lying and sitting in every conceivable posture; praying, shouting, and singing indiscriminately with all their might.

They were there to listen to Miller: "The performances commenced at nine o'clock in the morning with a hymn. . . . After this, and one or two more hymns, Father Miller and Brother Himes came in. Another hymn was sung, and Father Miller delivered a brief, but very commonplace address, comparing himself to St. Paul when about to leave the brethren, and the latter fell on his neck and kissed him. He said, he was about to leave them—to take the parting hand—never to see their dear faces again until the resurrection morning."

Miller described the scene in Washington, where "a goodly number of persons belonging to both houses of Congress" were among the listeners—the well of the House was often used for religious services, though Miller was not invited to deliver a sermon from the floor. "They throng us constantly for papers, books, and tracts, which Bro. Himes is scattering gratuitously by thousands, containing information on this subject. They send in from this vicinity and from 'old Virginia' for papers and lecturers; but the one-hundredth part of their requests can never be complied with. Never have I been listened to with so deep a feeling, and with such intense interest, for hours." Miller was tired from his travels, but Washington renewed his spirit. "Now in the capital of our country, the prospect is fair, yes, very fair; we shall triumph beyond our expectation," he said.

An Act of God

While Miller was working to prepare the capital, much of official Washington was focused on other things. The presidential election was already beginning to occupy people's minds and dinner conversations. President John Tyler, nominally a Whig, wanted to be reelected, but he was unlikely to be nominated by either side. It looked like a certainty that Henry Clay would be the Whig candidate; the Democrats appeared almost as certain to choose former president Martin Van Buren. So on the last day of 1843, Tyler had made Van Buren the offer of a seat on the Supreme Court that he hoped might get the New Yorker out of the presidential sweepstakes.

That gambit having failed, Tyler began casting about for other ways to rid himself of the Little Magician, a nickname Van Buren had well earned for his astute political sense. Tyler still thought he might be able to ride to victory in November on the popular idea of annexing Texas, and his subalterns were engaged in purportedly secret talks with the Lone Star Republic to that end. Secret or not—Van Buren's minions had already informed him of the talks—annexation was becoming a popular dinner party topic, although some people preferred to avoid talking about Texas at social occasions because it tended to set Northerner against Southerner, and why run the risk of spoiling a party?

But there was still plenty of time for (seemingly) nonpolitical and nonreligious diversion for the city's elite. Just before the Millerite camp set up shop, the USS *Princeton*, pride of the navy, had steamed up the Potomac and docked in the river's Eastern Branch (now the Anacostia River) at the Washington Navy Yard. The ship was the pet project of Captain Robert F. Stockton, and the vessel was named for his New Jersey hometown. The well-connected Stockton had even used some of his family's money to pay for its construction. Secretary of State Abel Upshur had been a patron of the project during his time as secretary of the navy; it was only one of the weapons systems he would back that would prove less than successful.

Stockton was a self-aggrandizing egotist, a political opportunist, and a pro-Tyler, pro-annexation expansionist. A contemporary described him as "a humbug sort of fellow, a speculator, intriguer, politician and popularity hunter." The grandson of Richard Stockton, who signed the Declaration of Independence, he added to the family fortune by investing in the transportation revolution, turning a handsome profit on railroads and canals. He might have been secretary of the navy, but he wanted to oversee construction of the *Princeton*, and then wanted to command it.

Stockton also fancied himself an inventor. He designed one of the two rotating guns on the *Princeton*'s deck, the twelve-inch cannon nicknamed "Peacemaker," which weighed more than twenty seven thousand pounds. The other gun was designed by Swedish-born John Ericsson (who would later gain fame for designing the Civil War–era ironclad *Monitor*). Ericsson's gun was originally dubbed "Orator" because, Ericsson said, its power would speak for itself. But Stockton, an avid expansionist, changed it to "Oregon." The craft was the first steam-powered warship to have an underwater screw propeller instead of an above-the-waterline paddlewheel; it ran quietly and relatively smoke-free on high-grade anthracite coal. In addition to the two big guns fore (Peacemaker) and aft (Oregon), the ship boasted two-dozen forty-two-pound short smoothbore, cast-iron cannons known as carronades.

Before Miller's arrival in Washington, Stockton had taken a collection of senators, House members, journalists, military brass, and other notables on brief excursions down the Potomac, the latest in a series of trial runs he had made while "parading with much ostentation from port to port." On one particularly cold day there was a thin sheet of ice on the river, which the *Princeton* had no trouble cutting through. To entertain his guests, Stockton decided to fire the Peacemaker—the fore gun of his own design.

"Now, gentlemen, fellow citizens and shipmates," he grandly announced to those assembled on deck, "we are going to give a salute to the Mighty Republic. Stand firm and you will see how it feels. It is nothing but honest gunpowder, gentlemen, it has a strong smell of the Declaration of Independence." The gun then hurled a 228-pound cannonball a couple miles downstream, creating a marvelous fountain for the onlookers to enjoy. If, as John Quincy Adams accused, the trip was designed "to fire their souls with patriotic ardor for a naval war," the design was working.

On February 28, the cruise was less business and more pleasure. Many of the participants had gathered at a White House reception the night before. The dinner and the cruise included a number of political dignitaries, Tyler among them, back for another day on the river. The president was joined by the slightly plump and quite attractive Julia Gardiner, whom the widower president was courting, and her father, Colonel David Gardiner, an attorney and onetime New York state legislator. Dolley Madison, former first lady and star of the Washington social scene for more than three decades, was a center of attention.

A retinue of congressmen and cabinet officials came along, including Secretary of State Abel Upshur, who just the day before had wrapped up annexation negotiations with Isaac Van Zandt, Texas's ambassador to the United States, who was also aboard, along with Mexican Minister Juan Almonte. Also aboard were Navy Secretary Thomas Gilmer, a former governor of Virginia and recent member of the House of Representatives who had been in the cabinet for less than two weeks, and Missouri senator Thomas Hart Benton, who was about to cause Tyler some heartburn over Texas. Adams had been invited but declined. He could not countenance, he would write, "the burning thirst for more and more of these infernal machines."

All told, about four hundred guests had come out on the warm midwinter morning to be ferried on steam launches to the 164-foot-long ship, which had a beam of 30½ feet, drew 21½ feet of water, and had a brilliant white oak hull. Gilmer took the opportunity to investigate every nook and cranny of the vessel that was the cornerstone of the department he now headed. Stockton, in full regalia, greeted each passenger as he or she came aboard. As the ship began the downriver journey at about 1 PM, Stockton ordered the carronades to fire a twenty-six-gun salute, honoring each state in the union. The steamer's sails were unfurled against a brilliant blue sky and the Marine Band played "The Star Spangled Banner" as the festive visitors began milling around the decks. Finally, as the vessel cast off, the ship's crew shouted huzzahs and the voyage was underway.

The ship, which could make thirteen knots but was going much slower today, sailed past Fort Washington, which was undergoing renovation at the time. It would not have its first mounted guns until 1846—compare that with the massive guns on the *Princeton* and one gets some idea of the priority placed on coastal defense and the protection of Washington. This was the second version of the fort, completed in 1824; the original, built in 1809, was destroyed by its own troops during the War of 1812 to keep it out of British hands.

South of Fort Washington, the ship's gunners loaded forty pounds of powder and a twelve-inch ball into Stockton's Peacemaker and sent a shot down the river, setting off a loud roar and giving a start to many of the visitors aboard the *Princeton*. The ball traveled two miles and skipped across the surface for another mile like a flat stone skimmed by a child. The gasps sparked by the gun's noise turned to cheers as the ball bounced out of sight. Never one to disappoint an audience, Stockton ordered the gun fired again as the ship sailed past Mount Vernon, where the band offered a rendition of "Hail to the Chief" in honor of George Washington.

As the day wore on, guests began to move below decks to enjoy some of the treats Stockton had stashed aboard before the ship left Philadelphia, including a selection of fine wines. Toasts were offered. Upshur offered one to the president, who had joined the other guests for the late afternoon luncheon. Tyler in turn raised his glass to "the three great guns: the *Princeton*, her commander, and the Peacemaker." The guests applauded and Stockton appreciated the presidential nod. But he felt his gun had done enough work, so when an officer told Stockton that one of the guests had requested another firing, his response was "no more guns tonight." Unfortunately for Stockton, the request had come not from just any guest, but from the new navy secretary, Thomas Gilmer. Stockton was no plebe: he knew that when a military superior makes a "request," it is safest to assume that "request" means "order." So Stockton commanded the gunners to once again load the Peacemaker and prepare to fire.

History can change in an instant, affected by the smallest of contingencies. John C. Calhoun's son, Patrick, had offered to escort a young lady to a closer view of the firing, but she demurred, complaining that the report of the gun was "disagreeable to her." Upshur decided to go on deck to see the

gun fired again. Tyler was headed in that direction, but stopped below deck
to listen to his son-in-law William Waller sing a patriotic song. As Waller
sang the word "Washington," and with Calhoun's son "only a few paces"
away, a deafening blast was heard as the Peacemaker exploded.

The ship shuddered as if it had been hit by enemy fire. "The scene upon
the deck may more easily be imagined than described," the *National Intelligencer* put it delicately to its readers. A congressman aboard was more
graphic, describing the "ghastly countenances of the dead, the shattered
limbs, the gashes in the wounded, the mournful moaning." As the ship sat
in the river about three miles below Alexandria, the guests were engulfed
in smoke. Huge chunks of iron and shards of razor-sharp filings were flung
across the deck. David Gardiner, father of the president's soon-to-be fiancée,
was dead. So was Tyler's valet (a slave named Armistead), and Navy Secretary Gilmer.

In all, six people died. Senator Thomas Hart Benton probably would
have been killed, but seconds before the gun exploded he had moved behind
it to get a better view of the arc of the shell. "I saw the hammer pull back,
heard a tap—saw a flash—felt a blast in the face, and knew that my hat was

EXPLOSION OF THE *PRINCETON. Library of Congress*

gone," he wrote, "and that was the last I knew of the world, or of myself, for a time of which I can give no account." The explosion flattened him and gave him a concussion. Stockton, who had positioned himself at the base of the gun for the evening's final demonstration, suffered powder burns and all the hair on his head was singed off, but he was otherwise uninjured. Tyler himself carried a dazed but unhurt Julia Gardiner off the ship.

But of all the destruction aboard the *Princeton*, none had such profound implications for the nation as the death of Secretary of State Upshur, who had left a copy of the Texas treaty, written in his own hand, sitting atop his desk the night before. His demise would wreck Tyler's Texas policy even more thoroughly than the *Princeton* itself had been wrecked.

Writing to Texas secretary of state Anson Jones, treaty negotiator Van Zandt said the disaster "will have, I fear, an unfavorable influence on our affairs here."

SLOW OF SPEECH AND TONGUE

The fault lay in Stockton's design of the Peacemaker. Ericsson's gun, forged in Liverpool, was stronger and better able to withstand the large charges necessary to fire heavy ordnance long distances. Ericsson, a true genius, had designed his gun with a breech reinforced with bands of wrought iron that were shrunk in place on the tube. "The lousy Stockton," as Ericsson referred to him, merely thought he was a genius, and so had tried to copy Ericsson's design without, apparently, fully understanding it.

An American chauvinist, Stockton bragged that his gun was "forged of American iron" in Philadelphia. That did no harm. But he did not reinforce the Peacemaker with bands shrunk in place; he simply added more wrought iron, making the gun thicker and heavier without making it any more able to withstand the stresses of firing. Stockton, Ericsson concluded, "lacks sufficient knowledge for the construction of a common wheelbarrow." Human error—indeed, one human's arrogance—had caused the disaster.

The Millerites saw other hands at work. "The dreadful catastrophe called all to a most serious consideration of preparation to meet God," Joshua Himes wrote. "The event has had a great influence upon the public mind, and has aided us essentially in our work." Miller wrote that the explosion had "added interest and solemnity to the [Washington] lectures, and caused them to be more fully attended." The event might have been God acting in the affairs of man, Miller seemed to be saying, but it certainly served to focus the mind of man on the affairs of God.

Miller had not always seen the hand of God in the life of the world. Born in Massachusetts, he was devout as a child. As a teen he adopted deism before becoming a seeker in the mold of Joseph Smith, the founder of Mormonism who was a younger contemporary. Both had emigrated from New England and they lived 250 miles apart—one on each end of New York's "burned-over district," so called because of the religious fervor that swept the area during the Second Great Awakening. Smith's family lived on the western end, Miller on the eastern (first in Poultney, Vermont, then across the river in Low Hampton, New York). Miller, like Smith, was part of the generation of thinkers freed up to seek their own theological path by the democratization of American religion in the early years of the republic. Both men would take full advantage of the opportunity.

Miller's deist tendencies were severely tested by his experiences as a soldier in the War of 1812. For much of the war, he was on recruiting duty near his home in Poultney. Eventually his persistent requests for front-line duty were answered, and he found himself confronting the British navy on Lake Champlain. Although he probably never directly engaged the enemy from his shore position, men were wounded within his sight and he witnessed the horrors of war up close, the "roaring of cannon, the bursting of bombs, the whizzing of balls, the popping of small arms, the cracking of timbers, the shrieks of the dying, the groans of the wounded."

Facing the reality of death in wartime pushed him away from the deism of the revolutionary generation and toward a more conventional view of Christianity. The conversion was personal, but also was reflected in his view of the external world. Miller came to believe, for example, that God had intervened in the Battle of Plattsburgh (the naval fight that took place on Lake Champlain during the War of 1812), on behalf of the Americans, certainly a very non-deist way of looking at things. "At the commencement of the battle, we looked upon our own defeat as almost certain; and yet we were victorious. So surprising a result against such odds did seem to me like the work of a mightier power than man," he wrote.

By 1816, the year that brought an influx of New Englanders—including the family of Joseph Smith—to upstate New York, Miller's conversion was complete. He set aside deism and began a personal religious exploration that, for the most part, rejected conventional church structure in favor of Bible-based learning, a common motif among seekers during the Second Great Awakening.

Within two years, Miller had reached the conclusion that Christ would return about the year 1843, based on his close study of the Old Testament book of Daniel and Revelation in the New Testament. He would spend almost five more years studying to satisfy himself that his thesis was sound. Finally, in September 1822, he committed to paper a twenty-point statement that summed up his conclusions based on the matching up of Biblical prophecies with earthly events, along with simple math.

Daniel 2:39–45 tells of Daniel interpreting King Nebuchadnezzar's dream of four earthly kingdoms that will be crushed by the arrival of God's everlasting kingdom. And in Daniel 8:14, the prophet recounts his own vision: "And he said unto me, Unto two thousand and three hundred days; then shall the sanctuary be cleansed." Literal biblical scholars had long interpreted these passages to mean that Christ's second coming would occur twenty-three hundred years after the Jews returned to Jerusalem following the Babylonian captivity, dated to 457 BC. Thus 2,300 minus 457 came to 1843. Miller affixed other earthly mileposts to biblical prophecies, such as the entry of Napoleon's army into Rome in 1798. He would make adjustments over time, and was reluctant to commit to a specific date, but Miller never deviated from the certainty of his underlying theory, which the movement displayed visually in a "prophetic chart."

After writing up his paper, Miller began talking about his ideas with neighbors, friends, and family. He still refused to do any formal preaching, feeling himself inadequate to the task, and sought a preacher to carry the message. But, in the words of his most recent biographer, "this intimate world bound by blood and mutual obligation" that "had long nurtured Miller's spiritual growth" had finally "midwifed the Millerite movement."

PROPHETIC CHART OF THE
MILLERITES. *Jenks Collection*

"The more I presented it in conversation, the more dissatisfied I felt with myself for withholding it from the public," Miller wrote. "I tried to excuse myself to the Lord for not going out and proclaiming it to the world. I told the Lord that I was not used to public speaking, that I had not the necessary qualifications to gain the attention of an audience, that I was very diffident and feared to go before the world, that they would 'not believe me nor hearken to my voice,' that I was 'slow of speech, and of a slow tongue.' But I could get no relief."

He continued to talk about the coming end times, and wrote a fuller dissertation—"A Few Evidences of the Time of the 2nd Coming of Christ to Elder [Leman] Andrus"—in 1831, as a deliberate attempt to recruit a messenger. When that failed, he at last went public, making his first appearance in the home of his brother-in-law, family Bible propped in his lap, in August 1831.

He was a plainspoken, plain-appearing man. His preaching that a loving, forgiving God and a personal relationship with Jesus were the solutions to the world's and individual problems might have been rare before the Second Great Awakening but was unremarkable by the 1830s. What set Miller apart was his premillennialism—his determination that the second coming was nigh.

These first public appearances were followed by a series of articles published in the *Vermont Telegraph*, a Baptist paper, beginning in May 1832. Miller thought the pieces would be published anonymously, but his authorship became known and the people who had begun gathering around him became persuasive enough to get him away from his relatives' living rooms and out on the stump.

Miller began traveling, though not too far, and he took no wages from his preaching and no profits from the many books and tracts his movement began producing in great numbers. Before 1836 he refused even to take travel expenses, and got by on income from his farm and from his savings, though he often faced critics who accused him of profiteering. His selflessness seemed to yield little in terms of a following in the first years of his ministry. But disasters are handy recruiting tools, and Miller, like public figures of every era, hated to let a crisis go to waste. Just as the explosion of the *Princeton* would provide the movement with fresh recruits on the eve of the predicted end time, the economic depression known as the Panic of 1837 had earlier served to bolster Miller's credibility with those already converted and to help persuade others that he might be onto something.

Not everybody was convinced. "We hope ministers or churches will not encourage such a madman or deceiver as Miller is," proclaimed Reverend T. F. Norris. "He is probably mad, and ought to be put under the care [of] the State Lunatic Asylum. If not a lunatic he is a dangerous man, and his attacks on Christianity are of the most insidious character." One fellow Vermonter suggested that "were Satan permitted to delude the people with an error in the garb of religion, it is believed he would adopt Millerism."

Newspapers liked to poke fun, and gave the movement considerable attention because it made good copy. The *Utica Daily Gazette* took note of a *New York Herald* report that put "this, Father Miller's recovery, and that, the warm weather, together, and asks what the end is to be?"

The *Brooklyn Eagle* ran an item from another paper complaining that while one Millerite planted "sixteen acres of rye, though claiming fully to believe that the world will certainly come to an end," another "cut away all the bushes, and removed all the combustible rubbish around his house, with the hope that it will escape the general conflagration. Truly there is no uniformity among the sect."

A letter writer to the *Times and Seasons*, a newspaper in the Mormon stronghold of Nauvoo, Illinois, had attended a Springfield meeting of the "strange deluded sect," concluding that "Balaam's ass was not a Millerite, for he could speak the truth, and talk plain Hebrew, and this Millerite could not do it."

The editor of the *Westfield News Letter* in Massachusetts was somewhat supportive, writing that he remained "personally an infidel on the Second Coming in 1843," but knew of "a number of influential citizens who had embraced the doctrine." This inspired a flood of letters from readers, including one writing as "Anti-Millerite" who demanded the names of any supposedly respectable citizens who had fallen for the Millerite line, for fear "the sentiment to go out from this town that the Westfieldanians are composed of fools or dupes, as I conceive the Millerites to be."

A writer in the *Lowell Courier* at the opposite end of Massachusetts was just as derisive and no less definitive. "This Miller does not appear to be a knave, but simply a fool, or more properly a monomaniac. If the Almighty intended to give due notice of the world's destruction, He would not do it by sending a fat illiterate old fellow to preach bad grammar and worse sense." The *Courier* did not explain how its correspondent knew what God would do, and in any case Miller—who could give as good as he got—more often than not took a sticks-and-stones attitude toward critics: "I have heard lions roar, and jackasses bray, and I am yet alive."

One man Miller could not dismiss as a braying jackass was Charles Grandison Finney, the foremost preacher of the Second Great Awakening and a leader in many of the social reform movements—collectively known as the Benevolent Empire—that grew out of the religious revival. When Finney encountered Miller in Boston in 1842, he found "it was vain to reason with him and his followers." Finney listened to Miller's lectures and attended his Bible classes.

> I invited him to my room, and tried to convince him that he was in error. I called his attention to the construction which he put on some of the prophecies, and as I thought showed him that he was entirely mistaken in some of his fundamental views. He replied that I had adopted a course of investigation that would detect his errors, if he had any. I tried to show him that his fundamental error was already detected.

But Miller, even while acknowledging that Finney had a convincing argument, was unmoved. "Believing, as they most certainly did, that the Advent of Christ was at hand, it was no wonder that they were greatly excited, and too wild with excitement to be reasoned with to any purpose," Finney wrote in his autobiography.

Joseph Smith, who by 1844 led a flourishing if still persecuted new religion, felt threatened enough by Miller's movement that he took steps to protect the Church of Jesus Christ of Latter-Day Saints from the enticements of anyone else's end-of-the-world beliefs. Because God had not given him any sign the end was near, the Mormon prophet reassured his followers that "the Lord will not come to reign over the righteous in this world in 1843."

In Constant Expectation

There was a time when Miller could not have imagined people like Charles Grandison Finney and Joseph Smith taking the time to worry over what he was saying. Miller might have plodded along forever, preaching his particular brand of the gospel and urging a few folks here and a cluster of believers there to prepare for the second coming, if he had not encountered Joshua Himes.

In many ways, Himes was a mirror image of navy captain and *Princeton* commander Robert Stockton—an enthusiast and a promoter, he had a genius for publicity and an eye for the main chance. Unlike Stockton,

Himes was aiming not at self-aggrandizement but at saving souls. He was certain he had found the vehicle through which to achieve that aim when he met William Miller. Miller had launched a personal quest. Himes would convert it into a national crusade.

The man who would come to be considered Miller's "son in the spirit" took a different path to the movement than the man who began it. Himes gave up cabinetmaking to become a full-time minister in Boston in 1830. Where Miller was relatively uninterested in the earthly realm, Himes, like Finney, was active in multiple social reform groups: education reform, women's rights, temperance, and abolition. William Lloyd Garrison, the radical publisher of the antislavery newspaper the *Liberator* and a severe critic of Millerism, called Himes "a remarkably active and zealous man."

It was Himes's experience in the social reform activities of organizations of the Benevolent Empire that helped him develop the public relations skills that would prove so valuable to the Millerite movement. He understood that the revolution in communications and transportation that was taking place in America in the 1830s and '40s opened up new avenues for sharing the Word of God. Himes was instrumental in developing the movement's first newspaper, *Signs of the Times*, in 1840, soon after he met Miller, and he was the driving force behind a vast array of tracts, pamphlets, and books. He came up with the idea of producing temporary local editions of the *Midnight Cry*, another Millerite newspaper. Himes was also instrumental in organizing the movement's general conferences. Miller was adamant about Millerism not being a separate denomination—he believed in ecumenism and wanted his followers to remain loyal to their own churches. But the general conferences served a similar purpose, providing an organized structure to a loosely affiliated group of believers that allowed the movement to function in the absence of any official hierarchy.

In much the same way Brigham Young complemented Joseph Smith, Himes was the mover and shaker to Miller's thinker and theologian. Where Miller patiently plodded, Himes pushed aggressively ahead. Without Himes's promotional skills—his marriage of "organizational modernity" with "ideological archaism," as one historian of the Adventist movement put it—Miller would never have turned his apocalyptic notion into a national movement, never would have addressed congregations of thousands, and certainly would never have spoken to members of Congress in the nation's capital.

After the explosion aboard the *Princeton*, Miller preached another four days in Washington. "We have advocates of our views, in the circles of the high and low," Himes reported. As the day of reckoning approached, Miller was eager to return to his farm in Low Hampton, New York, to await the return of Christ. He declined a number of invitations from followers in the South—rather than travel down the coast to Charleston and Savannah, on March 3 he turned northward, toward home.

But he wasn't done preaching. Miller spent several days in Baltimore, moved on to Philadelphia, Newark, New York, Brooklyn (then an independent city), and Williamsburg. The *New York Tribune*, which had regaled its readers with tales of the Millerites' camp on his previous visit, this time limited itself to a simple, sarcastic announcement that he would be preaching at Franklin Hall on Chatham Square, "providence permitting."

With Miller on his way home, another bizarre bit of violence struck the capital city, although this was more comic opera than Princetonian tragedy. Major Samuel Ringgold's horse artillery—the first such unit in the US Army—conducted a demonstration on the grounds of the Capitol. The firing of the cannon broke a number of windows along the East Front and left every pane of glass in the Supreme Court's chambers shattered, disturbing a case that was then being argued. The Senate chamber and some committee rooms also fell victim to the explosion. No one was injured, except perhaps Ringgold's ego and reputation. But following so closely on the *Princeton* explosion, some were beginning to worry that the US military might not be up to the task if the controversy over Texas led, as many believed it would, to war with Mexico. For his part, Miller was three days from home and would not be able to add any converts based on this latest military misfire.

On March 14, one week before the appointed day, he arrived in Low Hampton, an upstate village nestled against the Poultney River, the border between New York and Vermont. As something of a valedictory, Miller noted in his journal that over the past dozen years he had delivered thirty-two hundred lectures. During the past three summers a half-million people had attended Millerite camp meetings. He could claim more than

twenty-five thousand adherents, with perhaps that many again loosely affiliated with the movement. In the years since Himes had joined up, Adventists had distributed four million pieces of literature, in a country of about
twenty million people.

Miller was at peace with the moment, but anticipation was great among
the believers as March 21 approached. The skeptical and the curious also
cast an occasional eye heavenward, just to be safe. Some of Miller's followers had been preparing for this day for years. They came from most every
walk of life—farmers and small-town shopkeepers, the working and middle
classes. A host of denominations contributed to the Millerite ranks, but the
vast majority came from evangelical backgrounds, mostly Methodist or Baptist. The economic depression that had dragged on since the Panic of 1837
helped feed the notion that the end times were approaching. The broader
ferment of the Second Great Awakening also contributed to a cultural atmosphere that encouraged extreme religious experiences. But every individual
had his own reasons for coming to the movement, and each reacted to the
approaching millennium in his own way as well.

Some had quit their jobs or closed their businesses in anticipation of
the end. Others gave away their earthly possessions. Newspapers tended, as
they do now, to zero in on the extreme cases, or in some instances to simply
invent cases, such as the unsubstantiated rumors about believers donning
white ascension robes. A number of Millerite preachers, including prominent abolitionist Elon Galusha, resigned their positions so as to be "free to
preach the whole truth."

For people accused of being "solemn as eternity," they could show a
lighter side. A twelve-year-old boy in Ohio's Miami Valley who had been
swayed by a Millerite hired hand refused to chop wood, telling his father
that winter was not going to arrive, so what was the point?

Others took the subject more seriously. "Do you think, supposing it
to be true, that Christ will soon appear in the clouds of heaven and the
world destroyed," Millerite abolitionist Angelina Grimké Weld asked her
husband, "that it is a matter of no consequence whether we believe it or
not—that altho' God has taken so much pains to point out the time of the
great event, we may innocently be ignorant of it?"

Joel Buttles, an Episcopalian banker and postmaster, and one of the richest men in Ohio, believed the Millerite case "to be conclusive and yet I do not assent to his conclusions. But the time is at hand which will decide the matter." In any case, Buttles reasoned, "No one will lose anything by being prepared for that event."

But the time of the great event passed, and Christ did not appear. The faithful were not taken up, and no infidels were burned. Those who had prepared for the end were alternately disappointed and bewildered.

The general reaction of outside observers was that Miller, whom they had assumed was a fool anyway, had troubled them for the last time. Under a headline reading THE DANGER PASSED, the *Oneida Whig* reported that "we shall probably hear no more of Millerism now. The grand catastrophe did not come off on the day which was fixed for it."

Miller had always been somewhat uneasy with the setting of a hard date, but he remained convinced that his calculations were correct. When the sun rose on March 22, he was at first uncertain about how to proceed. On March 25 he wrote to Himes that he was "still looking for the Dear Savior . . . and I expect every moment to see the Savior descend from heaven. I have now nothing to look for but this glorious hope." On April 5 he wrote to another follower that he was still "looking every day and hour for Christ to come."

Five days later, Joshua Himes felt compelled to address the flock publicly, releasing a statement that was published in the *Advent Herald* (successor to the *Signs of the Times*) and the *Midnight Cry*.

It has been our sincere and solemn conviction, for three years past, that the *second* glorious and blessed Advent of the Savior of the world, would have taken place before the present time. I still look for this event as being nigh; and cannot avoid the entire conviction which arises from the consideration of the prophetic periods, fulfillment of the prophecies, and signs of the times, that it is the next great event, and must transpire within a very short time. It is not safe, therefore, for us to defer in our minds the event for an hour, but to live in constant expectation, and readiness to meet our Judge. With such views, we can make no certain arrangements for the future; except in conformity with these views of the shortness and uncertainty of time.

On the other side of the country, Mormon leader Joseph Smith used the occasion to poke his fellow premillennialist. The two American-born movements shared some beliefs about the second coming but not about the exact interpretation of "soon"—not before 1890 at least, Smith said. They also were often confused for one another, particularly by foreigners who were targeted by missionaries of both. In a sermon delivered March 10, less than two weeks before Miller's predicted date, Smith assured his listeners,

> I take the responsibility upon myself to prophesy in the name of the Lord, that Christ will not come this year as Miller has prophecyed. . . . And I also Prophecy in the name of the Lord that Christ will not Come in *forty years* and if God ever spake by my mouth he will not come in that length of time, and Jesus Christ never did reveal to any man the precise time that he would Come. Go and read the scriptures and you cannot find any thing that specifies the exact [time] he would come & all that say so are fals teachers.

The appointed time had come and gone. But hope was not extinguished. Miller and his followers would soon be readying themselves for another ethereal deadline. Others—including Joseph Smith—were pressing ahead with their plans for November, just in case.

{ 2 }

A Prophet for President

Mormon prophet Joseph Smith, a man of certainties, was befuddled. In the late fall of 1843, he had written to five of the likely presidential candidates—Whig Henry Clay and Democrats Lewis Cass, John C. Calhoun, Martin Van Buren, and Richard Mentor Johnson. "What will be your rule of action," Smith asked, "relative to us, as a people?" The Mormon newspaper, the *Times and Seasons*, published an editorial at about the same time titled "Who Shall Be Our Next President?"

> We as a people have labored, and are still laboring under great injustice from the hand of a neighboring state. The Latter Day Saints have had their property destroyed and their houses made desolate by the hands of the Missourians; murders have been committed with impunity, and many in consequence of oppression, barbarism, and cruelty, have slept the sleep of death. They have been obliged to flee from their possessions into a distant land, in the chilling frost of December; robbed, spoiled, desolate, houseless, and homeless; without any just pretext of shadow of law; without having violated the laws of that state, or of

the United States, and have had to wander as exiles in a strange land, without as yet, being able to obtain any redress for their grievances.

The newspaper's answer to its own question was that the next president should be "the man who will be the most likely to render us assistance in obtaining redress" for those grievances.

If Smith seriously expected the candidates to offer rousing defenses of his persecuted sect, he was sorely disappointed. "I can enter into no engagements, make no promises, give no pledges to any particular portion of the people," Clay wrote in response, although he had been making such promises to other portions of the people for the better part of three decades. He did note that "it is not inconsistent with this declaration to say, that I have viewed with a lively interest, the progress of the Latter Day Saints; that I have sympathized in their sufferings under injustice, as it appeared to me, which has been inflicted upon them; and that I think, in common with all other religious communities, they ought to enjoy the security and protection of the constitution and the laws."

Cass, Van Buren, and Johnson didn't bother to write back. But states' rights champion Calhoun—the man who would soon claim a political benefit from the destruction aboard the *Princeton*—did, and his response riled Smith. "The case does not come within the Jurisdiction of the Federal Government, which is one of limited and specific powers," the South Carolinian wrote.

On January 2, 1844, Smith took pen in hand and responded. "If the General Government has no power, to reinstate expelled citizens to their rights, there is a monstrous hypocrite fed and fostered from the hard earnings of the people!" the prophet wrote indignantly. And he offered a novel (for its time) interpretation of federal authority: "that Congress, with the president as Executor, is as Almighty in its sphere as Jehovah is in his." His response to Clay was equally caustic, inspiring an anti-Mormon newspaper in Warsaw, just down the river from Nauvoo, to say that "a more scurrilous, low, blackguard production, we have seldom seen."

Smith was rowing upstream and had to know it. Calhoun and John Quincy Adams agreed on very little, but both were of the same mind on the question of federal assistance to address the Mormon persecution. "The

Joseph Smith. *Library of Congress*

power of Congress to interfere is questionable," Adams would write after meeting with a delegation of saints. "The right is doubtful."

Like William Miller, Smith was a seeker, who had founded Mormonism after coming to the conclusion that no other existing religious group met his spiritual needs. Now he reached a similar conclusion about politics. Mormons tended to vote as a bloc, but they shifted their allegiances from Whig to Democrat and back to Whig as circumstances dictated. If no presidential candidate would address the concerns of the Latter-Day Saints, Smith would have to run for president himself. And so on January 29, one day after Miller had begun the East Coast tour that would take him to Washington, the Quorum of the Twelve Apostles—as the council of Smith's top advisers was known—and other church leaders met at the office of the mayor of Nauvoo, Illinois, the wandering saints' latest home base. It was a friendly venue: among Smith's many titles was mayor. A motion was made that Smith should run for president and that those in attendance should employ "all honorable means . . . to secure his election."

"If you attempt to accomplish this," Smith told those gathered, "you must send every man in the city who is able to speak in public throughout the land to electioneer and make stump speeches, advocate the 'Mormon' religion, purity of elections, and call upon the people to stand by the law and put down mobocracy."

The Mormon newspaper took up the call. "Our interests, our property, our lives and the lives of our families are too dear to us to be sacrificed at the shrine of party-spirit, and to gratify party feelings," the *Times and Seasons* reported. "Under existing circumstances we have no other alternative, and if we can accomplish our object well, if not we shall have the satisfaction of knowing that we have acted conscientiously and have used our best judgment; and if we have to throw away our votes, we had better do so upon a worthy, rather than upon an unworthy individual, who might make use of the weapon we put in his hand to destroy us with."

The cause of the Mormon consternation with the political and legal process went back to the founding of the movement with the publication of the Book of Mormon in 1830. At each stop where the church hoped to set up its Zion, mobs—unofficial and official—had hounded members and, in many cases, committed violence, personal and legal. Fleeing from their first Zion in Ohio, the saints relocated to Missouri, where locals objected to their religious practices and to their communitarian spirit, which included the habit of voting as a unit. Sporadic violence increased along with the number of Mormon émigrés to the Show Me State and erupted into the "Mormon War" of 1838. The blame lay mostly with anti-Mormon locals, but Democratic governor Lillburn Boggs blamed the saints and issued his infamous Executive Order 44, which called for Mormons to be "exterminated or driven from the State."

Smith and other church leaders were arrested and their followers began fleeing into Illinois. They settled on a spit of land along the Mississippi River that had once been the site of a Sac and Fox village and was described by one writer as "a malarial riverbottom swamp," although another described the surrounding country as "really beautiful, the land being of the best quality, with an abundance of timber, &c." They changed the town's name from Commerce to Nauvoo, which Smith said was a Hebrew word meaning "beautiful place," and began rebuilding their lives once again. After four months' confinement in Missouri, Smith, his brother Hyrum, and three others escaped, with a little help from their guards. A week later, they were in Nauvoo.

Six months after fleeing Missouri justice, Joseph Smith headed for Washington, hoping to enlist the aid of the federal government in protecting his people's constitutional rights. Smith and Elias Higbee, the official church historian, arrived in the capital on November 28 and wasted no time. After setting up shop at the National Hotel, they went the next day to the White House. In those days, no appointment was necessary and security was all but unheard of. The two Mormon leaders were accompanied by Illinois Representative John Reynolds, a Democrat who introduced the pair to President Martin Van Buren. After a few pleasantries, the men got down to business.

Smith found Van Buren less than sympathetic. Like most Americans, the president considered Mormons to be, at best, peculiar, certainly heretical, and maybe worse. But their greatest sin, as far as Van Buren was concerned, was that coming to the aid of their relatively small group might cost him some votes. "What can I do?" he asked plaintively. "I can do nothing for you. If I do anything, I shall come in contact with the whole state of Missouri." Missouri's four electoral votes might prove decisive in what was expected to be a close fight for reelection in 1840.

Nauvoo. *Library of Congress*

Having found no friend in the White House, Smith and Higbee turned to Congress. In meetings with the Illinois delegation, they were afforded the respect any influential constituents might expect. They were given a fair hearing and allowed to present a petition, with 678 signatures, seeking compensation for the losses they suffered in Missouri, estimated at about $2 million. The lawmakers helped the religious leaders prepare their case. But all the effort was to no avail. The Senate Judiciary Committee ruled that Congress could not act, and the Mormons needed to seek redress in the Missouri courts, a step Smith knew would be futile. The saints would have to look elsewhere for justice.

"Give Every Man His Constitutional Freedom"

Though the appeal to official Washington proved fruitless, for the most part Illinois state officials gave the Mormons wide latitude to set up their own institutions, a freedom they pursued with great vigor. A liberal city charter granted by the state legislature allowed them to establish friendly courts and organize a militia—headed by General Joseph Smith—called the Nauvoo Legion. Smith continued to operate under the cloud of possible extradition to Missouri, though the local Mormon-dominated court system was effective in blocking those efforts.

But, just as had happened in Ohio and Missouri, suspicious and bigoted local residents began to agitate against the saints, aided by Mormon apostates—"a few artless villains," the *Times and Seasons* called them—who didn't like the way Smith was running things or what they knew or had heard about the practice of polygamy. "A chosen people is probably inspiring for the chosen to live among," Wallace Stegner noted, "but it is not so comfortable for outsiders to live with." Even if Smith might have agreed with that sentiment, he would not have considered the discomfort of outsiders reason enough to surrender his people's constitutional rights.

The agitation would come to a head by the summer of 1844, but first Smith had to put together a presidential campaign. He began with a manifesto, presented in public for the first time on February 8 and published in pamphlet form as *General Smith's Views of the Powers and Policy of the*

Government of the United States on February 24. Fifteen hundred copies were mailed to prominent citizens, including Van Buren and his cabinet, the US Supreme Court, members of Congress, and major newspapers. A mix of utopian idealism and practical American politics, with a dash of biblical-inspired skull-cracking, *General Smith's Views* was reprinted in the May 15, 1844, edition of the *Times and Seasons*.

> We have had democratic presidents; whig presidents; a pseudo demo-cratic whig president, and now it is time to have a president of the United States; and let the people of the whole union, like the inflexible Romans, whenever they find a promise made by a candidate, that is not practised as an officer, hurl the miserable sycophant from his exaltation, as God did Nebuchadnezzar, to crop the grass of the field, with a beast's heart among the cattle.

Despite the ecumenical tone, Smith took some controversial stands that crossed party lines. He called for slavery's abolition not through force but through gradual, compensated emancipation. He would pay slave owners for their surrendered property out of proceeds from the sale of public lands. His calls for prison reform went far beyond any others of his day, urging voters to "Petition your state legislature to pardon every convict in their several penitentiaries: blessing them as they go, and saying to them in the name of the Lord, go thy way and sin no more." He wanted imprisonment to be replaced by public works performed by convicts. He backed creation of a national bank, but with limited powers and branches in the states.

Penal policy aside, most of that was more or less in the mainstream of American political thought in the middle of the nineteenth century, although the compensated emancipation plank would gain few if any adherents in the South. But on the question of the role of the federal government, Smith was a true outlier, anticipating by more than a century the expanded power of Washington to enforce constitutional rights against violations by states and individuals.

> Give every man his constitutional freedom, and the president full power to send an army to suppress mobs; and the states authority to repeal and impugn that relic of folly, which makes it necessary for the

governor of a state to make the demand of the president for troops, in
cases of invasion or rebellion. The governor himself may be a mobber
and, instead of being punished, as he should be for murder and treason,
he may destroy the very lives, rights, and property he should protect.

General Smith's Views, indeed his entire presidential campaign, represented a convergence of the prophet's theological and political opinions.
"In the millenarian mood of the early years," Smith's best biographer,
Richard Lyman Bushman, writes, "the nation's destiny, its elections, even
its history meant little in light of the Second Coming." Starting from the
same eschatological position as William Miller, Smith had taken a turn
and moved into American political life, eschewing end-of-the-worldism in
favor of fix-the-worldism. Miller's predicted end had not come in March
1844. At the same time Smith was shifting his quixotic presidential race
into gear, Miller and his followers were adjusting their calculations and
preparing a new date for the end of the world. Miller, looking heavenward,
thought the world was doomed and was preparing for its demise. Smith
thought the world—and America—eminently savable, and he meant to
save them.

One question on which Smith deviated little from the prevailing political winds was westward expansion. Even as he was planning and executing
his presidential campaign, Smith was in the early stages of developing a
plan for moving the Mormon people once more, this time to Oregon, California, or Texas. Two weeks after the Quorum of the Twelve Apostles had
nominated him for president, Smith empowered them to mount an explor-
atory visit to find a new home where they might "have a government of our
own." This was not yet an exodus; Smith wanted more than one base for
the Mormon people, but he saw the unfettered West as an outlet, and Texas
was included in the list of possibilities. "The whole of America is Zion" was
Smith's view. Brigham Young, one of the Twelve, looked at his task as finding "the best manner to settle our people in some distant and unoccupied
territory, where we could enjoy our civil and religious beliefs without being
subject to constant oppression and mobocracy." An envoy was sent to Texas
to talk things over with Texas president Sam Houston, who was enthusiastic
about the possibility of new recruits.

But this was not in the interest of fleeing from US jurisdiction. If Smith wanted the Mormons in Texas, he wanted Texas in the union. In *General Smith's Views*, the prophet supported the annexation of Texas and hoped to see "the union spread from the east to the west sea; and if Texas petitions Congress to be adopted among the sons of liberty, give her the right hand of fellowship."

"ROUSED AND MADE OF ONE MIND"

Outside Smith's manifesto, there was little fellowship to be had on the question of Texas annexation. His reference to "sons of liberty" was crucial. Smith wanted Texas in the union, but as a free state. That was a pipe dream. For the nonutopian presidential candidates, and for the members of Congress and of Tyler's cabinet who would have to make the decision, the question was much simpler. Texas would remain a slaveholding empire. Would it be that inside the union or out?

Talk of annexation predated Texas's independence from Mexico in 1836. Some hardliners claimed the area was part of the Louisiana Purchase, a claim that was bargained away in exchange for the Floridas by Secretary of State John Quincy Adams in the Adams-Onis Treaty between the United States and Spain in 1819. After Moses Austin received his 1821 land grant from the Mexican government and his son Stephen began colonizing the region along the Brazos River with American settlers—almost 150,000 by 1844—the idea of Texas joining the union quickly began to take hold. The heroic defense of the Alamo in 1836, the subsequent declaration of independence, and the ultimately successful military revolt against Mexican rule turned the idea of annexation into something more than a goal for the distant future. Texans were for it. The Democrats who ran the national government in Washington, especially President Martin Van Buren, were wary. Yet continued violations of Texas's hard-won sovereignty provided an emotional element. Americans sympathized with their national brethren against the depredations of the former Mexican masters.

But until 1844, the issue never fully took hold of the public imagination. That's one reason the annexation negotiators were able to keep their talks secret, which most likely aided in their success. Andrew Jackson wrote to his old friend Sam Houston that keeping the talks behind closed doors "prevents that arch fiend, J. Q. Adams, from writing memorials and circulating them for signatures." Negotiator Isaac Van Zandt kept his boss, Texas secretary of state Anson Jones, informed of the progress. Jones responded by dismissing the idea. Annexation would mean war with Mexico, he told Van Zandt. Houston backed annexation, but assumed for much the same reason as Jones that it would not win Senate approval.

Despite these warnings from above, Van Zandt soldiered on. He continued his talks with US secretary of state Abel Upshur through the autumn of 1843 and into the following winter. Like Van Zandt, Upshur had received warnings against proceeding. Juan Almonte, the Mexican minister to the United States, got wind of the talks and told Upshur point-blank that annexation would bring war. A worried Houston decided to send James Pinckney Henderson, an experienced diplomat who had negotiated trade deals and foreign recognition for Texas, to supplement the delegation. The night before the explosion aboard the *Princeton*—before Henderson's arrival—Upshur had concluded the negotiations with Van Zandt. All that remained now was the signing of a formal treaty, which would then have to be approved by the Senate.

Official Washington had been hearing rumors of the negotiations for months, and Whigs—along with a few Northern Democrats—were beginning to grumble. But Upshur had reason to believe that the ratification process would go smoothly: he interpreted his easy Senate confirmation as tantamount to support for annexation; Jackson was confident; Upshur could mine a deep vein of anti-British feeling (England had been meddling in Texas affairs almost from the moment of its independence from Mexico); and there was wide support for territorial expansion among the people and in Congress. In a January 1844 letter to the American chargé d'affaires in Texas, Upshur asserted that annexation was favored by two-thirds of the Senate.

Unfortunately for Upshur and supporters of annexation, the expectations of smooth sailing were blown to pieces aboard the *Princeton*. Upshur, a Virginian like Tyler, had been an ardent sectionalist. He backed John C. Calhoun for president and believed that Texas was the key to uniting

Southerners behind Calhoun's candidacy. He was committed to bringing Texas into the union for a variety of reasons, including the expansion of slave territory. But he was also pragmatic enough to know that nationalism, not sectionalism, was the way to sell annexation.

On March 6, a week after Upshur's death, Tyler chose Calhoun to take over the State Department—"the only man in the country who could meet all the exigencies of the crisis," according to Virginian Henry A. Wise. Fellow South Carolinian George McDuffie, who would play a central role in the coming Senate debate on Texas, carried Tyler's request for Calhoun to join the cabinet. "The President is very anxious that you should accept and come on immediately as the Texas negotiation admits of no delay," he wrote.

Like Tyler, Calhoun was a man without a party. A onetime proto-Whig who had become a Democrat and then resigned the vice presidency in a dispute with Andrew Jackson, Calhoun had moved from being a states-rights advocate to the more extreme position of Southern separatist, leaving him outside the mainstream of both political parties. Historians have puzzled over why Tyler chose the mercurial South Carolinian to be the key man on the issue upon which the success or failure of his presidency now rested. Calhoun's friends assumed Tyler would subtly suggest a quid pro quo—the State Department in return for Calhoun's support of Tyler's reelection.

That certainly would have been in keeping with the president's method of operation. A desire to derail another potential contender might have played a part in another of Tyler's post-*Princeton* machinations. To replace Thomas Gilmer at the Navy Department, he quickly settled on fellow Virginian John Y. Mason, a former House member and now district court judge. Mason waffled, so Tyler directed an operative to approach former Speaker of the House James K. Polk to gauge the Tennessean's interest in the job. Polk had served seven terms in the House in the 1820s and '30s and one term as Speaker, and lost two races for governor. Now he was angling to be chosen as the number-two man on a presidential ticket with Martin Van Buren. On March 10, Theophilus Fisk, a Virginia newspaper editor loyal to Tyler, wrote to inquire "whether it would meet with your approbation to be tendered a place in his Cabinet." Noting the "melancholy death" of Gilmer,

Fisk asked Polk if he would "consent to take it if tendered to you without any pledge, shackle or trammel being asked of you?"

Polk's eyes were cast in another direction, which turned out to be a good thing, because three days after the offer was extended, Fisk had to withdraw it when Mason decided he did want the job. No matter. Before Polk received the second Fisk letter, he humbly responded to the first, allowing that "there are many others, whose services the President can command, who could render more service to the country than I could."

Polk's phantom appointment would become an ironic historical footnote. Not so Calhoun's. Whatever Tyler's reasons for selecting the South Carolinian, he would quickly come to regret the choice. Tyler's message was national—extend American influence across the continent and end British interference in Texas, Oregon, and beyond. The most celebrated defense of this position came in a pamphlet by Mississippi senator Robert Walker, which argued that Texas annexation was an unadulterated good. There was something for everybody in it—more land, harbors for trade, a diminution of British power. And, Walker wrote, the addition of Texas to the union would dilute slavery, pushing it south and west, so that states of the middle border and perhaps even the upper South would eventually see the end of the peculiar institution. Others had made a similar argument with seeming sincerity. Whether Walker actually believed it or not was irrelevant. It was a shrewd way to make the case for Texas annexation to wary Northerners, and a fund established by well-off Southerners paid to have hundreds of thousands of copies of Walker's letter distributed in the North.

Calhoun might have believed Walker's argument about the dilution of slavery, but he didn't believe it would be a good thing. He wanted to deliver a different message. The South, the new secretary of state asserted, was under assault, which meant slavery—a positive good, in Calhoun's eyes—was also threatened. The North was growing in population relative to the South. Abolitionists, who not too many years earlier had been considered a lunatic fringe, had begun to make serious inroads in the political system. Most immediately, the years-long congressional debate over the so-called gag rule, which barred discussion or referral to committee of antislavery petitions in the House, was coming to a head.

"Why Will You Not Discuss This Question?"

The year 1831 had been a propitious one for the embryonic abolitionist movement. William Lloyd Garrison founded the newspaper the *Liberator*, abolitionists in Boston founded the New England Anti-Slavery Society, and slaves led by Nat Turner rose up against their masters in Virginia. Southerners were annoyed by Garrison and the fledgling society. They were scared to death by Turner.

Two years later, the American Anti-Slavery Society was founded. Its leaders soon launched a campaign to petition Congress to end slavery. Petitions poured in by the thousands. Congress had not seen anything like it since the efforts in the 1810s and '20s to repeal an 1810 law that required post offices to remain open on Sundays, an exercise in civics that served as a sort of dress rehearsal for the religious-infused abolitionist efforts of the 1830s and included many of the same activists.

By 1836, pro-slavery Democrats were complaining that Congress could hardly get its work done for all the time devoted to dealing with abolitionist petitions. This was a specious argument, but it worked, with an assist from Whigs who saw political peril in discussion of slavery and preferred that the issue simply go away. Under the leadership of Speaker James K. Polk, a Tennessee slaveholder, this coalition adopted a rule that automatically tabled all antislavery petitions—in blatant violation, opponents argued, of the First Amendment guarantee of the right to petition the government for a redress of grievances—and extended the ban in succeeding Congresses.

Each new Congress brought a renewed effort, led by former president and now Massachusetts congressman John Quincy Adams, to repeal the gag rule. Adams would pound and pontificate, deliver sermons on the sanctity of the right of petition and denounce the "slave power" that dominated the House of Representatives. Often he did it with a sense of humor, but laughter—earned or offered—never buried the outrage.

> Gentlemen of the South, why will you not discuss this question? Do you fear the argument? If not, why do you refuse to enter into it? If you are so firm, so confident, so immovably resolute, why will you not speak? I call upon you to speak; explain this subject to us who do not

understand it. Show us the "blessings" of this institution. Let us look at them. I believe some of you think that slavery is a blessing which we ought to take ourselves. If so, give your reasons; show us how it will be for our interest, and how it can be made to conform to our sense of duty. Perhaps we shall come round; who knows but you may convert us? I do not resist; I am open to conviction. Suppose you try it.

But the louder Adams protested, the less the Democracy, as the Democratic Party and its adherents were often called, seemed to listen. Year after year he challenged the gag rule and, while victory on occasion seemed to be at hand, year after year he failed. Even when the Whigs captured control of both houses of Congress in 1840—the only time they would do so in the brief life of the party—he could not win assent to a change in the rules. When Democrats regained control of the House by a whopping 142–79 margin in 1842, the cause seemed lost.

In those days, a Congress elected in November would not begin meeting until December of the following year. The ousted Congress would return a month after Election Day for a lame-duck session that lasted until they concluded their business in late spring or early summer. Upon adjournment Washington, under normal circumstances, would then be free from the ravages of Congress until the newly elected members gathered. The twenty-eighth Congress convened on December 4, 1843. Unhappy with Tyler, voters thirteen months earlier had tossed out the Whigs and turned Congress back over to the Democrats.

Adams estimated in April 1844 that "the standing supremacy of the slave representation is 112, a bare majority of the House, consisting of 80 slave-holders and thirty-two free-trade auxiliaries." Adams aimed to target the auxiliaries, some of whom sensed that the sands were shifting beneath their feet. Northern Democrats were growing increasingly uneasy about appearing to the public as being in favor of such an undemocratic proposition as the gag rule. Their party brethren from the South had bigger, Texas-sized fish to fry. It might be better to ungag the House, some reasoned, than to risk splitting the party at such a crucial moment.

When the new Congress convened, the motion was made to renew the rules from the twenty-seventh Congress. Adams, referring to the "life-and-death struggle for the right of petition," moved to delete the gag rule from the package. Procedural votes early in 1844 went Adams's way. But, as had happened on several other occasions, supporters of the gag rule marshaled their forces for the decisive confrontation, and again they prevailed, this time by a single vote, 88–87. Adams laid the blame at the feet of the New York delegation, whom he accused of supporting the gag rule to protect Southern support for Van Buren. Later that same day, the Peacemaker exploded on the *Princeton*.

Lawmakers opposed to the gag rule took some comfort in those numbers, and knew they would have another chance after the election was settled and, they felt certain, Clay was in the White House. They had waited this long. They could wait a few more months.

Calhoun was a radical, but he was not delusional. And he could count. The slow ebb of Southern power in Congress was not a figment of his imagination, as the close vote on the gag rule demonstrated. He saw the addition of Texas to the union as a way to stanch the flow of power northward. Further, he saw the public debate over annexation as a forum in which to rally the South to defend its prerogatives. Winning wasn't enough. They had to win for the right reasons. Southerners, Upshur had written to Calhoun six months before his death, were "far too lethargic upon the vital question. They ought to be roused and made of one mind." Calhoun intended to rouse them.

Adams and his allies saw the battles over the gag rule and Texas annexation as two fronts in the same war, just as Calhoun did. But while Adams possessed the loudest Whig voice in Congress on both issues, his was not the Whig voice that mattered most on Texas. That belonged to a man who had resigned from the Senate in 1842—and he was not yet talking, at least not in public.

Fed up with Tyler's apostasy to the Whig faith, demoralized with his inability to move the debate, and worn out by his declining health, Henry Clay had left Congress to rest, recuperate, and plan his presidential campaign. When Texas reared its head on the national political scene, Clay would rather have been talking about almost anything else. As a candidate for the White House, the Kentuckian wanted to debate the tariff, a national bank, internal improvements. Texas, he sensed, was a trap, and he would put off formally

addressing the issue as long as he felt he could, although he had been expressing his opposition privately for some time. When he finally decided to go on
the record, just before Tyler sent the annexation treaty to the Senate, Clay did
so against the advice of friends and advisers, who feared he could do himself
little good and plenty of harm. Clay, as always, was supremely confident in
his ability to finesse controversy by splitting the difference. It had worked for
him many times before, but it would not work on Texas.

Whigs not running for president did not have to be so circumspect. The
annexation of Texas, wrote Ohio congressman Joshua Giddings, "would be
a transfer of our political power to the slaveholders and a base and degrading surrender of ourselves to the power and protection of slavery. It is the
most abominable proposition with which a free people were ever insulted."
Adams was just as overwrought. "The treaty for the annexation of Texas was
this day [April 22] sent in to the Senate and with it went the freedom of the
human race," he confided to his diary.

The treaty Upshur and Van Zandt had negotiated was, with a few minor
changes, the treaty Calhoun and Henderson signed off on. The Calhoun-led,
post-Upshur stage of the talks was largely uneventful. Henderson and Van
Zandt feared that sending a note back to Texas for final instructions might
delay action and doom the chances for ratification, and they may have been
right. Jones and Houston were privately unhappy with some of the provisions—no statehood, no guarantee of defense from Mexican violence—but
they kept their complaints out of the public view. Van Zandt and Henderson signed the treaty April 12 on their own authority, just two weeks after
Calhoun took over. "The voice of the country," Calhoun wrote the next day,
"is so decidedly in favor of annexation that any hesitancy on the part of the
doubtful will probably give way to it." Ten days later, Tyler submitted the
agreement to the Senate, where the debate would be anything but uneventful.

"In My Cauling and Duing My Duty"

While the politicians in Washington were preparing to consider Texas,
William Miller was considering a new deadline for the second coming and
Joseph Smith was preparing to expand his presidential campaign.

After the disappointment of Christ's non-appearance, confused and depressed Millerites looked to Miller and other leaders of the movement in search of what would come next. Some drifted away and "walked no more with us," as Miller put it. But most still believed and were looking for guidance. In the days and weeks immediately following what came to be called "the spring disappointment," Miller was ambivalent. He admitted his error, but couldn't say exactly how or why it had happened. "I can't see where I'm wrong," he wrote. He could say, though, that he was as certain as ever of Christ's soon coming.

"I confess my error, and acknowledge my disappointment; yet I still believe that the day of the Lord is near, even at the door; and I exhort you, my brethren, to be watchful, and not let that day come upon you unawares. The wicked, the proud, and the bigot will exult over us. I will try to be patient. God will deliver the godly out of temptation, and will reserve the unjust to be punished at Christ's appearing," Miller wrote. As always, he urged followers seeking answers to resort to the Bible, not to man, for solace.

While Miller reassessed, others stepped in to fill the vacuum. Among the most colorful of these characters was John Starkweather, Joshua Himes's assistant pastor at the Chardon Street Chapel in Boston. He differed from Miller, who considered premillennialism the distinguishing tenet of his movement and was not interested in deviating from other Bible teachings (and believed that premillennialism was itself not a deviation). Starkweather, on the other hand, preached not only that one had to take Christ into one's heart in order to be saved, but also that a physical manifestation—a bodily weakness or some other outward sign—was necessary to gain God's favor. He attracted a following among the more extreme elements of Millerism, while the leadership quickly moved to disown him. Himes called his practices "abominations" and sent him packing from Chardon Street. Starkweather kept right on. Some of his antics bordered on the ridiculous, even in the context of the sometimes bizarre rituals associated with some evangelical and perfectionist elements during the Second Great Awakening. He would wave a tree branch over the heads of his crowds to determine who was saved, for example. He urged his congregations to eschew things of the world, including their sets of false teeth.

After the spring disappointment, Starkweather made a final attempt to shave off a sizable portion of the Millerite contingent for his own by bringing together a host of disappointed and disaffected believers. But, as tends to happen with gatherings of people who are already up in arms, the meeting devolved into chaos. "No two were of one mind," wrote Himes's friends. "Each wished to lead off in his own direction."

And so they did. Starkweather was never able to bring the disparate groups together and he would fade away rather quickly. But a modified brand of his fanaticism would reemerge for one last demonstration later in the year, thanks in large part to the work of another Millerite leader, who claimed to have found the error that Miller himself could not divine.

As early as February 1844, Samuel S. Snow had argued in the pages of the *Midnight Cry* that the spring date for the second coming was wrong. Miller had always been softer on the date than many of his lieutenants, but was not yet ready to accept that Snow had found the final answer. Editors added caveats to Snow's article in the *Midnight Cry* and again when it was reprinted in the *Advent Herald* on April 3. By May they were beginning to come around, though it would take another four months for Snow's new date to receive any kind of official endorsement, and even longer for Miller to lend his wholehearted support.

Snow's argument, like so much of Millerite theology, was arcane. His interpretation of Daniel 8:14 was that the twenty-three-hundred-year period ended in 1844 rather than 1843. That pushed the second coming back seven months to October 22, in conjunction with the Jewish Day of Atonement. Snow had already begun preaching the new date before the spring disappointment. After, he picked up the pace, traveling to Philadelphia, New York, and Boston, receiving enthusiastic notices from Millerites happy to have a renewed vision.

As Snow's ministry began to take hold of the Millerite imagination in the late spring, Miller was beginning to regain his footing. He planned a tour of the west, to commence in July, that would take him across New York to Canada and Ohio. But even as these plans were being laid, it was becoming clear that other personalities would carry the Millerite melodrama to its final act.

Joseph Smith's act, meanwhile, was kicking into high gear. If his campaign was symbolic, it was a symbol filled with substance. He employed the ready-made Mormon missionary force as campaign foot soldiers, proudly proclaiming "there is oratory enough in the Church to carry me into the Presidential chair." More than three hundred volunteers joined up. April saw forty-seven campaign events scheduled across fourteen states to deliver the message. All told, campaigners were assigned to every state—New York got the most, with forty-seven—and to the Wisconsin Territory, which got one. The Mormon newspaper the *Times and Seasons* covered the campaign extensively, reprinting Smith's policy manifesto, his correspondence with the major party candidates, and other campaign news.

Non-Mormon newspapers also took notice, more often than not in considerably less flattering terms than those of the *Times and Seasons*. A *New York Tribune* correspondent wrote of Smith: "none who know him can respect him. They cannot respect him for his sincerity—for he cannot be sincere; he cannot be the victim of his own delusion. They cannot esteem him for his piety—for he does not even profess to be pious—and he is notoriously the greatest blasphemer and railer in the country." Hancock County's *Warsaw Signal* published a letter to "Jo Smith—Prophet—Candidate for the Presidency—Mayor of the City of Nauvoo—Lieutenant General of the Legion—President of the Church—Tavern Keeper—Grog Bruiser—&c., &c." Claiming the "unalienable right of an American Citizen" to ask questions of presidential candidates, the paper wondered "what would you do with the State of Missouri? Would you pluck out the eyes of her sovereignty? Or would you take her up in your expanded arms, and giant-like stride across the Western Prairies—leap the Rocky Mountains and hurl her headlong into the angry Pacific, there to remain until purged of every Anti-Mormon sin? Or Jo, would you Xerxes-like muster your myriads, and every man armed with a hoop-pole, march across the icy bridge in winter time, and give her Sovereign Highness, a most transcendent drubbing?"

Such prejudices were to be expected. To counteract them, Smith sent ten members of the Quorum of the Twelve, including Brigham Young, out on campaign missions. "I am in my cauling and duing my duty," Young wrote to his wife, Mary Ann. He and his compatriots preached and politicked in

St. Louis, Cincinnati, Pittsburgh, Boston, and the saints' former home base in Kirtland, Ohio. Wilford Woodruff, another of the Twelve, left Nauvoo on May 9 with three colleagues on a nine-week electioneering mission. He delivered speeches at a half-dozen political meetings, often in schoolhouses, always being meticulous about separating his preaching from his politicking—the political speeches tended to come the night before the religious services he conducted on the trip. Others also typically did their politicking either the day before or the day after the religious meetings, which proved successful. During the campaign season, newspapers reported on mass Mormon conversions in Mississippi and Alabama, without mentioning any political activity.

Smith was officially nominated by the Illinois state convention of his supporters—largely Latter Day Saints but including a sprinkling of Gentiles—which he organized and hosted in Nauvoo on May 17. Even though it was characterized as a state convention, delegates came from all twenty-six states. Ten Illinois counties were represented, but most of the attendees lived in Nauvoo. Two non-LDS delegates, G. W. Goforth and John S. Reid, were given prominent speaking roles. Reid, Smith's onetime attorney, offered the colorful hope that the prophet would "live to put his foot upon the neck of his enemies in love and meekness." Smith had at first sought to include James Arlington Bennett, a New York lawyer who had been baptized into the faith by Brigham Young, as his vice presidential candidate. But Bennett had been born in Ireland and was thus ineligible. He looked next to Colonel Solomon Copeland, one of the leading saints from Tennessee, but ultimately settled on Sidney Rigdon, an early Mormon convert and Smith's fellow escapee from the Liberty Jail in Missouri. Having concluded their business, the state-level delegates planned a truly national convention to be held July 13 in Baltimore.

So, while Joseph Smith and his followers were engaging humanity, William Miller and his flock were planning for humanity's earthly destruction. Many people considered both to be fools. Neither cared much what other people thought. Miller trudged along as always, defiant in his simplicity. Smith, too, knew he was not on a fool's errand, and he had not sent his lieutenants on one. The prophet understood fully that he would not be elected president, but that didn't mean he was not a serious candidate. The campaign afforded him a chance to spread the word about Mormonism and put its case before the people and their leaders. Pointing toward a time when Mormonism would stand inside the big tent of American culture, Smith's focus was relentlessly on the future. That is more than could be said for the man most people believed would win the White House in 1844.

{ 3 }

"ANNEXATION AND WAR...
ARE IDENTICAL"

U nlike Andrew Jackson, his great rival for the political affection of westerners, Henry Clay was not a military hero. Clay's appeal was in his personal connection to voters, his sense of humor and ability to spin a yarn, his gilded oratory. To make the most of those advantages, he spent more time personally stumping for votes than any presidential candidate up to that time, and probably more than any would until William Jennings Bryan a half century later.

When Clay embarked on a winter/spring 1844 tour that would take him from New Orleans to Washington, it was part campaign swing, part royal progress, during which he traveled across the landscape holding court. He had lately completed a trip through the Southwest, to Alabama, Mississippi, and Louisiana. Now he would embark on a pre-convention sojourn through the Southeast, to Georgia, the Carolinas, through Virginia, and up to the capital city ahead of the May 1 Whig convention in Baltimore. The trip got him away from the Kentucky winter, which would be good for his health. And it gave him a chance to talk about his favorite subject, the American System, his decades-old program to build canals and roads, protect industry with tariffs, secure the currency with a national bank, and otherwise use the power of the federal government to boost the economy. It seemed never to occur to Clay that people were tired of listening to his litany and might have other things on their minds.

In December 1843 he traveled from his Kentucky estate, Ashland, toward New Orleans. On the way his party encountered an enthusiastic Democrat, who was invited to meet with the candidate. He was such an ardent party man that he refused to meet Clay or shake his hand. When informed that even Martin Van Buren had shaken Clay's hand, the incredulous Democrat refused to believe it. He backed up his doubt with a wager, and even consented to meet with Clay just to prove the untruthfulness of the slander against the Little Magician. This was rousing good fun for Clay, who recounted for the man Van Buren's 1842 visit to Ashland—a visit that would, by the end of the trip, cause Clay no small amount of grief—successfully demonstrating to the Whig basher that Clay was a "clever gentleman, with neither horns nor hoofs, as he had been represented."

Clay had been a frequent visitor to New Orleans—he liked to enjoy himself, and the Crescent City was, then as now, a good place for that. He

HENRY CLAY. *Library of Congress*

arrived two days before Christmas and spent two months resting, imbibing, and politicking. He pointed to the Tariff of 1842, which he had supported, as being a major reason the cotton economy of the state had improved. And he promised moderation in all things. His hosts ate it up because it directly affected their livelihoods. He found, though, that when he talked about the bank or other aspects of his system, people were less interested. The papers were full of news about neighboring Texas and voters wanted to hear about Clay's views on the subject. Privately he expressed opposition. "I consider the Union a great political partnership," he wrote to a supporter, "and that new members ought not to be admitted into the concern at the imminent hazard of its dissolution." Publicly he dismissed the issue as a distraction. Just as most Democrats didn't want to talk about slavery because it was too divisive, most Whigs, particularly Clay, didn't want to talk about Texas for the same reason.

But Clay didn't get all his information from the newspapers. General Charles F. Mercer, a longtime Whig member of Congress, had recently left Texas and met with the Kentuckian in New Orleans, delivering "intelligence which has greatly surprised me," Clay reported. He was especially surprised to hear "that 42 American Senators are in favor of the annexation of Texas, and have advised the President that they will confirm a treaty to that effect." Writing to Kentucky ally John J. Crittenden back in Washington, Clay asked incredulously, "Is this true?" It wasn't, but neither Crittenden nor Clay knew that at the time.

From New Orleans, Clay traveled to Mobile, Alabama, where a ball was given in his honor. He spent a week in the coastal city, trying to shake a bad cold he had caught just before leaving New Orleans. He "entertained no hopes" of carrying Alabama in the coming election, but was heartened by the friendly reception. Then he moved inland to Columbus, Georgia, then Macon, and the capital, Milledgeville. He spoke outdoors for more than an hour at each stop, which did nothing to help his cold and left him "hoarse as a circuit rider."

Fifteen hundred people met Clay at the railroad station when he arrived in Savannah, where he gave a two-hour speech on bank policy. Now, for the first time, he wrote to Crittenden suggesting that he was considering addressing Texas annexation once he reached Washington. Voters were writing to him on Texas as well as Oregon. Perhaps they cared more about it than he previously thought? If so, Clay would waver on his determination not "to introduce at present a new element among the other exciting subjects which agitate and engross the public mind." Ever certain of his own superior intellect, Clay was sure he could "treat the question in a manner very differently from any treatment which I have yet seen of it, and so reconcile all our friends, and many others, to the views which I entertain." Crittenden must have cringed.

Moving on to Augusta, Clay encountered a farmer who was mindful of one of the other great movements of the time. He feared the Millerites might be right. With the second coming of Christ at hand, the man wanted a chance to shake Henry Clay's hand before the end was upon them. He missed the candidate on his first day in town—Clay was delivering an hour-and-a-half-long speech on the steps of city hall. But the next day the farmer caught up with Clay at the Masonic lodge and his wish was granted.

Before leaving Georgia, Clay met with freshman congressman Alexander Stephens, who would one day go on to become vice president of the Confederate States of America. But in 1844 Stephens was a strong union man and no sectionalist. He sounded like Clay when he declared annexation "a miserable political humbug got up as a ruse to divide and distract the Whig Party at the South," and he advised the candidate to avoid the trap.

Beginning to weary of all the activity, Clay canceled stops in Madison, Georgia, and Greensboro, North Carolina, and begged out of any speeches, receptions, and public events in Columbia, South Carolina. Recharged a bit after his rest in the capital city, he progressed to Charleston, which greeted him with a military salute and a parade. He reciprocated by delivering a two-hour speech and attending a festive dinner and ball.

Up the coast he went to Wilmington, North Carolina, for more speechifying, then on to Raleigh, where thousands turned out to welcome him on April 12, his sixty-seventh birthday. It had been a successful tour. Clay felt confident that he had achieved his goal of uniting Northern and Southern Whigs behind his candidacy, and that he had set the stage for a sweeping electoral victory.

Others in the party were equally sanguine. They believed that voters preferred their economic program and that Clay was a superior candidate to anyone the Democrats might offer, especially Van Buren. This was the year, they were certain, that the differences between the parties would be the starkest, and voters would have a clear choice between two vastly different futures. True, voters had largely rejected the Whigs in local and congressional elections in 1841, '42, and '43, but the larger turnout expected for the presidential contest, as in 1840, would bring out all those who shared their vision. "We have always insisted that the Whig party has only to place its great distinctive principles fairly and fully before the People, advocate them fearlessly and frankly, *and stick to them*, to secure their hearty and early adoption by the great mass of the People. We have new confirmation of this view almost daily," Whig newspaper editor Horace Greeley confidently declared.

Clay certainly concurred in Greeley's assessment. But all the good he had done himself during the more than two months of campaigning across the South would be undone in North Carolina's capital city.

"IF WE CANNOT BEAT VAN BUREN, WE CAN BEAT NO ONE"

The Democrats had a frontrunner, too, but Martin Van Buren's position atop his party's heap of potential presidential candidates was considerably more tenuous than was Henry Clay's atop that of the Whigs.

The root of Van Buren's problem could be traced back to his selection as Andrew Jackson's vice presidential candidate in 1832. John C. Calhoun had resigned as vice president over a host of differences with Jackson. Van Buren thus succeeded Calhoun as Jackson's heir apparent. The move solidified the Democrats as a national party with wings in both North and South, with Calhoun on the outside looking in. His animus toward Van Buren would only grow over the years.

As 1844 had approached, Calhoun was still entertaining thoughts of making a run for the presidency himself, and he had the support of several supposed allies of President Tyler, including Abel Upshur. Calhoun had been a driving force behind Upshur's policy of challenging the British over Texas, and of US overtures to the Lone Star Republic. They viewed the challenge in the same Southern light. But the support of Upshur and other like-minded Southerners (and a few New York free traders) was not enough. And Calhoun, unlike Clay, would not campaign. He remained sentimentally attached to an earlier age and considered the type of campaign trips on which Clay regularly embarked to be demeaning. In this, Calhoun was misreading the electorate, which was increasingly democratic (small *d*) and wanted to see and hear the candidates.

As the new Congress assembled, anti–Van Buren forces set up a test of strength in the House, moving to require a two-thirds majority for the election of various party leadership posts. They felt sure they could block the chosen candidates of the Little Magician, damage his power base, and reveal his weaknesses. They failed mightily. That failure, John Quincy Adams averred, proved "there is no schism in the Democratic party, and not the shadow of a party for the election of John Tyler." Van Buren's success in this public forum, coupled with support he won at a dozen state conventions in all regions of the country, gave him the appearance of invincibility. It also scared off a number of second- and third-tier hopefuls, including former vice president Richard Mentor Johnson and future president James Buchanan, whose December 14, 1843, announcement was "dictated by an anxious desire to drive discord from the ranks of the party." (Buchanan was another potential candidate that Tyler would try, without success, to nominate to the Supreme Court to get him out of the way.) The scattering did nothing to guarantee Van Buren's inevitability, despite appearances.

Lewis Cass of Michigan was among those not scared off, and he won some early anti–Van Buren backing. Cass was a man of the West, of long accomplishment, with a military and diplomatic record. He had been hailed as a hero by expansionists when he resigned as minister to France in protest over the Webster-Ashburton Treaty, which settled a number of outstanding disputes between the United States and Great Britain but left in place the joint occupancy of Oregon that the countries had agreed to in 1818. Expansionists objected to the lack of progress on the Oregon question, and Cass felt he could carry their banner.

But Cass had never been elected to anything and had little political infrastructure in place. Cass's main qualification seemed to be that he "had, during a longer period, perhaps, than any other member of General Jackson's cabinet, except Mr. Van Buren, been linked with him in social and political intercourse," according to a campaign biographer. Unfortunately for Cass, Jackson at this point was still solidly behind Van Buren. When the time came for him to abandon his protégé, the old general had someone other than Cass in mind.

Personalities aside, Van Buren also faced fissures in the party over policy. On expansion, the party was divided mostly over means and timing, although Northern Democrats were increasingly wary of lining up with the South on anything that might expand slave territory. Without Jackson's stern hand, some (again, mostly Northern) Democrats had begun moving toward the Whigs on the tariff, the bank, even internal improvements, the sine qua non of Henry Clay's American System and the great dividing line between the Jacksonian and Whiggish visions of the role of the federal government. The 1842 tariff, of which Clay was so proud and for which he credited the economic recovery, was supported by a number of Van Burenite Democrats. An attempt to lower the tariff in May 1844 failed, with twenty-eight Democrats siding with all but one Whig to kill the effort.

A *Harper's Weekly* cartoon early in the campaign season summed up Van Buren's plight. Literally jockeying for position, Van Buren is one of several horses representing various candidates, ridden by Missouri Democratic senator Thomas Hart Benton, who says, "I am afraid my Poney has been too badly beaten by old Tip ever to run again," a reference to Van Buren's crushing defeat at the hands of William Henry Harrison in the "Tippecanoe and Tyler Too" campaign of 1840.

Whigs were sure that Van Buren would be the weakest possible candidate the Democrats could field. "If we cannot beat Van Buren," wrote North Carolina's Willie P. Mangum, "we can beat no one."

Calhoun seemed to be more worried about Van Buren winning than losing the nomination himself. The growing apostasies on the bank, the tariff, and federal spending, and the hesitancy on expansion, helped confirm for the South Carolinian that Northern Democrats could never be fully trusted to protect Southern prerogatives. Faced with Van Buren's demonstrated strength, Calhoun had all but decided by the turn of the year that he would not be a candidate for president, although he had won a delay—until late May—in the timing of the party's convention. A friend, Robert Barnwell Rhett, suggested it might be time to stand back from the worries of this world and begin to think about the next. "Let me implore you, my aged friend and political father, to seek God in Christ," Calhoun was advised in December. A month later, Calhoun withdrew his name from consideration for the Democratic nomination. But he did not withdraw from public life. The "aged" nullifier had plenty of energy left, and he saw one more crucial task in front of him: ensuring that Van Buren would not be the nominee.

Four Letters

Because of Abel Upshur's death aboard the *Princeton*, Calhoun was perfectly positioned to make good his vow to deprive Van Buren of the nomination. When Tyler sent the Texas annexation treaty to the Senate on April 22, his secretary of state sent along with it a compendium of documents related to the negotiations. Included among these papers was a letter Calhoun had written four days earlier to Sir Richard Pakenham, Britain's minister to the United States, that explained the American justification for annexation— or, at least, Calhoun's interpretation of that justification.

Typically, such interbranch sharing of diplomatic communications remained private. The letter would have caused a considerable stir among lawmakers even as a privileged Senate document. But Calhoun's letter was so explosive that Benjamin Tappan, a Democratic senator from Ohio and the brother of abolitionists Arthur and Lewis Tappan, leaked the contents to the *New York Post*. The newspaper ran what came to be known as the "Pakenham Letter" on April 27. Tappan was no abolitionist like his brothers, but he was also no fan of Tyler or the way he had handled Texas. The chairman of the Foreign Relations Committee, Virginian William Archer, wanted Tappan expelled from the Senate. His colleagues settled for a lesser punishment, voting 38–7 to censure Tappan on May 10. But the damage to the pro-annexation forces—and to Van Buren—was done.

The Pakenham Letter was Calhoun's way to settle all scores: with the self-righteous Brits for what he saw as their hypocrisy on emancipation and their interference in Texan and American affairs; and with Northern Democrats (and Van Buren in particular) for what he knew was their (and his) perfidy on the question of slavery. For as long as there had been a Democratic Party, with Northern and Southern wings, its members had tried to finesse the question, leaving the South to its own devices for the most part. Van Buren, as vice president and then president, had been the crucial figure in this game, a Northern man with Southern sympathies, protected from Southern radicals by the shield of Jackson. But Calhoun saw the future—a stronger, more populous North that would be less and less willing to defer—and he wanted his Northern party brethren, at long last, to take sides before time ran out. Framing Texas annexation as a question of Southern rights would put Northern Democrats on the spot in a way nothing else could.

The letter itself is a compendium of virulent racism (even for its own time), bad statistical analysis, and anti-British paranoia, "expressed in the most awkward, inelegant, and bungling manner." Calhoun accused Britain of plotting to fund the purchase of Texas's slaves with the purpose of freeing them—an idea that Calhoun might have actually believed but that Britain could neither afford nor hope to accomplish.

"So long as Great Britain confined her policy to the abolition of slavery in her own possessions and colonies, no other country had a right to complain," Calhoun wrote. "But when she goes beyond, and avows it as her settled policy, and the object of her constant exertions, to abolish it throughout the world, she makes it the duty of all other countries, whose safety or prosperity may be endangered by her policy, to adopt such measures as they may deem necessary for their protection." He used outdated and otherwise questionable numbers in assessing the health and welfare of free blacks versus slaves. And he included the usual arguments claiming the inferiority of blacks versus whites. Adams said Calhoun's analysis "betray[ed] so total a disregard for all moral principle that it can be attributed only to the alternative of absence of honesty or of mental sanity."

Calhoun risked alienating Northern Democrats more than they already were, although his arguments would not have been a novelty to them. They had heard them before, from Calhoun and others. He did not yet know it, but Calhoun had an important ally. Andrew Jackson's confidant, the Washington editor Francis P. Blair, had warned Jackson that Calhoun was up to no good. If Calhoun was paranoid about Britain's motives, Blair was paranoid about Calhoun's. The South Carolinian, Blair told Jackson, would "drive off every Northern man from the reannexation," part of his design to split the union and "make himself the great man of this fragment which he expects to tear from the embrace of our glorious Govt."

Jackson for the most part agreed with Blair. Like Van Buren, he had avoided the Texas question during the later years of his presidency because he feared it would mean war with Mexico and a splitting of the party. Now, though, he thought the time might be ripe. He had a dim view of Calhoun's rationalization: "How many men of talents want good common sense," was his commentary. But on the central argument—that Texas was a question that now required immediate attention because of the threat from Britain—Jackson was all in. While Whigs generally, and Clay in particular, dismissed the possibility of Britain making a power play on Texas, the idea had been born not in the mind of Democratic annexationists but in the mind of Sam Houston. An envoy from Houston to Jackson had suggested that, if annexation were not forthcoming, the Lone Star Republic "may look to a better reception from the grandmother" country than the mother country. Houston had also made a similar pitch to the British themselves. So Jackson was urging "immediate annexation as not only important but indispensable." That was not good news for Van Buren.

The Pakenham Letter helped give Calhoun something he had lost by late 1843—a modicum of control over the agenda of the Democratic Party. Jackson had no intention of collaborating with his old enemy, even in the cause of annexation. But Van Buren, who would have preferred to remain silent or at least neutral on Texas, would now have to speak. "The Texian question is exciting deep feelings here [Washington] & Clay & Van are both in a quandary," noted Representative Cave Johnson, a close confidant of James K. Polk. Anything Van Buren said would run the risk of alienating enough Democrats to deprive him of the nomination. No one could predict how many would abandon him, or how many he needed to keep on board to preserve his nomination. But that was theory. In practice, the number of alienated Democrats necessary to bring on Van Buren's demise was only one, if his name was Andrew Jackson.

On the same day the *New York Post* ran the Pakenham Letter, two Washington papers—the Whig-aligned *National Intelligencer* and the Democratic *Globe*—ran letters from Henry Clay and Martin Van Buren explaining why each man was opposed to immediate annexation.

An unpledged delegate to the Democratic convention, Representative W. H. Hammet of Mississippi, had written to Van Buren in March to
inquire about his views on annexation. Other letters had also come. This
was a common practice of the day, a way to get candidates on the record on
important issues. Usually such letters came from political opponents, trying
to draw out a response that might serve the candidate badly. Allies advised
Van Buren to dodge. New York senator Silas Wright told Van Buren that
"the excitement [Texas] will produce will surpass any I have witnessed." Van
Buren ignored the doomsaying and on April 20 answered Hammet. Unlike
Clay, Van Buren seemed to have a firm grasp on the importance of the issue.
"It is not only a question of intense interest to every part of the country, but
is unhappily also one in regard to which we may not promise ourselves that
unanimity in opinions which is so important when great national questions
like this are to be decided," he wrote.

Like Clay, though, Van Buren had absolute confidence in his ability to
split the difference on any issue, no matter how divisive. In what one historian dubbed a "long-winded, complex and typically cautious argument," Van
Buren sought to keep open the possibility of annexation without making any
commitments about timing. He worried about Mexico's reaction and saw the
likelihood of war. Texas, Van Buren argued in his inimitable style for intrigue,
should be held in abeyance until the United States needed it for some other
purpose, such as leverage in some unnamed negotiation in the future.

Reaction was swift and hostile to the Hammet Letter. Thomas Ritchie,
editor of the *Richmond Enquirer* and an important and long-standing supporter of Van Buren, jumped ship immediately. He mailed to Van Buren
a collection of the letters the newspaper had received in protest, and a personal letter that, in effect, called on Van Buren to get out of the race. Van
Buren's continued presence as a candidate, Ritchie told the New Yorker,
would "insure beyond the probability of a doubt, the triumphant election
of the profligate politician perhaps in our country." Senator William H.
Roane, another key figure in the so-called Richmond Junto (the Democratic powerbrokers who led the party in Virginia) had once kept Van Buren
informed about the secret Texas negotiations. Roane had referred to Texas
as the "Botany Bay for all the human refuse of the Southwest." Now he, too,
told Van Buren that the Old Dominion was a lost cause for the New Yorker.

Ritchie's imploring and visions of Clay victorious didn't move Van
Buren, nor did the protests from virtually every other corner of the Democracy. But one man's objection would gain Van Buren's ear. "I have shed
tears of regret," wrote Andrew Jackson upon hearing of the Hammet Letter.
"I would to God I had been at Mr. V. B. elbow when he closed his letter.
I would have brought to his view the proper conclusion." To Van Buren
directly he wrote that it was now "impossible to elect him."

Combined with the deviations from orthodoxy that Van Buren and
some of his congressional supporters had already espoused, standing apart
on the immediate annexation of Texas—and losing the essential support of
Jackson—doomed Van Buren. Somewhere, Calhoun was smiling.

Clay had written his letter on April 17, during his campaign stop in
Raleigh, North Carolina. The "Raleigh Letter" was classic Clay. He would
be happy to welcome Texas into the union if it could be done with Mexico's
assent. Clay knew as well as anyone that such assent would not be forthcoming. He saw in annexation the evil designs of sectionalists. "I conceive that
no motive for the acquisition of foreign territory would be more unfortunate
than that of obtaining it for the purpose of strengthening one part against
another part of the common confederacy," Clay wrote, anticipating Calhoun's
Pakenham Letter. "Such a principle, in practical operation, would menace the
existence if it did not certainly sow the seeds of a dissolution of the union."

In tone and substance, Clay's letter echoed Van Buren's. The similari-
ties were so great that many suspected collaboration. Van Buren had gone
to Ashland in 1842 to meet with Clay. The two wily politicians must have
cooked up an agreement to keep Texas out of the 1844 campaign, many
supposed. This was not hard to believe. Van Buren's reputation for skulldug-
gery and lack of principle was widely accepted, "the exemplar and chief
of sordid politicians—of men who recognize in the party strifes of a Free
People no great and generous purposes, no idea of improving, informing
and elevating the mass of men, but a mere game in which voters are the
dice, and the most skilful or least scrupulous player must win," as one Whig
newspaper put it. And for those with long memories, such a deal recalled
the supposed "corrupt bargain" of 1824 between Clay and John Quincy
Adams that handed the New Englander the presidency and Clay the State
Department, and blocked their hero, Jackson, from his rightful spot in the

White House. But there was no deal, shifty or otherwise; only two cautious politicians who feared, for reasons that mirrored one another, that talking about Texas would ruin their chances of election.

Clay's objections to annexation went beyond the spread of slavery and fears of disunion. He didn't want the United States to take on Texas's $13 million in debt. He pooh-poohed the notion that Great Britain was interfering in Texas or with slavery. The onetime advocate of conquering Canada—it could be accomplished by the "militia of Kentucky . . . alone"— now foresaw a future in which an independent Canada and an independent Texas would join with the United States to buttress North America against European meddling. He argued that the country didn't need to get any bigger. "We have been seriously charged with an inordinate spirit of territorial aggrandizement; and, without admitting the justice of the charge, it must be owned that we have made vast acquisitions of territory within the last forty years," he pointed out. And, because he didn't care much, Clay thought nobody cared much. This rush to annexation, he concluded, was "not called for by any general expression of public opinion." Texas, in short, was not worth fighting for. "Annexation and war with Mexico are identical," Clay explained. "Now, for one, I certainly am not willing to involve this country in a foreign war for the object of acquiring Texas. I know there are those who regard such a war with indifference and as a trifling affair, on account of the weakness of Mexico, and her inability to inflict serious injury upon this country. But I do not look upon it thus lightly."

The War Hawk of 1812 who had urged a fight against the richest, most powerful empire on Earth—on dubious grounds—now opposed Texas annexation because it might mean war with a poor, weak neighbor. The man who in 1810 had boldly declared that he would "prefer the troubled ocean of war, demanded by honor and independence of the country, with all its calamities, and desolations, to the tranquil, putrescent pool of ignominious peace," now had come to "regard all wars as great calamities, to be avoided, if possible, and honorable peace as the wisest and truest policy of this country."

Days before he was to be nominated by the Whig Party convention, Clay had, it appeared, mortally wounded his own candidacy. Except that, on the same day, in the capital city's Democratic organ, Martin Van Buren had committed the same sin. In fact, for Van Buren, it was an even graver one. Clay, at least, had a substantial and vocal element in his party that opposed annexation. While many Northern Democrats resisted the temptation of Texas, they were quickly becoming a minority in their own party. Clay had injured himself in a way that would affect him in the general election. Whigs were not so much upset about what Clay had said, but that he had spoken at all on the subject. Democrats were upset about the substance of what Van Buren had said, all but guaranteeing he would never get to the general election.

Four days before the Pakenham, Hammet, and Raleigh letters appeared in print, another precinct was heard from, but hardly anybody noticed.

James K. Polk, former Speaker of the House, was running for vice president, not president. He had maneuvered all spring in hopes of landing himself on the ticket with Van Buren. As a potential national figure, though, like Clay and Van Buren he had received letters asking for his opinion on the great question of the day. On April 23, Polk responded to one from a group of antislavery Ohioans that included Salmon P. Chase. "I have no hesitation in declaring, that I am in favour of the immediate reannexation of Texas to the territory and Government of the United States," he wrote. Polk went on to provide his version of the history of the loss of Texas, "most unwisely ceded away" by John Quincy Adams in the Adams-Onis Treaty that won Florida from Spain. Going beyond the scope of Chase's question, Polk called for bringing Oregon as well as Texas into the American orbit. "Let the fixed policy of our Government be, not to permit Great Britain or any other foreign power to plant a colony or hold dominion over any portion of the people or territory of either." Unlike Calhoun, he didn't mention slavery. Unlike Clay and Van Buren, he didn't equivocate. Unlike all three, Polk's letter didn't cause much of a stir when it appeared. But it wouldn't be too long before people began paying attention.

"Still Born into Oblivion"

The possibility of war with Mexico was on every politician's mind. It was also on the mind of Samuel Colt.

Concurrent with the final pre-convention maneuverings in Washington, the National Institute for the Promotion of Science was conducting the nation's first major scientific convention at the Treasury Department. The event was conducted under the auspices of the president, and members of the cabinet and diplomatic corps were in attendance. Benjamin Butler, a prominent supporter of Martin Van Buren, had come to town to attend the conference (and do a little pre-convention hobnobbing with the president and others). Among the subjects under scientific scrutiny that week was the "Origin, Duration and End of the World," the title of a lecture by one Dr. E. Nott. Also in attendance was Samuel F. B. Morse, who had earned a reputation as a fine painter before turning his attentions to inventing, along with a host of other inventors and would-be inventors who had come to demonstrate their wares.

Like his friend Morse, by 1844 Samuel Colt was already famous. His revolver had begun to revolutionize the use of firearms—they were especially popular in Texas—although his inability to persuade the US Army to adopt his design proved economically disastrous for his manufacturing company (and proved to Colt that the army lacked both imagination and good sense).

In truth, the youthful and arrogant Colt had tried to sell his guns to the army before they were fully ready. When the government balked after faulty trials in the late 1830s, he blamed his family, his colleagues, and the army. Eventually, he admitted the truth, confessing in 1840 that the prototypes of his Peacemaker—the same nickname Robert Stockton would apply to his faulty gun on the USS *Princeton*—were "got up in a great hurry" and "very imperfect."

Eventually, he would do better with firearms. But for now, Colt had another idea. In April 1844, less than two months after the explosion aboard the *Princeton*, he was ready to test that idea on a five-hundred-ton schooner anchored in the East Branch of the Potomac, off the Washington Navy Yard.

Getting to that point had been a struggle for the inventor, who had seen supporters back out, lose their influence, or die. He was chronically short of money because his business was failing and the government would not provide him working capital. This was, to a great extent, because Colt refused to divulge many of the details of his proposed weapon.

Colt's secretiveness about his "submarine battery"—an electric-powered underwater mine—was somewhat understandable. Having been jilted by

the government on his revolver and, he felt, abused again by bad production of a trial lot of his tinfoil cartridges by the Washington Arsenal, he was
suspicious of the capital city's ways. When he first approached the government to seek financing for the submarine battery in June 1841, therefore,
he vowed to avoid the Army Ordnance Office, which would have been the
usual route. Instead, he took into his confidence, at least partially, New
Jersey senator Samuel L. Southard, a Whig and former secretary of the navy
who had sponsored Colt's efforts to sell the revolver to that service branch,
and Major William Gibbs McNeill, a former member of the Army Corps
of Topographical Engineers. Southard, who could claim the late President
James Monroe as a personal friend, bypassed the army and wrote straight to
Tyler on behalf of Colt.

Colt then followed up with his own letter a few days later, writing to
Tyler that his invention "if adopted for the service of our Government, will
not only save them millions outlay for the construction of means of defence,
but in the event of foreign war, it will prove a perfect safeguard against all the
combined fleets of Europe, without exposing the life of our citizens." Colt
suggested a demonstration, and asked for $20,000 to pay for his expenses,
along with guaranteed future payments "as a premium for my secret."

Southard persuaded Congress to appropriate $50,000 for the develop-
ment of naval ordnance. There was no specific line item included for Colt's
work, but both Southard and Navy Secretary George E. Badger were oper-
ating under the assumption that some of the money would go to their pet
project. Unfortunately for Colt, on September 10, Badger and the rest of
Tyler's cabinet, except for Secretary of State Daniel Webster, resigned over
dissatisfaction with Tyler's swing away from Whig policies. Seven months
later, Southard died. For the moment, Colt was left without a patron.

But not for long. McNeill interceded on Colt's behalf with the new navy
secretary, Abel P. Upshur, in November 1841. Colt and Upshur must have
hit it off, because the inventor opened up with the secretary as he had with
no one else, revealing "the whole plans and secrets of my inventions." This
worked. Now all that was needed, Upshur told Colt, was a demonstration
showing that the weapon was capable of "blowing up a vessel at a distance
beyond the range of an enemy's shot." Upshur gave Colt $6,000 out of the
$50,000 naval ordnance appropriation to get started, and Colt used this

seed money to persuade private investors, including McNeill and Southard, just months before his death, to pony up more.

The ever-secretive Colt still filed no patent application. This allowed him to continue developing the device, and probably more important from Colt's point of view, kept it away from the curious gaze of army officialdom. The Corps of Engineers' job was to build things. Colt knew they'd rather be building and arming forts—recall the ungunned Fort Washington on the Potomac below the capital—than helping to develop weapons that he believed would make such forts redundant. The more the brass knew, Colt feared, the more likely it would "excite the jealousy of the officers of the Army & Navy (particularly that portion of them that are exeld in putting together stone and mortar)" and the more likely Colt's "invention will be still born into oblivion."

With money in hand, Colt spent two years developing the system. He worked with Morse, a New York neighbor, to improve the underwater cable that delivered the charge to the gunpowder-powered mine. Colt got another congressional appropriation to continue his work in 1842, and may have been aided in his quest for respect for innovation by the continuing success Morse was enjoying. In any case, after three years of work, in April 1844 he was ready for his submarine battery to be put to the test.

The city was abuzz in anticipation of the "blow up," as the newspapers were calling it. While the president, members of Congress, clerks, and cooks found their way to good viewing spots on rises above the Navy Yard, no military professionals bothered to note where Colt had set up his observation post, or detailed his preparations, or recorded for posterity a time line that could prove useful in judging the work. Apparently, Colt had arrived early enough to get set up before they noticed. The navy provided anchors, boats, timber, mooring line, and navigational charts, and by April 1 Colt had "fortified the river leding to the Navy Yard & the ship is to be got under way with all her sails set & blown up while at her greatest speed." And, while Colt didn't want to tell the brass what he was doing, he kept the press informed enough that they were able to warn onlookers away from the path of danger.

On April 13, the day of the test, a skeleton crew boarded the ship the *Styx* and set sail. From his vantage point (his exact location is lost to history, a victim of Colt's secretiveness), Colt fired a pistol shot to signal that he was ready to begin. The crew aboard the vessel then lowered the topsail three times and hauled down the American flag, to cheers from the crowd of onlookers, and took it with them as they loaded into a smaller boat and rowed away.

Thousands of people were watching from shore, including much of official Washington. It was sunny and warm, late in the afternoon, and the anxious crowd had been gathering for some time, pushing closer to the water as it lapped against the bank. In addition to the people standing along the shore, the heights surrounding the Eastern Branch were populated by men on horseback, families in carriages, and mothers trying to keep their children from straying down the embankments. Despite the newspapers' warnings, several boaters were in evidence, trying to get as close a view as possible from out in the river.

Paddling furiously to get away from the target vessel, the crew fired a signal flare to alert Colt that they had reached a safe distance. Two decoy explosions disappointed the crowd, and a murmur arose. "Ah, what a pity, it is a failure," was the cry as the first of the two went off, then the second was followed by "Oh, he has missed her!" Now that Colt had their attention, he was ready for the main event. The crowd buzzed as the crew rowed to safety, and then heard "a low and peculiar sound" and saw "a most beautiful jet, of mingled water, fire and smoke." The jet shot high into the air, then "fell back in white translucent masses, the smoke, colored by the sun's rays with all the dyes of the prism, slowly melted into the air, while the grains of wet powder, ignited and smoking, fell in soft showers upon the bright surface of the river." The *Styx* was wrecked, "shattered to atoms," as one newspaper reporter described it. "The fore part of the vessel was lifted up almost out of the water, and then immediately sank, while the stern continued above water, and the mizzenmast was left still standing, though in an inclined position." It was, all agreed, "a wreck in the highest degree picturesque."

The weapon did what Colt said it would do, at least under the controlled circumstances of a more or less static test in calm waters. But Colt's furtiveness was wearing on those who would have to make a decision about funding the project further and making it part of the plan for national defense.

And again, as had happened with Southard, tragedy intervened. Upshur's death on the *Princeton* had not only cost Colt a high-level supporter, but also the only man in government with whom Colt had trusted his secrets. Upshur might have been an effective advocate for Colt with his former department, the army, and Congress. Now that he and his knowledge were gone, all that was left was Colt's sense of defensiveness. He was suspicious of the motives of the army and the congress, and of their ability to make an informed decision.

Lawmakers and executive branch officials were suspicious right back. Secretary of War William Wilkins wrote to the distinguished chemist Robert Hare, a professor at the University of Pennsylvania, asking for Hare's "views in reference to the claims which Mr. Colt's methods may have to originality."

Hare couldn't claim, as did McNeill, to be a close friend of James Monroe. But he did claim that as a child he was dandled on the knee of George Washington, an indication that he was lacking in neither self-confidence nor ego. He quickly replied to Wilkins, leaving no doubt as to his position, which was that the "galvanic process employed by Mr. Colt has not the slightest claims to originality." Hare went on to cite several instances of his own work and that of others disproving, he was certain, any claims of originality or invention by Colt. Magnanimously, he did consider himself "ready to admit that Mr. Colt must have been judicious and skillful in availing himself of the means which he has owed to the invention of others." As for using any such device as a weapon against "movable bodies like ships of war," Hare considered such a proposition to be "very precarious," echoing Wilkins's own concerns.

Joseph Henry, another eminent scientist polled by Wilkins, told the secretary much the same thing. "The method now generally used was made public in 1832, and is the invention of Dr. Hare, of Philadelphia," Henry wrote. Like Hare, though, Henry credited Colt with some originality of application, and for the "industry and practical skill with which he has brought them before the public."

Colt never claimed originality, and specifically gave credit to others for the underlying technology as early as May 1843. It was his application of the technology for which he claimed credit and wanted to be paid. But it was not to be. Hare's and Henry's opinions carried great weight with law-makers. Colt's secrecy and stubbornness did not. Not even the crisis atmosphere surrounding the Texas annexation and perceived threats from Great Britain could sway the decision makers. Wilkins rejected Colt's proposal, delaying for a generation the development of effective underwater mines for the US Navy.

{ 4 }

"WHO THE DEVIL IS POLK?"

The Whig convention assembled at 11 AM on May 1 at Baltimore's Calvert Street Universalist Church. After a few preliminary housekeeping motions and a scripture reading (the fifth chapter of Ephesians), the delegates got right to the point.

Benjamin Watkins Leigh, a delegate from Virginia and one of Clay's closest friends, rose to say that the choice for president was so obvious that no formal nomination process was necessary. He offered a resolution "that this convention do unanimously nominate and recommend to the People of the United States, HENRY CLAY, of Kentucky for next President of the United States."

The motion was greeted by enthusiastic cheering, the tossing of hats into the air and the waving of handkerchiefs. When order was restored after several minutes, Leigh's resolution was put to a vote, with shouted "ayes" resounding through the hall, and nary a "nay" to be heard. Another demonstration broke out, again lasting several minutes. When quiet finally prevailed, a committee was appointed to inform Clay of the honor that had been bestowed upon him and, in a break with protocol, to invite him to attend in person.

Clay, "weather beaten" and "hoarse" from his recent travels, declined the invitation to accept the nomination in person, displaying a rare case of reticence for fear of offending his own and the nation's "sense of delicacy and propriety." He thereby missed the opportunity to go down in history as the first candidate to address his party's convention.

The remaining business was to select a vice presidential candidate and write a party platform. The platform was easy. In about a hundred words, the Whigs resolved what they had always resolved: a well-regulated currency; a tariff for revenue to pay the expenses of government and to protect selected industries; distribution of the revenue from the sale of public lands; and a weaker executive branch, with a single term for the president. There was no mention of Texas, annexation, or slavery. Whigs wanted to build up the country that existed, not diffuse economic growth westward, a position party historian Daniel Walker Howe called "qualitative development" over "quantitative extension."

The vice presidency was a bit more complicated. Clay disavowed any interest in dictating the choice to the convention. But he had been thinking about a running mate for the better part of a year. His favorite was John Clayton, a former (and future) senator from Delaware. But Clayton publicly declined any interest in the number-two spot, and Clay began to look at other options: former New York congressmen Millard Fillmore and Francis Granger, General Winfield Scott, John Davis of Massachusetts, who had served in the House and Senate with Clay, and John Sergeant, another former House member from Pennsylvania. Even Daniel Webster's name came up, but the simmering rivalry between the two giants—both men had seen themselves as presidential material for almost three decades—made such a combination impractical.

Fillmore, Davis, and Sergeant would have their names placed in nomination, along with Theodore Frelinghuysen of New Jersey, a former senator and mayor, current chancellor of New York University, and a leading light of the Benevolent Empire.

Frelinghuysen led on the first ballot, with 103 votes, to 83 for Davis, 53 for Fillmore, and 38 for Sergeant. Without a majority, a second ballot was required. Frelinghuysen picked up ten votes, mostly from Delaware and South Carolina, at the expense of all three of the other candidates. On the third ballot Sergeant dropped out, Frelinghuysen won the majority, and the convention then nominated him by acclamation.

It was a remarkable move, considering Whig history. Once again, the party had chosen a vice presidential candidate almost as an afterthought, a process that had not served the Whigs well in 1840. As the list of candidates suggested, a Northern man was needed to balance Clay. It's also likely that many delegates and party leaders felt a conspicuously moral man was needed to balance Clay. If Clay was the beau ideal of Whiggery, a man of the people with a streak of impishness, Frelinghuysen was its conscience.

No man better personified the political/religious culture of the party than Theodore Frelinghuysen. Clay was known as something of a religious non-practitioner, if not exactly a skeptic, as a man who enjoyed a drink and who attended horse races and bet on them, and there were always whispers about Clay and the ladies. No such vices attached to Theodore Frelinghuysen, a descendant of Revolution-era patriots and of New Jersey's most prominent revivalist of the First Great Awakening. He had learned law from the father of Robert Stockton, commander of the *Princeton*. He was the type of politician mothers named their children for. Frelinghuysen was an active member or a leader in a host of moral improvement groups—the American Board of Commissioners for Foreign Missions, the American Bible Society, the American Tract Society, the American Sunday School Union, the American Temperance Union—that tied together political activism with the religious spirit of the Second Great Awakening. He had been a vociferous and eloquent opponent of Andrew Jackson's plan to remove the Cherokee and other southern Indian tribes to the west, a cause to which Clay was a latecomer. He was not an abolitionist but, like Clay, had been a supporter of the American Colonization Society, which hoped to win gradual emancipation and send the freed blacks to Africa. He stood first, in the words of his biographer Robert J. Eells, as "representative of a culturally transforming Protestant Whiggery in antebellum America."

Clay had many of the same reforming impulses, but his was a political rather than a religious affiliation. This dichotomy would follow reform movements all through American history. While Frelinghuysen believed in using moral suasion to make people want to live better lives, many of Clay's political followers, and occasionally Clay himself, wanted to change the law to require them to live better lives. The premier historian of the Whig Party said Frelinghuysen "personified the reform impulse of American Protestantism."

For one slice of the electorate—recently arrived Irish Catholic immigrants concentrated in the Northeast—that was just the problem. Even if they accepted that Frelinghuysen was not personally bigoted, his close ties to some who were—and his participation in organizations that were honeycombed with anti-Catholic sentiment—made him an easy target, one the Democrats would make full use of in the fall campaign.

For Whigs, those worries lay in the future (though not as far in the future as they may have thought). At the conclusion of their harmonious one-day convention, Whigs were sanguine. With the Kentuckian Clay—good old Harry of the West—at the top of the ticket, the God-fearing Frelinghuysen in second place, and Texas casting the Democrats into turmoil, the Whigs left Baltimore in a state of electoral giddiness. But it wouldn't last long.

LIBERTY AND BIBLES

In 1844 abolitionism was still more political irritant than juggernaut. Despite the fears of Calhoun and others that abolitionists were gaining ground, the political arm of the movement, the Liberty Party, had won a paltry 7,069 votes in the 1840 presidential contest, less than one-third of one percent of the total.

The Liberty Party—"conceived in frustration and self-delusion," as one historian of the abolition movement put it—was the mainstream antislavery movement's answer to William Lloyd Garrison's 1839 call for the North to secede and leave the South to its slaveholding self. Unlike Garrison, who saw the Constitution and the American union as fatally flawed because of slavery, Liberty Party joiners were not yet ready to take such a radical step. Rather, like other Whiggish members of the Benevolent Empire, they believed that American society was, if not perfectible, certainly not beyond saving.

The party's dismal showing in 1840 did not discourage its small band of dedicated adherents. Salmon Chase, one of the instigators of the Texas letter to Polk, hoped to persuade a well-known figure to take up the party's banner, and appealed to John Quincy Adams, former New York governor William H. Seward, and William Jay, a judge and son of Founding Father John Jay. But in late August 1843, a thousand delegates from a dozen states, including leading Millerite Elon Galusha, gathered in Buffalo, New York. As had their predecessors four years earlier, they nominated James G. Birney, a native of Kentucky, scion of a wealthy slave-owning family and a former slaveholder himself, for president, and former Ohio Democratic senator Thomas Morris for vice president. An early supporter of colonization, like Frelinghuysen, Birney abandoned that philosophy in 1834 and aligned himself with the more radical Kentucky Anti-Slavery Society. Not surprisingly, he encountered considerable local opposition. Mobs confronted him; his mail was pilfered. Birney soon moved across the river to Ohio and became editor of an antislavery newspaper, the *Philanthropist*, before moving on to New York.

A few party members had hoped to broaden the movement's appeal by moving the party beyond the issue that had birthed it. Rejecting "with a strong hand" all efforts to write a broad-based platform, the Liberty Party would enter the election season focused solely on slavery.

Galusha was a delegate to the convention and other Millerites—including Gerrit Smith and William Miller himself—were strong advocates of abolition. In Miller's case, he was simply too single-minded to spend much time on such earthly concerns, and he saw the squabbling among antislavery factions as counterproductive. If Garrison saw Birney and the Liberty Party as too impure, and party members saw men such as Seward as too much a part of a corrupt system, Miller saw the whole lot as imperfect vessels. "While the pretended friends of the slave are expending all their ammunition on each other, the release of the captive will be little thought of," said Miller, to whom the true deliverer of the slave was clear. "God can and will release the captive. And to him alone we must look for redress."

Birney and his party mates believed God would help those who helped themselves. In August 1843 they had no idea how crucial a role slavery and its ancillary issues would play in the next election. In New York, one of the party's strongest states, Democrats would claim victory in the fall 1843 elections in large part because abolitionist voters abandoned the Whigs. In the coming presidential election of 1844, seven thousand votes shifting nationwide from antislavery Whigs to Birney probably wouldn't mean much in the grand scheme of things; they certainly hadn't hurt William Henry Harrison in 1840. But if that vote total grew by any substantial amount—and who knew what sort of trouble the agitation over Texas might brew—it could cost Clay a state or two. In a close election, that would make all the difference.

The Liberty Party posed a potential problem for the Whigs, though no one could yet say how much of a problem. A far more threatening portent arose just days after Clay's nomination in Baltimore, when anti-Catholic nativists held a rally in Philadelphia, only one hundred miles away, sparking a running street battle with working-class Irish immigrants in the Kensington neighborhood on the city's north side.

The proximate cause of the confrontation was Catholic opposition to the mandatory use of Protestant Bibles in the city's public schools, where the influx of Irish immigrant children was crowding the classrooms. But deeper resentments were percolating. The violence that was about to explode owed more to the clash of civilizations that was taking place in urban areas all over the Northeast than to a dispute about what version of the Bible school children would be required to read.

Two day after Clay's nomination, on Friday, May 3, nativists took to the streets of the Irish enclave. Their immediate goal was the construction of a speaker's platform from which to deliver a series of harangues. Work began in the early afternoon, with the platform being built against a fence in the schoolyard across the street from St. Michael's Church. Organizers had planned to start their outdoor meeting at 3 PM, but by that hour only about a hundred people, including some immigrants, had gathered around the construction site. But a small, steady stream of listeners kept arriving, so rather than wait any longer, the first speaker to address the crowd—newspaper editor Samuel R. Kramer—climbed up on the wooden platform and began.

"A set of citizens, German and Irish, wanted to get the Constitution of the United States into their own hands and sell it to a foreign power," Kramer bellowed. He was a member of the American Republican Party, which had been founded in the previous decade, then all but disappeared, only to be revivified in this presidential election year. The party's two stated goals were a twenty-one-year residence requirement for immigrants to vote and a constitutional amendment to block non-naturalized foreigners from holding public office. The party's unstated goal was to deny any political power to recent— mostly Catholic—immigrants, preserving such authority for themselves.

It didn't take long for the locals in the crowd to fire back at Kramer. "Come down here, you old son of a bitch," one yelled. Another appealed to an age-old Irish animosity, shouting that "it was not Americans speaking but the money of British Whigs." Others joined in. The crowd surged forward toward the rickety platform. Kramer and his compatriots on the stage sensed they might be in danger. He shouted out an invitation for an opposing viewpoint to meet him in debate. This garnered some hoots, and shouts of "Go on, boys!" as the assembled Irishmen pushed against the stage and began ripping it apart.

Kramer and the other nativists decided discretion was the better part of valor at that point, jumping down from the platform as it was dismantled and rapidly retreating to a nearby temperance hall. A few locals feigned pursuit, but most stayed behind to finish destroying the speaker's platform, claiming the lumber for firewood.

No one had been injured, but tempers remained raw over the weekend. Nativists, claiming the right to speak in public when and where they chose, rescheduled their meeting for Monday, May 6. They spent the weekend getting the word out, hoping to draw a much larger crowd of supporters that would outnumber the Irish.

Their canvassing paid off. On Monday afternoon, three thousand people filled the schoolyard and spilled into the surrounding streets. Kramer was back, determined to finish the speech he had begun on Friday. Another nativist, Peter Sken Smith, a local pol and brother of noted abolitionist and Liberty Party member Gerrit Smith, followed him. Halfway through Smith's oration, an Irishman pulled his horse and wagon into the middle of the assembled throng and dumped a load of manure (some said dirt) ten feet in front of where Smith was speaking. Undeterred by the filthy provocation, Smith finished his speech and handed the rostrum over to Lewis Levin, editor of the *Philadelphia Sun* newspaper, a temperance lecturer, and a leading light in the American Republican Party. Levin, who was Jewish, would soon parlay his anti-Catholic sentiments into a seat in the next Congress. On this day, aligned with the overwhelmingly Protestant nativists, he bemoaned the abuse of the vote by "foreign" elements. His next objection—to religious influence in politics—surely sounded tinny to the ears of his fellow temperance advocates, sons and daughters of the Second Great Awakening and foot soldiers in the Benevolent Empire.

Perhaps God, too, disagreed. Suddenly, a fast-moving thunderstorm swept over the city and interrupted Levin, forcing the speakers and the crowd down the street toward the Nanny Goat Market, the commercial and social center of the Irish Catholic neighborhood. This added a sense of disorder to an already tense situation as people began to scatter to get out of the rain.

Moving from the open space of the schoolyard into the partially enclosed market would doom any chance that Friday's relatively peaceful conclusion would be repeated.

As the mob moved toward the market, pushing and shoving broke out. About thirty locals were waiting at the entrance to the open stalls. "Keep the damned natives out of the market house," one yelled. "This ground don't belong to them, it's ours!" But most of the crowd—both nativist and Irish—made it into the market. Levin climbed up on one of the stalls and tried to restore order and resume his speech, but he was drowned out by cries of "now let's make a noise so he won't be heard." That led to more pushing and shoving, then to punching, then to stones, bricks, and clubs being wielded. Clearly, both sides had come prepared for violence.

A few potential peacemakers tried to intervene, but ended up joining the melee. Then a young nativist pulled a gun out, and an intemperate Irishman dared him to shoot. He did, and the fire was returned by another Irishman from the crowd. The outnumbered Irish hurled rocks and bricks in defense; the nativists appeared to be better armed and, at least inside the market, had numbers on their side. But, as in any pitched battle, those fighting on their home turf had a decided advantage. The covered, open-face stalls of the Nanny Goat Market provided protection from the rain, but did not afford much protection from an outburst of musket fire from the houses across the street.

As general mayhem erupted, noncombatants scattered. "Men with their wives, and often six or seven children, [were] trudging fearfully through the streets, with small bundles, seeking a refuge they knew not where," a contemporary chronicler noted melodramatically. "Mothers with infants in their arms, and little ones following after them, [were] carrying away from their homes whatever they could pick up at that instant, passing along with fearful tread, not knowing where to turn."

Facing gunfire from secure positions, the nativists dashed out of the market. But once in the street, their numerical advantage disappeared. Confronted by a superior force wielding bricks, stones, and broken glass, they quickly retreated back into the market. Their position, they realized, was becoming untenable. If they stayed here and fought, they'd be shot to pieces. If they tried to flee, the Irish mob might massacre them. So they huddled against the onslaught as best they could while a handful of hardy souls snuck out to get reinforcements.

In short order, eighteen men with muskets and rifles hurried to the scene, and the tide of the battle began to turn. The reinforced nativists broke out of the market and rushed up Cadwalader Street, where most of the Irish gunfire was coming from. They fired at the houses and assaulted doors and windows with clubs and bricks. The violence had reached a deadly equilibrium, with neither side able to dislodge the other. Finally, at about five o'clock, after almost two hours of fierce combat, the police arrived and the shooting stopped.

But gangs of both locals and nativists continued to mill around, and the bonfires lit by the Irish heightened the sense that this was no longer a city street but a battlefield. The sheriff, Morton McMichael, knew he couldn't keep the two sides apart with his scanty force, and so sent for the local militia, led by his friend, General George Cadwalader, commander of the City Division of the First Brigade of the Pennsylvania Militia. But friend or not, Cadwalader was reluctant to act, fearing that without proper executive approval, he or his men might be legally liable if someone ended up dead at their hands. After some haggling, he agreed to join McMichael, but only as an advisor and observer.

Overnight, most of the locals who had not already fled the neighborhood did so. Roving nativist mobs continued to attack houses, breaking windows and smashing in doors. The undermanned and ineffectual deputies could do little to stop them. The largest group of nativists set up shop outside the abandoned seminary of the Sisters of Charity. The sisters had relocated to Iowa, leaving the building in the hands of a Mrs. Baker. When she saw the crowd outside, silhouetted against the bonfire they had started, she came to the door and appealed for calm. Someone standing near the fire threw a rock that hit her, and she retreated inside. As the door closed, shots were fired from an open window in St. Michael's across the way. The nativists around the bonfire scattered, but two were lying in the street, bleeding. One was dead. The other would die a few weeks later.

More Irishmen, armed with rifles, shotguns, and pistols, headed for St. Michael's, which seemed to be the new defensive bastion. Nativists tried to regroup. They offered a reward for the capture of any Irish shooters, and spread the word about a meeting to be held the next afternoon in the State House Yard (known today as Independence Hall National Historic Site). Handbills were prepared that included the phrase "Let every man come armed to defend himself." Periodic gunfire was heard throughout the Kensington neighborhood all night long, but no more running battles were fought. As the sun rose on Tuesday, no one was sure what to expect. But few were expecting peace to return.

By Tuesday afternoon at three thirty, more than three thousand people assembled at the historic State House. Appeals for a peaceful demonstration led the proceedings. Thomas R. Newbold, publisher of the *Philadelphia North American*, pleaded for order and respect, the better to contrast with the "irrational" and "unpatriotic" behavior of the heathen Irish. The spirit did not last. The next speaker, militia colonel Charles J. Jack, a lawyer, reminded the crowd of their cause, to end "the influence of foreigners in the elections," and called for "a regiment of Native American volunteers to sustain the native citizens and the laws against the aggressions of foreigners."

When Pericles spoke, the people said, "How well he speaks." When Demosthenes spoke, the people said, "Let us march!" Newbold's Periclean appeal to reason stood little chance against the marching orders from Jack. Cries of "Let's go up to Kensington now!" arose from the crowd, and a file formed with Jack at its head, moving military-style out of the State House Yard.

The nativists figured the Irish were storing guns at Hibernia Hose House, the neighborhood fire station next to the Nanny Goat Market, so that became their first target. They pulled the hose carriage out and set about wrecking it, but before they could finish the job marksmen from surrounding houses opened fire and once more drove the nativists back into the cover of the market. Again fighting on their home ground, the Irish had the advantage, "little fellows scarce able to carry a musket, who laughed and hurrahed when shots were directed at themselves without effect." They also had a fresh cache of guns, and fired freely into the market from every conceivable angle. "Women, too, were busy, as in the French Revolution, cheering on the men and carrying weapons to them," according to a contemporary account. Nativist casualties mounted quickly.

But, just as had happened the previous day, the nativists found a way to counterattack. Several small groups broke out of the market and began setting homes on fire. The smoke and flames drove the Irish gunmen away from their cover. In a tragicomic irony, the flames spread to the Hibernia Hose House, leveling the neighborhood's fire protection. Again, the forces of civil order were slow to respond. None had been stationed in the neighborhood, a dereliction of duty considering the likelihood of trouble. When Cadwalader and McMichael finally arrived at the market with several companies of militia at about five o'clock, they put a quick end to the shooting, the militia leader having apparently decided that he would restore order and deal with any legal repercussions later.

The area around the market, the communal heart of the Irish neighborhood, was charred and abandoned. The only people left by evening were the militia. By Wednesday morning, militia leaders had concentrated their forces around St. Michael's, the highest-value target still standing. The curious had come to gaze at the destruction, adding another potentially dangerous element to the situation. More troops were pouring in all morning. Fire companies were hosing down the ruined remains of Irish homes, and some boys were sifting through the wreckage. But no shots were being fired, and no mobs were assembling.

However, small gangs of nativists were slipping back into the neighborhood and starting small fires. The militia, dominated by men generally sympathetic to the anti-Irish mobs, was reluctant to intervene in the absence of confrontational violence between the warring factions. The Irish, having largely abandoned the field, had effectively surrendered the right to have their property protected by civil authorities. Attempts by some locals to safeguard their homes by writing "No Popery Here" or "Native American" in chalk on their doors in hopes of keeping the wolves at bay proved futile.

Seeing that they could use the veneer of order and the militia's ambivalence to their advantage, the nativists moved against St. Michael's. They set two fires around the corner to draw away troops guarding the church. With the defenders distracted, nativists broke into the rectory and the church proper and set multiple fires. By the time the troops knew they had been duped, the church was ablaze. People who had been milling about the area flocked to the street in front of St. Michael's. When the steeple toppled and the cross atop it fell, nativists cheered and began singing the Orangemen's anthem "The Boyne Water," celebrating the victory of the Protestant William of Orange over the Catholic James II at the Battle of the Boyne in 1690.

> So praise God, all true Protestants, and I will say no further,
> But had the Papists gained that day, there would have been open murder.
> Although King James and many more were ne'er that way inclined,
> It was not in their power to stop what the rabble they designed.

Tasting success against the "rabble" and liking it, the mob moved on to the Sisters of Charity seminary and burned it to the ground as well. Another Catholic church, St. Augustine's, would also be felled by fire that night, although a nearby German Catholic church was spared, indicative of the nationalist as well as the religious aspect to the violence.

For the third day in a row, Cadwalader and McMichael were late to the scene. "Nothing was done on the part of the authorities to prevent these outrages," a witness wrote. "Mayor and sheriff are universally censured." Firefighters could do little more than hose down surrounding buildings to keep the fires from spreading. Finally, the mobs dispersed with the arrival of two units of militia from Germantown and an order from Mayor John M. Scott (who had stayed out of the conflict so far because Kensington was technically not within the city limits) barring civilians from the streets. That order was made effective by its accompanying order, delivered in the delicate language of the day, authorizing the militia to "employ such force of arms as may be necessary to compel obedience." In other words, they were ordered to shoot to kill any mobbers. Standing by just in case were crewmembers of the USS *Princeton*, lately recovered from the February explosion, "armed to the teeth, and ready to do battle, if their services should be required," a contemporaneous report noted.

Six people were known dead, all nativists, although some Irish residents who were never officially accounted for were likely burned to death in the ruined homes of Kensington. More than twenty from both sides had suffered serious injury. Hundreds of thousands of dollars' worth of property had been destroyed. The governor arrived and martial law was declared and maintained for a week. Volunteers were stationed at various hot spots, including a Catholic seminary where "there were about 40 of us, all very young, perfectly undisciplined," one of the civilian troops wrote. "I doubt much whether we could defend the building against a large number." And, at least in his case, it was "the first time in my life [I] had a musket on my shoulder." Fortunately, the green volunteers were not called on to defend the seminary. Catholic church services were suspended for May 12, but Mass was resumed a week later. A guarded stillness fell over the city. It would last less than two months. "An excitement has been roused which will be difficult to allay," a local diarist recorded, predicting that "our riots in future will assume a more dangerous character."

The political implications of the Bible Riot, as the incident absurdly came to be known, were not immediately apparent. The nativists complained that their right to peaceably assemble had been violated by Irish ruffians. The Catholic residents of the neighborhood were more interested in restoring peace and rebuilding their homes, but knowing they were the targets of organized political violence, they seemed unlikely to take it lying down. And Kensington was not an isolated incident. Only a month earlier, "quite a serious riot" had broken out in Brooklyn in which several people were wounded. It took gunfire from local militia, headed by the mayor, to quell the uprising. Irish wards in Manhattan were the scene of similar confrontations in April, the same month a nativist candidate was elected mayor of the city.

Again, the political fallout was not the first thing on anybody's mind. But the violence and the underlying causes of the hostility—economic, cultural, and religious—were bad news for a Whig ticket that included Protestant icon Theodore Frelinghuysen. John Quincy Adams confided to his diary that the situation had been "much aggravated by the pernicious factious influence of these Irish Catholics over the elections in all the populous cities." The Democratic paper in the capital city of James K. Polk's home state, the *Nashville Union*, said such anti-Catholic Whig rhetoric was the "true cause" of the disorder, a clear signal that Democrats were going to attempt to exploit the violence in the coming campaign.

European immigration in the eighteenth and early nineteenth centuries had built the United States. But that was almost exclusively a Northern European, Protestant phenomenon. As the century wore on, more and more Catholic immigrants from the German states and Ireland poured into America. Almost all ended up in the North. This population influx was part of what fueled John C. Calhoun's worries about declining Southern power.

But Calhoun and his fellow slave-owning Southerners were not the only ones worried. Northern Protestant workingmen who had seen their economic well-being destroyed by the Panic of 1837 and the ensuing depression resented the newcomers for driving down wages and filling the jobs they had once held—although the ranks of the nativists included not just workingmen but also professionals and artisans, lawyers and shopkeepers. The noneconomic elements mattered, too. Nativists despised the immigrants' Catholicism and feared supposed Popish plots to direct the political activities of the immigrants. Such fears were groundless, but concerns that immigrants would sign on as loyal Democrats and vote as a bloc were more firmly rooted in reality.

"The natural ally of [the nativist] party are the Whigs," wrote Sidney George Fisher, a Philadelphia diarist who was both a nativist and a Whig. "Their object harmonizes with the instincts and secret wishes and opinions of the Whigs."

"Tumbled About Their Ears"

While only a few days passed between publication of Clay's Raleigh Letter and the Whig convention, Democratic discontent with Van Buren's Hammet Letter would have a full month to simmer before the party gathered in Baltimore on May 27. "Vans opponents & the friends of Texas are outrageous & the chances now seem to be, that his nomination will be defeated," assessed Polk fixer Cave Johnson.

When Andrew Jackson got wind of Van Buren's missive on Texas, he was crestfallen, expressing "deep regret" at Van Buren's "fatal error." Whatever his personal disappointment with his New York protégé, Jackson moved swiftly to summon his home-state protégé, James K. Polk, to the Hermitage, Jackson's home in Tennessee, to discuss the next moves for "Young Hickory." Polk's plan all along had been to secure the Tennessee delegation's support for Van Buren, thereby making himself the logical choice to balance the ticket. If Van Buren's forces looked elsewhere for a vice president, then Polk would shift his delegates to Lewis Cass. Polk showed that he had control of the delegation at the state party convention in November 1843—at least so far as the vice presidential nomination was concerned—when Democrats endorsed Polk for VP and refused to cast their lot with Van Buren. That left their options open, which is what Polk needed them to be.

The strategy carried certain risks. Men like Pennsylvanian James Buchanan and Missouri Democrat Thomas Hart Benton, who saw themselves as potential future presidents, wouldn't want another future president in line behind either Van Buren or Cass. They saw Alabama senator William R. King as an acceptable alternative—a lesser light and no threat to their future plans. They couldn't come right out and say this, of course, so they couched their opposition to Polk in terms of his inability—refusal, in reality—to deliver Tennessee's delegation for Van Buren. Things got worse for Polk in January when Ohio, a state he considered crucial to his success, endorsed Richard Mentor Johnson for vice president.

But Van Buren's blunder on Texas altered the landscape. Now, Jackson insisted, Polk must put aside his carefully crafted plans to become vice president and instead make a run at the top of the ticket. Ideally, Van Buren would recognize the error of his ways and get out of the race. If not, Polk should challenge him directly. "General Jackson says the candidate for the first office should be an annexation man, and from the Southwest, and he and other friends here urge that my friends should insist upon that point," Polk wrote to Cave Johnson.

Polk, whose back-to-back losses in races for governor gave him legitimate reasons to be humble, called such a proposal "utterly abortive." Or perhaps he was being disingenuous. In truth, Johnson had broached the subject with the candidate and his wife, Sarah, as far back as January, writing to

Mrs. Polk that her husband was "now encountering the very identical difficulties as to the Vice that he would have to do for the first office of the
government and if he can overcome the one he could have done the other."
Polk knew that to prevail for either office, he would need Van Buren's delegates. So he listened attentively to Jackson, but kept his own counsel about
how he would proceed.

Doubts about Van Buren were creeping into the popular consciousness ahead of the convention. A cartoon in *Harper's Weekly* on May 22, five
days before the confab was to get underway, imagined Van Buren's funeral
with John Tyler as the hearse driver and Andrew Jackson as the nag pulling
the cart. The doubts were about more than Texas. Van Buren, having been
around for a long time, seemed to many to represent the past. He had loy-
ally served Jackson and non-radical Southern interests, but Southerners were
increasingly wary of any Northerner. "This undercurrent existed long before
Van's position as to Texas was known," observed Cave Johnson.

Alabama's William R. King, about to head to France as US minister
and no longer a vice presidential possibility, complained that "discontent,
division, despondency, seem to have taken complete possession of a large
portion of our prominent men; and, with a decided majority of the people
in our favor, we are about to be shamefully beaten, from a want of harmony,
and concert of action."

The Democrats convened at noon on Monday, May 27, meeting in the
cramped Egyptian Saloon on the top floor of the Odd Fellows Hall at 30
North Gay Street in Baltimore. It was quickly moved that this meeting
operate under the same rules that had existed at the previous party gatherings. It seemed to the uninitiated an unremarkable suggestion. But the
entire convention rested on the question. The tradition among Democrats
was to require a two-thirds vote to gain the nomination. If the rule stood,
it was easy to see that Van Buren would not be the nominee. It was much
harder to see who would be.

Just as the Democrats were getting down to business, forces loyal to John
Tyler were meeting across town at Calvert Hall, to lend an official imprimatur to the president's half-formed non-party candidacy. Tyler supposed that
about a thousand delegates were there. *Niles' Register*, a weekly magazine,
said the "room was not crowded and a large portion of the persons within

were spectators." Texas was the theme, at least as much as Tyler. Behind the speaker's rostrum were banners proclaiming "Tyler and Texas" and "Rannexation of Texas—Postponement is Rejection." After some introductory speeches, a proposal was made to wait and see whom the Democrats nominated, in the forlorn hope that a deadlocked Democracy might turn to Tyler as a compromise candidate. But the motion was rejected by acclamation and the delegates swiftly nominated Tyler. The whole thing took about an hour.

Over at the Odd Fellows Hall, things were not proceeding at quite the same brisk pace. Most of Monday afternoon was taken up with debate on the two-thirds rule and complaints about the small size of the room—it was the largest in the city but still too small for the number of attendees. Beyond the delegates, there were the usual hangers-on, the press, office holders, and office seekers. Bad acoustics, heat, and a lack of organization also plagued the event. In short, it was a typical party convention. By evening, deal making between delegates and campaign minions was in full flower. "There is so many rumors, so much excitement, that it seems impossible to come to any correct conclusions for the future," Cave Johnson reported to Polk. "Every thing is in doubt."

All those opposed to Van Buren were making direct appeals to state delegations, telling each what it wanted to hear. Michiganders were reassured that Cass, who actually was the focal point of anti–Van Buren activity ahead of the convention, would be the candidate if they all stuck together. But others received the same sorts of assurances for their favorite sons, all of whom had long since renounced any interest in the nomination on the assumption that Van Buren was a shoo-in: James Buchanan of Pennsylvania, Richard Mentor Johnson of Kentucky, Levi Woodbury of New Hampshire. Polk's people were included in this appeal, but his hired hands—Cave Johnson and Gideon Pillow—insisted, per Polk's instructions, that they remained with Van Buren. Two delegates from Massachusetts offered up another suggestion to Cave Johnson—that after Van Buren fell short of two-thirds on the first ballot, Tennessee would move en masse to support another New Yorker, Silas Wright. In that circumstance, Wright would pick Polk as his running mate. To make this work, Tennessee would have to support the two-thirds rule (working against Van Buren), then vote for Van Buren on the first roll call.

The first part happened. On Tuesday the convention backed the two-thirds rule on a vote of 148–118. All thirteen delegates from Tennessee supported the rule. The ever-shifty James Buchanan, with the presidential gleam still in his eye, worked with Calhoun supporters to undermine Van Buren in Pennsylvania. It was, as the pro-Whig *New York Tribune* gleefully reported, a disaster for Van Buren, whose months of machinations in pursuit of the nomination "have all come to nought, and their house of cobs, which it has cost them so much toil and care to construct, has tumbled about their ears, burying the pigmies beneath its insignificant ruins." With the two-thirds rule in place, the convention took a lunch break before reconvening at 3:30 PM to begin the balloting for the presidential nomination.

To win the nomination, a candidate would need 178 of the convention's 266 delegate votes. On the first ballot, Van Buren got 146. Lewis Cass was next with 83, Richard Mentor Johnson got 29, and a sprinkling of votes were cast for James Buchanan, John C. Calhoun, Levi Woodbury, and Charles Stewart, who had commanded the USS *Constitution* during the War of 1812. Tennessee, which had pledged as part of the bargain on the two-thirds rule to cast its first ballot votes for Van Buren, went unanimously for Cass. This was a demonstration both of Polk's loose hold on the delegation and of Van Buren's weakness.

Things would eventually look brighter for Polk. They would only grow darker for Van Buren. His totals sank progressively, to 127 on the second ballot, 121 on the third, 111 on the fourth, 103 on the fifth. It was here that he gave up the lead for the first time, to Cass, who garnered 107 votes on the fifth ballot. Van Buren's decline continued, to 101 on the sixth, then 99 on the seventh. But Cass peaked at 123, far less even than Van Buren's first ballot total, and not approaching the 178 needed for nomination. Johnson and Buchanan won only regional or state support. Calhoun got a consistent 1 vote. Clearly, if a Southerner was going to win the nomination, it was not going to be the Old Nullifier Calhoun. Worst of all for the sweaty, tired delegates, none of the also-ran candidates was showing enough strength to be in a position to carry the convention even if they could unite behind a single man.

But Van Buren's backers could read the writing on the wall. If the Buchanan and Johnson delegates began moving to Cass, the Michigander

JAMES K. POLK. *Library of Congress*

would soon enough be the nominee, the unfriendliest of possible outcomes as far as Van Buren was concerned. Van Buren had observed Cass up close in the Jackson administration and considered him to be unprincipled and opportunistic. During the bank crisis of 1834, when Jackson decided to shift the federal government's funds from the Bank of the United States to "pet" state banks, Cass equivocated, demanding that he not be held responsible in any way for the move. As secretary of war Cass was already safely removed from such financial decisions, but his insistence on distancing himself irritated Jackson, whom it was unwise to get on the bad side of. Worse, after the shift of funds proved popular, Cass tried to associate himself with the move. The episode proved the undoing of Cass's hopes for advancement in the party as long as Jackson—and later Van Buren—had anything to say about it.

So in the tried and true practice of parliamentary desperation, the Van Buren forces moved to adjourn in order to avoid, in the words of one supporter, a victory by "the damned rotten corrupt venal Cass cliques." The adjournment maneuver didn't work, though, so they staged a mock melee as an Ohio delegate, Samuel Young, tried to make a motion to dump the two-thirds rule and declare Van Buren the nominee.

Pandemonium ensued. Young shouted that he would not be "kept here for all eternity," and insulted Tyler, Calhoun, and other annexationists. Southerners shouted back, and it seemed for a moment that violence was about to erupt. Then a Pennsylvania delegate rushed to the podium and shouted out that he was nominating Andrew Jackson for president. For Democrats, that was as close to invoking the name of Jehovah as they were likely to come. The proposal earned a hearty round of applause and laughter, which calmed the convention sufficiently that the chairman was able to restore enough order to adjourn for the night.

Although dismissed from the crowded hall, the delegates' work was hardly done. Historian George Bancroft, a Van Buren delegate from Massachusetts, had been a longtime admirer of Polk and had considered him vice presidential timber in 1840. Now, with the convention deadlocked and Bancroft's man frozen out, Bancroft thought it might be the time to reach out. Van Buren had instructed his floor manager, Benjamin Butler, to allow his delegates to shift to Silas Wright if the convention deadlocked. But Wright was steadfastly refusing to make himself a candidate so long as Van Buren had breath. "Never before or since has an American politician so clearly thrown away a presidential nomination that was so certainly in his grasp," Polk biographer Walter Borneman wrote of Wright. Perhaps, Bancroft suggested to Gideon Pillow, the list should be turned upside down, with Polk at the top and Wright in the second slot. Bancroft reasoned that Wright could hardly say no to that, once it became a certainty that the nominee would be Polk and not Van Buren.

Maybe, came the reply from Pillow. But if that were to be the case, the move would have to come from a Northern delegation, lest Yankee Democrats see the elevation of Polk as a Southern plot. If Bancroft could manage that, Pillow was sure he could bring along the Southwest.

The combination served all interests. Van Buren men would get Wright and, perhaps more importantly to them, stop Cass. Southern men and annexationists would get Polk. The fly in the ointment was Wright, who had the same position on Texas as Van Buren and who steadfastly refused to alter his stance about being a candidate for either office. That left Benjamin Butler, Van Buren's lead convention operative, at something of a loss. With his favored candidate dead in the water and his preferred alternative stubbornly eschewing involvement, Butler had little choice.

On the first ballot of Wednesday morning—the eighth ballot overall—New York stuck with Van Buren. But Massachusetts cast 7 votes for Polk, Tennessee jumped in with its 13, and a smattering of others gave him a total of 44, to Van Buren's 104 and Cass's 114. The die was cast. On the ninth ballot, Butler withdrew Van Buren's name and released the New York delegates to their own devices. With that the sluice gates opened and Polk rode the wave. All but two Van Buren delegates switched to Polk, who also picked up a number of Cass men, giving the Tennessean a convincing total of 233. "Deafening" cheers resounded about the room, and one reporter noted that he "never heard or saw any thing like it, and don't want to again."

It was all harmony and merriment inside the hall. Outside, the reaction was a bit more muted. "When the announcement was made in the street, numbers in the crowd called out 'Polk—Polk—who the devil is Polk?'" This was something new in American politics. Never before had the Democrats taken more than one ballot to nominate a candidate. Never had any party nominated someone who was not widely known. Polk had been Speaker of the House and governor of his state—although he had also lost two races for governor—but it would be an understatement to say merely that he was not of the stature of a Washington, Adams, Jefferson, or Jackson. As Whigs would spend the next five months gleefully pointing out, he was not even of the stature of Clay.

"Certainly the man beaten twice in succession by a stripling of his own State, would seem hardly the man to pit against Henry Clay!" exclaimed one pro-Whig reporter covering the convention. Polk was "certainly not more than a third rate politician—who never devised a measure nor said a thing worth remembering." In the days to come, others would express much the same sort of condescension. The Whig newspaper in Polk's own state capital, the *Nashville Republican Banner*, gave the Whigs their slogan: "Who is James K. Polk?"

A *Harper's Weekly* cartoon portrayed a hapless Polk sliding down a pole while Clay easily ascends to the top to claim the "civic crown," despite the exhortations of Jackson and attempts by Calhoun and Benton to boost Polk up the pole. "With ease I reach the goal, when the hearts of my countrymen are with me," says a grinning Clay.

"Polk is a fourth-rate partisan politician, of ordinary abilities, no eminence or reputation," a Philadelphia Whig concluded with self-satisfaction. "With such leaders, the Democratic Party is to go before the country. . . . Fortunately, they have but little chance of success."

Experienced politicians, who should have known better, were just as exuberant. William Seward, assessing the outlook in his crucial state, argued that Polk's position on Texas would keep the Whigs "safe and right" in New York.

Clay's own analysis was just as upbeat about his chances, and even more derisive of Polk. "Are our Democratic friends serious in the nominations which they have made at Baltimore of candidates for President and Vice President? We must beat them with ease if we do one half of our duty," he wrote a friend.

But Democrats from all factions seemed satisfied with their choice and eager that the battle be joined. The *Washington Spectator*, a Calhoun outlet, cheered that "the great mass of the people wanted a man pure in morals, sound in political principles, and in favor of the immediate annexation of Texas, and such they have in James K. Polk." Representing the Van Burenites, Silas Wright called Polk "very, very far my choice over all the other candidates" other than Van Buren himself. Theophilus Fisk, who had approached Polk on behalf of Tyler as a possible navy secretary in the wake of the *Princeton* explosion, said "you are the *only one* upon whom the friends of John Tyler could unite with their whole souls." Mississippian William M. Gwin, a Calhoun supporter who would later represent California in the Senate, noted that "Men who have been enemies for months met shook hands & pledged themselves to fight shoulder to shoulder through this contest." A speaker at a Virginia Democratic rally made a most salient rejoinder to the question "Who is James K. Polk?": "Young Hickory, of Tennessee—a pure and thrifty shoot from the old stalk." Democrats felt confident they could never go wrong invoking the name of Jackson. Summing things up was Old Hickory himself, in a letter to Polk's wife: "Daughter, I will put you in the White House if it costs me my life!"

Democrats being Democrats, they couldn't simply nominate their candidate, finish up the remaining business, and quietly disperse. After a short recess for lunch and to soak in the news of Polk's nomination, the delegates returned to anoint a running mate. They quickly settled on Silas Wright, who was notified by a new invention—Samuel Morse's telegraph—connecting Baltimore to Washington.

The telegraph was new, but Wright's answer was the same old one. He didn't want the job, and the new technology allowed him to inform the convention in a mere ten minutes. Van Buren floor manager Benjamin Butler refused to take no for an answer, and he telegraphed Wright again. And again. And again. But Wright's answer never changed. Perhaps he thought this newfangled device was not properly conveying his message. So he went low-tech, asking a pair of Democratic congressmen to ride the forty miles to Baltimore to make it clear to Butler and everyone else that he was not going to join the Polk ticket.

That settled who was not going to be Polk's running mate. Who it would be was still up for grabs. When the convention reconvened on Thursday morning with the intention of writing the party platform, delegates were surprised and disappointed to learn that they had to choose a new vice presidential candidate. The first ballot of the morning was a bad portent, with regional candidates splitting the vote and casting a pall over the proceedings as delegates feared they might be in for another marathon balloting session like the process that chose Polk. But on the second ballot, Southerners who had backed Cass and Woodbury on the first united behind George M. Dallas, a lawyer, diplomat, former mayor of Philadelphia, briefly a senator, a relative of Robert Walker, and an enemy of Buchanan.

With the ticket set, delegates turned their attention to the platform. It was, for the most part, an unremarkable document that strayed not at all from Jacksonian orthodoxy—no bank, no internal improvements, a low tariff, and no messing with "the domestic institutions of the several states"—the last being code for slavery. But on the twin questions of territorial expansion—Oregon and Texas—the Democrats went high and hard on the first while throwing a bit of a curve on the second. The platform proclaimed "that our title to the whole of the Territory of Oregon is clear and unquestionable; that no portion of the same ought to be ceded to

England or any other power, and that the reoccupation of Oregon and the reannexation of Texas, at the earliest practicable period, are great American measures, which this convention recommends to the cordial support of the democracy of the union."

The emphatic position on Oregon was not new, but its prominence in the platform was, and its pairing with Texas was construed correctly as an attempt to woo queasy Northern Democrats away from worrying excessively about Texas. That was especially true in light of the qualification on the Texas plank, which did not align with the candidate's stated position. "At the earliest practicable period" was considerably milder than Polk's declaration in his letter to the Ohioans that he favored "immediate reannexation." No matter what Polk had said before on the subject, he now had a party platform to run on that hedged ever so slightly on Texas and offered the North an equally grand prize.

The outcome of the election would not rest solely on the debate over the future of Texas. But the future course of the American experiment would be irrevocably altered by the outcome of the election.

The Annihilation of Time and Space

News of Polk's nomination took several days to reach the candidate in Columbia, Tennessee. But, as the back and forth with Wright had shown, the news was spread instantaneously to eager politicians in Washington by means of the telegraph.

Samuel F. B. Morse, already well known as a painter, had spent much of the previous decade developing the technology, and much of the previous year leading a project to string a telegraph line between Washington and Baltimore, along the right of way for the Baltimore & Ohio Railroad. At first workers tried burying the lines. But the insulation for the wires—based on a similar insulation developed by Morse's friend Samuel Colt for the underwater explosives he was working on—proved unreliable. After nine miles and several failed transmissions, Morse tore up the underground line and switched to hanging the wires along wooden poles. The project was paid for by a $30,000 appropriation from Congress. It wasn't the first federal money Morse had been given. He had won appropriations to develop the telegraph itself, and had run demonstrations during the Van Buren admin-istration. This latest money survived an attempt by scoffers, including Polk ally Johnson, to give half the funding to a mesmerist to conduct experiments that the skeptical politicians believed would parallel Morse's.

Before the news of Polk's nomination was speeded down the wire, Morse had conducted a smaller experiment—a "dramatic stunt," one biographer called it—earlier in the month at the Whig convention. Alfred Vail, Morse's assistant, was posted at a train stop about midway between Baltimore and Washington, where he was to intercept the news of Clay's nomination as it was being delivered to the capital by train, and to telegraph the results down the partially completed line. Vail did as he was instructed. At the other end of the line, Morse waited on one side of a cramped, dingy room in the Capi-tol, with a window affording a view of Pennsylvania Avenue and the B&O station across the way. On the other side of the room were the containers filled with nitric acid that composed the primitive battery that powered Morse's invention. Outside, people were milling about, many waiting for the train to arrive with news from the convention.

Late in the afternoon, a full seventy-five minutes before the train from Baltimore arrived, Morse's machine began clicking. This version, described as "simple & plain" by a contemporary witness, was more refined than the one he had developed in the 1830s, an "almost ludicrous-looking assem-bly of wooden clock wheels, wooden drums, levers, cranks, paper rolled on cylinders, a triangular-shaped wooden pendulum, an electromagnet, a battery, a variety of copper wires, and a wooden frame of the kind used to stretch canvas for paintings." Inside the little office, "the paper halted, moved ahead, stopped, and moved again in an irregular way," a witness remembered, "till finally Morse rose from his close scrutiny of the paper, stood erect, and looking about him, said, proudly, ' . . . the Convention has adjourned; the train for Washington from Baltimore has just left Annapolis Junction bearing that information, and my assistant has telegraphed me the ticket nominated.'" Morse held up the paper dramatically and announced "the ticket is Clay and Frelinghuysen."

On May 24, three days ahead of the start of the Democratic convention, Morse was ready to go live with the completed line. To enhance the drama of the moment, Morse set up his machine in the chamber of the Supreme

Court, then located inside the Capitol building. Vail was at the other end of
the line, at a Baltimore train depot. As a reward for being the person who
delivered to him the happy news of Senate passage of the appropriations
bill, Morse let Annie Ellsworth, the seventeen-year-old daughter of Henry
Leavitt Ellsworth, first Commissioner of the US Patent Office and an old
college friend of Morse's, choose what the first message would say.

Annie's choice, from the Book of Numbers, was, at once, profound and
prophetic: "What hath God wrought." Morse, a devout man, was willing to
share the credit. "It is *his* work, and he alone could have carried me thus far
through all my trials, and enabled me to triumph over the obstacles physical
and moral which opposed me," he wrote to his brother.

The timing also worked out well for Morse. Political conventions were a
relatively new thing and had quickly become a primary source of entertain-
ment for the masses. The Democratic convention followed by three days the
opening of the Baltimore-Washington telegraph line. Newspapers had paid
some attention to the first telegraph message, but they covered the conventions in detail. Voters were hungry for news of the proceedings, and it often
took several days for reports to filter out into the hinterlands. The uncertainty of the Democratic conclave added to the desire of voters—and readers—to know quickly what was going on. "The conventions at Baltimore
happened most opportunely," Morse understatedly observed.

Vail sent regular updates to the Capitol, which were then hung up on
the walls of the rotunda. At both ends of the line, people mobbed the teleg-
raphers just to get a peek at the new technology. "Hundreds begged and
pleaded to be allowed merely to look at the instrument," Vail told Morse.
"They declared they would not say a word or stir and didn't care whether
they understood or not, only they wanted to say they had seen it." At the
other end of the line, Morse was inundated by an "expectant throng of politicians" more interested in the results than the technology.

"The enthusiasm of the crowd before the window of the Telegraph
Room in the Capitol, was excited to the highest pitch at the announcement
of the nomination of the Presidential Candidate," Morse wrote. While the
startling technology improved the speed with which news was transmitted,
it also speeded up the delivery of misinformation. One of the early messages
sent on the first day of the convention noted that "at half-past 11 o'clock

a.m. the question being asked here, 'What the news was at Washington?' the answer was almost instantaneously returned—'Van Buren Stock is rising.'"

That same day, the *Baltimore Patriot* became the first newspaper ever to print a story transmitted by telegraph, reporting not on the convention but on a decision by the House of Representatives not to begin debate on a motion related to the occupation of Oregon. "So that," the paper reported, "we are thus enabled to give to our readers information from Washington up to two o'clock. This is indeed the annihilation of space."

Despite the erroneous view that Van Buren's stock was rising, the telegraph provided news to people at a distance almost as quickly as to those who were in attendance. Morse and Vail were effectively conversing across forty miles in real time, asking questions and all but immediately getting answers. Vail kept a running tally of the balloting, and as the move toward Polk picked up steam he tapped out "Illinois goes for Polk . . . Mich goes for Polk. Penn asks leave to correct her error so as to give her whole vote to Polk." Morse sent back "Intense anxiety prevails to . . . hear the result of last Balloting." And then, the result, from Vail: "Polk is unanimously nom." "3 cheers have been given here for Polk and 3 for the Telegraph," Morse proudly responded. The next day, the telegraph became more than a sender of news when it played a direct role in Silas Wright's refusal of the vice presidential nomination.

Those who had doubted the efficacy of the telegraph quickly began to fall into line. "Even the most inveterate opposers have changed to admirers and one of them Hon. Cave Johnson who ridiculed my system last session by associating it with the tricks of animal magnetism, came to me and said 'Sir I give in, it's an astonishing invention,'" Morse wrote.

People seemed to realize at once that their world would never be the same, as if they had crossed a dividing line as momentous as that which divided the calendar between before Christ and after Christ. "All this is calculated to put us upon the inquiry into the future agency of the wonderful contrivance which thus, without metaphor, annihilates both time and space," opined the *New York Tribune*. Patent commissioner Ellsworth attributed almost mystical powers to the telegraph, arguing that people could "enjoy the earliest intelligence of the markets, and thus be prepared against speculation. Criminals will be deterred from the commission of crimes, under the hope of escaping upon the 'iron horse;' for the mandate of justice, outrunning their flight, will greet their arrival at the first stopping place."

Whatever the worth of the telegraph as a crime-fighting tool, the annihilation of time and space went hand in hand with other wonders of the age. The burgeoning manufacturing economy was creating opportunity for thousands to improve their lot. Better farming technologies meant more food. Better printing techniques made newspapers available to wider audiences. The railroad, "a heaven-sent deliverance from the tyranny of distance," as one historian called it, gave both manufacturers and farmers expanded outlets for their products.

These new tools served all comers. As Joseph Smith built his Mormon empire on the Mississippi, the steamship allowed his missionaries to quickly proselytize Britain and the Continent, bringing hundreds upon hundreds of new converts to the Illinois enclave. Advances in printing allowed for the rapid production of millions of pamphlets by Benevolent Empire organizations and, as Joshua Himes well knew, by Millerites. Railroads meant they could be distributed more widely and much faster.

It was a great irony that while the very idea of progress that was inspired and accelerated by the telegraph and other elements of the communication and transportation revolutions ran counter to Millerism, the movement never would have prospered as it did except for those revolutions. Most Americans saw the new technologies as gifts from God and believed they would enhance their lives as part of the steady forward progress of the United States. Millerites believed that progress was at an end, that it was time to say goodbye to the vanities of this world, even if advances in mass printing and rapid communication had made far-flung delivery of the Millerite message possible.

But most of those swept up in the Second Great Awakening and active in organizations of the Benevolent Empire made their peace with progress; many embraced it outright as an earthly manifestation of God's benevolence. Morse was convinced that the telegraph was divinely inspired. Others saw the telegraph and similar tools of the new age as a birthright, to be guarded and passed along. "We should so live and labor in our time that what came to us as seed may go to the next generation as blossom, and that which came to us as blossom may go to them as fruit," explained clergyman Henry Ward Beecher. "That is what we mean by progress."

Henry Clay thought the seeds and blossoms needed to be planted and tended by the government. Clay thought it too important to leave to private enterprise. He feared the telegraph would be used "to monopolize intelligence and to perform the greatest operations in commerce and other departments of business. I think such an engine ought to be exclusively under the control of government."

Although Congress had handed over $30,000 so Morse could build his telegraph line, in the inventor's mind, this did not give the government a claim on his technology. And despite the sound of it, Clay was no Marxist (although as Clay spoke, Friedrich Engels was busy writing *The Condition of the Working Class in England*). He would not seize Morse's miracle out from under him. "The object cannot be accomplished," Clay concluded, "without an appropriation by Congress to purchase the right of the inventors." For Clay, development of the telegraph was just like building roads and canals: another internal improvement that would be a bond of union. Morse, a nativist with Whig tendencies, happened to agree with Clay. He hoped to sell his patent to the government—his original asking price was $250,000—and have Washington foot the bill for stringing lines across the country. Then, in Morse's version of crony capitalism, the government would hire him to run the system.

"A Bad Reason for Doing a Good Thing"

It was an age of miracles. Morse, Colt, even Joseph Smith and William Miller—each in his own way—had made it seem so. But now John Tyler needed a miracle of a different sort, for it appeared only divine intervention could save the Texas annexation treaty from the missteps, deliberate and otherwise, of the president and his secretary of state.

Tyler sent the treaty to Capitol Hill on April 22. The Senate Foreign Relations Committee spent three weeks digesting the details, including the Pakenham Letter and other accompanying documents, then sent the treaty to the floor on May 10 without a recommendation. Around the country, in political gatherings and town hall meetings and the pages of local newspapers, the issue was already being contested.

"It is conceded on all sides that it cannot be ratified," the Whig press asserted in early May, a stark contrast with the assurances from Jackson, Upshur, and others that the Senate was strongly behind annexation.

At the Illinois Capitol in Springfield, an ambitious young Whig attorney named Abraham Lincoln addressed what was billed as "one of the largest meetings ever held by our citizens." Lincoln had spent much of the spring traveling from town to town in the Seventh Congressional District, laying the groundwork for what he hoped would be his own run for Congress two years hence, and campaigning for his boyhood idol, Henry Clay. That night in Springfield, he put his lawyerly skills to use opposing the annexation of Texas, which he considered "an evil."

He was not alone. Thomas Hart Benton thought so, too. But, where Lincoln was a self-effacing small fry in the small pond of Illinois state politics, Benton was a thunderous, bluff behemoth standing astride the national scene in Washington. At that point, few bothered to listen to what Lincoln thought. No one could afford to ignore Benton.

For as long as there had been a state of Missouri, Benton had been its senator. His life was, in many ways, a metaphor for the nation. Like the country, he had been born east of the Appalachians, in North Carolina, then migrated west to Tennessee, where he became a lawyer and a friend and military aide-de-camp to Andrew Jackson. A falling out with Jackson led to a frontier duel—really a running gun battle that was more of a barroom brawl—and Benton's self-exile to Missouri (where, four years later, he would kill a man in a real duel).

He and Jackson eventually reconciled—Benton wrote the resolution to expunge from the Senate Journal the resolution of censure against Jackson, and he became an ardent Jacksonian Democrat. He would joke about the encounter for years, explaining that "yes, I had a fight with Jackson. A fellow was hardly in fashion then who hadn't." Benton owned slaves but bemoaned slavery, demonstrating an ambivalence that again mirrored his country's. Mostly he bemoaned the way slavery had a way of seeping into and poisoning every political question. Like Clay, he would rather just not talk about

Thomas Hart Benton.
Library of Congress

it. "Silence such debate is my prayer," he would say, "and if that cannot be done, I silence myself."

A silent Thomas Hart Benton would have been difficult for most senators to imagine. But Benton was sincere in his desire to keep the question of slavery off the national agenda, because he knew its presence there would interfere with his agenda—westward expansion. Benton wanted Texas. But he didn't want it on John C. Calhoun's terms. Like everything else in his larger-than-life life, he wanted Texas on his own terms.

Tyler wanted the treaty and the debate on it to remain secret, to be sprung on the public only after the deal was done and the treaty ratified. Tappan's leak of Calhoun's Pakenham Letter had blunted that preposterous strategy. Benton, who never saw an argument he didn't think he could win or confronted an opponent he didn't think he could drown out, wanted the whole of the debate to be made public. On May 13, he moved that his own speech, at least, be released. The Whig majority was only too happy to agree to this demand, and quickly voted to include the record of the rest of the debate as well. They believed the public was with them, and they wanted to expose what they considered Tyler's duplicity and Calhoun's dangerous diplomacy. Benton just wanted to let everybody know what he thought.

He started by demanding the Tyler administration turn over letters from Duff Green, the "executive agent" Tyler had sent to England in early 1843 to deliver a private presidential message to the American minister in London, Edward Everett, and that Green himself appear before the Senate. The men were to gather information to be used in negotiations to settle outstanding territorial disputes over Oregon, California, and, to a lesser degree, Texas. During this fact-finding mission, Green claimed to have uncovered the British plot to lend money to Texas for the purpose of paying slave owners to set free the republic's slaves. When Green reported this discovery to Abel Upshur in July 1843, Upshur turned to Calhoun. The answer was obvious: the United States must annex Texas. When Lord Aberdeen, the British foreign secretary, told Parliament in August that his government was doing what it could to bring peace between Mexico and Texas and hoped that it would end with slavery abolished in the Lone Star Republic, Upshur, Calhoun, and Tyler took this as confirmation of Green's assertion, and set the wheels in motion that led to the annexation treaty.

Benton's motion:

Resolved, That the author of the "private letter" from London, in the summer of 1843, and addressed to the then American Secretary of State (Mr. Upshur), and giving him information of the supposed anti-slavery designs of Great Britain in Texas, and which information was the basis and moving cause of the American Secretary's leading dispatch to the American chargé in Texas to procure the annexation of Texas to the United States, be summoned to appear at the bar of the Senate to be examined on oath in relation to the subject matter of his said communication from London; and also to be examined by the Senate on all points that they shall think proper in relation to his knowledge of the origin, progress, and conclusion of the Texas treaty, and all the objects thereof, and of all influences and interests which may have operated in setting on foot and carrying on the negotiations for the conclusion and ratification of said treaty. Resolved, also, That the Senate will examine, either at its bar or by a committee, any other persons that it shall have reason to believe can give information on all or any one of the foregoing points of inquiry.

Tyler and Calhoun responded with a clever dodge, telling the Senate that a full review of State Department files found no such documents from Green. A broader request from the Senate for all of Green's 1843 correspondence was met with an assurance from Calhoun that there was "no communication whatever, whether to or from Mr. Green in relation to the annexation of Texas, to be found in the files of this department." Just so, since Green had been acting as an agent of the president, not the State Department, and had communicated privately with Tyler, Calhoun, and Upshur, not through the auspices of the department.

Benton and the Senate got no satisfaction on their request for Duff Green's appearance or his letters. They did a little better on getting a clarification from the administration about military activity. Benton wanted to know if

since the commencement of the negotiations which resulted in the treaty now before the Senate for the annexation of Texas to the United States, any military preparation has been made or ordered by the President for or in anticipation of war; and, if so, for what cause and with whom was such war apprehended, and what are the preparations that have been made or ordered? Has any movement, or assemblage, or disposition of any of the military or naval forces of the United States been made or ordered with a view to such hostilities?

Yes, came the response.

In consequence of the declaration of Mexico communicated to this Government . . . announcing the determination of Mexico to regard as a declaration of war against her by the United States the definitive ratification of any treaty with Texas annexing the territory of that Republic to the United States, and the hope and belief entertained by the Executive that the treaty with Texas for that purpose would be speedily approved and ratified by the Senate, it was regarded by the Executive to have become emphatically its duty to concentrate in the Gulf of Mexico and its vicinity, as a precautionary measure, as large a portion of the home squadron . . . as could well be drawn together; and at the same time to assemble at Fort Jesup, on the borders of Texas, as large a military force as the demands of the service at other encampments would authorize to be detached.

Sam Houston had been insistent on the point, writing to his negotiators in Washington that "if negotiation fails, our file is uncovered, the enemy may charge through our ranks, and we have no reserve to march up to our rescue."

The decision to defend Texas in the event of a Mexican attack had splintered Tyler's cabinet. The move was backed by Secretary of War William Wilkins, a Pennsylvania Democrat, who had to carry out the orders. But Treasury Secretary John C. Spencer, a New York Whig who had to write the check to pay for the operation, balked. When Tyler ordered Spencer to deposit $200,000 with an unnamed agent in New York City to fund the force being sent to the Gulf of Mexico, Spencer decided to resign rather than comply. To deposit such a sum without congressional approval, he argued, would be unconstitutional. Spencer's resignation salved his conscience, but it also paved the way for the payment to be made and the force to be deployed.

Armed with documentation confirming the deployment, Benton began a speech, which continued over three days, a tour de force in which he questioned the Tyler administration's motives, methods, and policies. He expounded at length on the history and geography of Texas, and excoriated the 1819 Adams-Onis Treaty that, in his mind and the minds of many of the people he was now debating against, started all the trouble in the first place. (Although not in the mind of Adams, who was watching the debate. He immodestly referred to the treaty as "the most successful negotiation ever consummated by the Government of this Union.")

Standing to his full height at his desk on the crowded Senate floor, Benton gazed up at the packed semicircular gallery, where Adams sat, that ran the entire length of the west wall of the chamber. Sunlight streamed in through windows on the opposite side, casting shadows against the tobacco-stained red carpeting beneath Benton's feet. He began slowly but clearly— the acoustics in the Senate chamber were much better than in the larger House, where members only a few feet apart often had trouble hearing one another.

"I—the first denouncer of the treaty of 1819—the first advocate for the recovery of Texas—the consistent, uniform, and disinterested advocate for this recovery: I go for it when it can be accomplished without crime and infamy . . . and I wash my hands of all attempts to dismember the Mexican republic by seizing her dominions in New Mexico, Chihuahua, Coahuila, and Tamaulipas," Benton thundered. All this, he asserted, could fall under the aegis of the treaty, which did not even bother to set a boundary for the territory that the United States was hoping to annex.

Calhoun had argued that the boundary was left unsettled to allow for a later negotiation with Mexico that would not be limited by any preset parameters. Benton called that nonsense. "Would we take 2,000 miles of the Canadas in the same way?" he asked. "I presume not. And why not? Because Great Britain is powerful and Mexico weak."

There were other speeches—ten considered important enough to be fully recorded in the *Congressional Globe*. James Buchanan, a treaty supporter, would prove a prophet when he declared on June 8 that Texas annexation was "a question of transcendent importance . . . more momentous than any question which has been before the Senate since my connection with public affairs." Buchanan espoused the Robert Walker argument that the acquisition of Texas would help dilute slavery by westward expansion. And he rejected the notion that Texas would become a British colony, but argued that a Texas-Brit commercial relationship would be "equally injurious to our peace and prosperity."

House members weighed in, although they didn't—yet—have a vote on the issue. Robert Dale Owen, a Glasgow, Scotland–born Indiana Democrat who helped his father found the utopian community of New Harmony, backed the treaty but chided Calhoun's pro-slavery presentation in language less colorful than Benton's but more to the point: "He gives a bad reason for doing a good thing," Owen said.

On June 8, with the raucous debate over, the Senate was ready to vote.

Andrew Jackson was convinced that Benton had lost his senses, perhaps a result of the injuries he suffered aboard the *Princeton*. He also thought Henry Clay might push Senate Whigs to support the treaty just to get the issue off the national agenda. From Jackson's point of view, this was a rational conclusion because it assumed Clay was being insincere in his maneuverings on the treaty; Jackson always assumed Clay was insincere. But in this instance Jackson misread his man. Clay wanted to avoid war with Mexico, and he genuinely feared annexation would mean war. He would not be doing any arm-twisting on the Texas treaty, and it turned out he didn't need to.

It wasn't even close. Needing two-thirds of the Senate for ratification, supporters of annexation couldn't muster even one-third. The treaty was defeated 35–16, though Benton was the only Southern Democrat to oppose ratification. But only one Southern Whig voted for the treaty. The vote breakdown was Whigs 27–1 against and Democrats 15–8 in favor. By section, Northern Democrats voted 7–5 against (with 1 abstention) and Northern Whigs voted 13–0 against. Southern Democrats voted 10–1 in favor of the treaty, with Southern Whigs voting 14–1 against. Upshur and Calhoun's desire that the South "be roused and made of one mind" on Texas had failed.

Tyler had lost, and John Quincy Adams opined that he had played his "last card for a popular whirlwind to carry him through." Once again, a political opponent had underestimated Tyler. On May 16 Tyler himself had written that "I entertain not the least doubt, that if annexation should now fail, it will, in all human probability, fail forever." Less than a month later he changed his mind, setting the stage for the next, extended round of debate over Texas.

Benton had won, but as always with Benton, there were still more horizons to explore. In the midst of the annexation debate, he had briefly paused from his bombast to make note of the other great question of the day concerning westward expansion. As he usually did, the Missourian personalized the cause, giving the rush to Oregon a home state cast.

"Some hundreds went a few years ago; a thousand went last year; two thousand are now setting out from the frontiers of Missouri; tens of thousands are meditating the adventure," he told the Senate on June 3, at the midpoint of the Texas debate. "I say to them all, Go on! The government will follow you, and will give you protection and land. . . . It is the genius of our people to go ahead, and it is the practice of our government to follow, and eventually to protect and reward the bold pioneers who open the way to new countries, and subdue the wilderness for their country."

This had been Benton's constant theme, since before he had come to the Senate, before Missouri was even a state. A lawyer by trade, he had also once been a St. Louis newspaper editor. In that role, he filled his columns with editorials espousing expansion, two decades before the first wagon train headed west. For emphasis, and to demonstrate his own foresight, Benton had the articles repackaged and published as a book in 1844 with an introduction—unsigned but probably written by Benton—that claimed the twenty-five-year-old writings demonstrated a "spirit of prophecy." "All obey the same impulse," he wrote, "that of going to the West; which, from the beginning of time, has been the course of the heavenly bodies, of the human race, and of science, civilization and national power following in their train."

For Thomas Hart Benton, the West was more than a political question. It was a state of mind, a matter of the heart, a national destiny. And it was personal. In the Benton clan, westward expansion was a family affair.

{ 5 }

THE MISSIONARY
AND THE PUBLICIST

On the day of the Texas annexation vote, Thomas Hart Benton's daughter, Jessie, had a severe headache. His granddaughter, Lily, was also ill, with a bad case of whooping cough. Jessie had been suffering for a couple of weeks. But neither her own infirmity nor her daughter's kept Jessie from her appointed duty. Each evening at dinnertime, as she had each night for all of 1844, she set a place at the table for her absent husband, readied his bed, and placed a lighted lamp in the window, hoping against hope that tonight would be the night he returned home.

Jessie Benton Frémont might have been worried about her father's exertions on Texas, but her illness was more likely a result of worry about her husband's exertions. John C. Frémont had left home more than a year earlier on an exploration of the Rocky Mountains and the Pacific Northwest. An officer in the Army's Corps of Topographical Engineers, Frémont was technically under the command of Colonel John James Abert, chief of the corps that had been created in 1838. But really, Frémont was under the command of no man. And, while his marching orders were delivered by Abert, they originated with his father-in-law, the senior senator from Missouri and chairman of the Military Affairs Committee, Thomas Hart Benton.

JESSIE BENTON FRÉMONT. *Library of Congress*

Frémont was already something of a celebrity. His first trek into the western wilderness in 1842 had yielded a bestselling official report, transcribed and rewritten by Jessie from John's dictation. It was a task she thoroughly enjoyed, taking full advantage of the fact that "second lieutenants cannot indulge in secretaries." The thousand copies the Senate ordered to be printed in March 1843 were eagerly snapped up by armchair travelers and by others whom it so inspired that they got out of their armchairs and began heading west themselves. More stationary types were nonetheless similarly moved. The poet Henry Wadsworth Longfellow, whose wife read the report to him while the couple holed up in a snowy Massachusetts winter, wrote that "Frémont has particularly touched my imagination. What a wild life, and what a fresh kind of existence." Longfellow, not only a poet but also a realist, added, "But, ah, the discomforts."

Newspapers reprinted large sections of the report. Some in the Topographical Corps wondered what the fuss was about, although Abert—knowing well where his bread was buttered—gave it an enthusiastic endorsement. Critics pointed out that Frémont had blazed no new trails, and the scientific contributions of the report were negligible. But, as the premier historian of army exploration in the West has noted, judging Frémont's contributions by his scientific acumen misses the point entirely. "He saw the West with the eye of an artist," wrote William H. Goetzmann, "and his narrative reveals the emotional quality of his experience in first penetrating the mountainous wilderness." Another interpreter of Frémont's first expedition insightfully observed that the report of that journey "seems to be the first official document of the Far West written by someone who had been trained to see that landscape beforehand and who liked what he saw." Frémont was more than an explorer. "I flatter myself that what is discovered, though not enough to satisfy curiosity, is sufficient to excite it," he wrote, "and that subsequent explorations will complete what has been commenced." He was a missionary for Manifest Destiny. His wife was his publicist.

Less than two weeks after the Senate received Frémont's official report of the 1842 trip, he got his orders from Abert—"to connect the reconnaissance of 1842 with the surveys of Commander Wilkes so as to give a connected survey of the interior of our continent." (Charles Wilkes had explored the northwest coast as part of a four-year Pacific expedition.) Frémont was to cross the Rockies, travel up to the Columbia River, and explore

JOHN C. FRÉMONT. *Library of Congress*

the Wind River country on his way back via the Oregon Trail. Beyond science, Frémont was to note the best locations along the way for campsites,
where wood and water were most plentiful, and where hostile Indians might
be expected. Not all of this was "our" continent yet, despite Benton's dream
and Abert's assertion, but that didn't seem to deter anybody involved in the
adventure. The orders contained no mention of California.

Two months later, the family—John, Jessie, Lily, who was not yet two,
the senator, and his wife, Elizabeth—were all gathered in St. Louis. John
made final preparations for the journey, buying supplies and hiring men
while Jessie stayed busy acting as clerk for both husband and father and
organizing dinner parties, an essential skill as part of the political and social
scene in which she had grown up. Frémont signed up legendary mountain men Tom "Broken Hand" Fitzpatrick as guide and Lucien Maxwell
as hunter. Back for another trip was the mapmaker who had accompanied
him the year before, Charles Preuss, a cantankerous German who hated
the West, didn't much like being outdoors, and complained incessantly
about nearly everything—the food, the weather, the landscape, the animals,
the company. "This morning we started out on our monotonous journey
through the prairie," was how he began his journal of the trip. But he was a
fine cartographer.

The core party consisted of thirty-nine men, only two of whom—Frémont and Preuss—had any kind of real scientific training. There would be
another dozen or so hangers-on who were not officially part of the exploring party but traveled with the group at different stages. A detail of wagons
was loaded with supplies, some of which had been hard to come by because
Frémont was competing with hundreds of Oregon pioneers who were outfit-
ting their rigs for the long journey at the same time. He also had a detail of
scientific instruments, including two telescopes, two barometers, two chro-
nometers, two sextants, six thermometers, and multiple compasses. Also
counted among the mound of goods was a twenty-foot-by-five-foot India-
rubber boat built by Horace Day, an industrial spy who had failed to make
off with the secrets of his competitor, Charles Goodyear, but succeeded in
selling some of his inferior wares to the Corps of Topographical Engineers.

Frémont departed St. Louis on May 13, 1843, and almost immediately
got into trouble. He had arranged with Benton family friend Stephen Watts

Kearny, an army colonel, to obtain a howitzer and ammunition, along with the usual complement of small arms, from army stores. The expedition was supposed to be a scientific endeavor. It would be crossing the territory of another nation, without any firm diplomatic permission to do so. A howitzer, army brass reasoned, might be considered provocative. Benton had told Frémont what he needed most was presents—in fact, however many he requisitioned, he couldn't get enough. The senator did not mention artillery in his advice. Frémont argued to his superiors that the artillery piece would be a most effective deterrent to any hostile Indians the group might encounter, and his men should have at their disposal "every means of defense which may conduce to its safety." Because of the press of time, Kearny told Captain William H. Bell, chief of the St. Louis arsenal, that Frémont should be given what he asked for without further checking with Washington. Bell did as he was ordered, then took the precaution of quickly writing a letter of objection to the Ordnance Office in Washington, getting his protest on the record, just in case.

When Abert received Bell's letter, he acted quickly. The colonel fired off a response that arrived at the Bentons' St. Louis home barely a week after Frémont had departed. When Jessie opened it, she was shocked to see that her husband was being recalled to Washington to explain why he had armed his scientific exploring party with a howitzer. Another Topographical Corps officer would soon arrive on the scene to take charge of Frémont's men, Abert wrote.

For Jessie, this was just the sort of envious nonsense she had come to expect in the three years she had been married to Frémont. The West Point–dominated officer corps could not countenance the success her husband had enjoyed, she believed. Her father pointedly referred to Frémont as "the young explorer who held his diploma from Nature, and not from the United States' Military Academy." Many in the Army did resent what they considered the favoritism shown Frémont by his father-in-law, a great irony as far as Jessie was concerned, considering the difficulties the couple had encountered from Benton when they eloped in October 1841.

The first of Frémont's powerful patrons, Joel Poinsett, a former US consul in Mexico, had seen something in Frémont during his South Carolina youth and made him a protégé. When Poinsett became secretary of war, he gave Frémont his commission in the Topographical Corps. Before entering the army, he went on an expedition of the Cherokee lands of the Southeast; after, he was engaged for a survey of the upper Midwest. In 1840, Poinsett introduced Frémont to Benton, who took the young lieutenant under his wing. But a year later, the senator thundered against his daughter's marriage to the bastard son of an adulteress and a ne'er-do-well French Canadian bon vivant. Confronted with the determination of his iron-willed favorite daughter, however, Benton eventually was forced to relent. Instead of continuing a pointless objection, he co-opted the new son-in-law for his own purposes. If this was the life his daughter wanted, he would have no reservations about making her husband his agent of destiny. "We could count on each other—my father, Mr. Frémont and I, as one," Jessie said.

Senator's pet or not, Frémont was now in real trouble. Abert had been taken to the woodshed by acting secretary of war James Madison Porter, who reprimanded Kearny and ordered Abert to get to the bottom of the howitzer business. He didn't know that Frémont had already left St. Louis. Abert had every reason to believe—and right to expect—that Senator Benton or Mrs. Frémont would forward his letter down the trail. But Benton had left town on a political tour around the state. Jessie had no intention of doing anything that would result in her husband not accomplishing what he set out to do. "I had been too much a part of the whole plan for the expeditions to put them in peril now," she wrote.

One of the voyageurs Frémont had engaged had chosen to stay behind to tend to his wife, who was ill. Jessie sought him out to deliver a message to Frémont. But not Abert's message. "It was in the blessed day before telegraphs," she would later write, so a man on a fast horse could still get there before officialdom. "I wrote urging him not to lose a day but start at once on my letter. That I could not give him the reason but he must GO. That I knew it would be bad for his animals, who would have only the scant early grass, but they could stop at Bent's Fort and fatten up. *Only trust me and go.*" The messenger caught up with Frémont at Kaw Landing on the Missouri River, not far from where state militia had attacked the Mormons and chased them into Illinois in 1838. It is a measure of the Frémonts' relationship and of the faith the thirty-year-old husband placed in his nineteen-year-old bride that he did not hesitate. Within a week of her letter going out, one came back. "Goodbye. I trust and Go."

Defying the War Department was a bold move for a teenager, but she operated under the umbrella of protection provided by her father, who endorsed her misdemeanor and interceded on her behalf with Abert. He also made sure that acting secretary Porter's nomination to fill the post permanently was "rejected contemptuously by the Senate." There were no immediate repercussions for Jessie and John, but the incident cemented in the minds of many in the Topographical Corps and the army generally that Frémont was a loose cannon—in this case quite literally—who was not to be trusted. It was a reputation that would follow him for the rest of his life.

"FRÉMONT CHANGES HIS MIND EVERY DAY"

Having got started quickly, Frémont moved methodically, feeling secure in the knowledge that Jessie was protecting his rear flank. The slow pace gave the grass more time to sprout and the rivers, which had flooded because of heavy rains, more time to recede. He marshaled his force at Elm Grove, Kansas, and, hard on the heels of about one thousand Oregon-bound pioneers, headed up the trail. After a short time among the crowds, though, Frémont and company veered off south to the Kansas River, then proceeded westward along the line of the Republican River, until the party struck the Arkansas at Big Timbers, in present-day Colorado, on June 16.

In need of supplies because of their rushed departure and the competition from those bound for Oregon and California, the party split here. The mountain man, Fitzpatrick, took two-dozen men and a dozen wagons northward toward the Platte and the emigrant trail. Frémont continued westward with the rest. As Frémont's party moved on, they found "wild flax three and a half feet high" and huge herds of buffalo that they used for target practice with the howitzer, a "cruel but arousing sport," as Preuss described it. Further along, they also found equally huge herds of diminutive prairie dogs, along with a high and dry prairie and treeless riverbanks. Frémont was convinced all the prairie dog holes were interconnected, so spent part of a day digging to prove his theory. As far as he dug, they were, but eventually he had to be on his way.

Frémont's party soon reached St. Vrain's Fort, "on the South Fork of the Platte, immediately under the mountains," as Frémont described the location on the Front Range of the Rockies. It had been built in 1837 as a fur trading post by Ceran St. Vrain and his partners, Charles and William Bent, and was managed by his youngest brother, Marcellin. Frémont arrived in time for July 4 celebrations, and "all hands were soon busily engaged in preparing a feast to celebrate the day." With a combination of foodstuffs brought from St. Louis and game taken on the route, they enjoyed "a large supply of excellent preserves and rich fruit-cake . . . macaroni soup, and variously prepared dishes of the choicest buffalo-meat, crowned with a cup of coffee." But St. Vrain could not resupply Frémont for the journey ahead, offering only minimal provisions of "a little salt and unbolted Mexican flour." After several days of hospitality, Frémont's party headed south in search of resupply at a ramshackle fur trading station in Pueblo, not far from Bent's Fort on the north bank of the Arkansas River section of the Santa Fe Trail.

Frémont sent Lucien Maxwell toward Taos, New Mexico, to buy mules and supplies, but Maxwell ran into an uprising inspired by the incursion of Texans seeking revenge for Mexican depredations. Taos was in an uproar, trade down the Santa Fe Trail was at a standstill, and the supplier that Maxwell had counted on provisioning him had seen his store looted by rampaging mobs.

Kit Carson, a mountain man extraordinaire who had been an integral part of Frémont's expedition the previous year, heard from Maxwell that Frémont was at Pueblo and rode the seventy miles from Bent's Fort to enlist. Maxwell having failed to get any supplies, Frémont took Carson up on his offer to go back to the fort, where William Bent provided him with ten loaded-down pack mules. Frémont didn't dally, but headed back northwest to blaze a new trail across the Rockies.

None of Frémont's original party knew the route, along the Cache de la Poudre River, and neither did Carson, one of the most experienced mountain men still living. Another mountain man who had joined the party, Alexis Godey, knew something of the country, so he went with Frémont while Carson backtracked to Bent's Fort. Although the mountain men he ran into at St. Vrain's had plenty of suggestions about how to proceed toward Long's Peak and the headwaters of the Cache de la Poudre, it soon became clear after fighting their way over broken country that even Godey could not help them find a way through. By early August they'd given up trying to find a southern route through the mountains and headed north, toward the one known reliable path over the continental divide, South Pass.

South Carolina Senator George McDuffie, enthusiastic supporter of Texas annexation but opponent of the colonization of Oregon, had once given thanks to God on the Senate floor "for his mercy in placing the Rocky Mountains there" to block the passage of west-bound pioneers. Undaunted, Frémont compared the ascent up South Pass to strolling up Capitol Hill. This might have been a bit of an overstatement, but he found that moving across the wide, gradual summit was certainly easier than cutting a new trail through unknown mountains.

Discovered by fur traders heading east in 1812–13, South Pass was a natural thoroughfare that opened western expansion to wagon travel. The trail that passed through the gap had been a commercial route for trappers and traders for several decades, like the Santa Fe Trail. The southern trail remained a route of commerce (and was old enough to have its first extensive history published in 1844), doing $200,000 worth of business in 1844. But the Oregon Trail evolved into an emigrant road, pretty dull stuff for Frémont. So at this point, he decided to detour from his orders and headed south once again, for an exploration of the Great Salt Lake. "Frémont changes his mind every day as usual," the perpetually dissatisfied Preuss recorded.

It took three weeks of rough going to get there, but the sight of the inland sea inspired Frémont toward one of his flights of lyrical exaggeration. "I am doubtful if the followers of Balboa felt more enthusiasm, when from the heights of the Andes, they saw the great Western Ocean," he reported.

Perhaps adding to Frémont's romantic notion was the mistaken understanding that his party was the first to explore the lake, which he believed "had been seen only by trappers who were wandering through the country in search of new beaver streams, caring very little for geography." He was wrong in this supposition. Mountain man Jim Bridger and a party of trappers had paddled around almost the entire circumference of the lake in 1826 and put to rest any theories that it was connected directly to the Pacific.

Frémont outfitted Horace Day's rubber boat and set off September 7 on a reconnaissance of the lake with Preuss, Carson, and two others. A year earlier, in a similar rubber craft, Frémont had twice met with near disaster, losing a cache of coffee and sugar while crossing the Kansas River, then losing most of the expedition's records when the boat flipped over coming down the Platte. Preuss, never one to withhold a negative judgment, wrote that "it was certainly stupid of the young chief to be so foolhardy where the terrain was absolutely unknown."

"The Instrument in the Hands of His Maker"

In addition to Frémont's foolhardiness, part of the problem was the boat and the material from which it was made.

Rubber, known to Europeans since the voyages of Columbus, was more curiosity than world changer in the first half of the nineteenth century. The reason was simple: while it was flexible and water-resistant under normal conditions, it was ruined by extreme heat or cold. In heat, it melted and stank. In cold, it turned hard and useless. Charles Goodyear spent his life, his health, and other people's fortunes trying to figure out why, and what to do about it.

Colt and Morse were celebrity inventors, with friends in high places. Goodyear was not. He had some friends, and had exhausted the patience and money of more than a few financial backers in his obsession to make rubber a practical material for personal and industrial use. Like Morse, he believed God had chosen him to do this great work. Like Colt, he had suffered humiliating setbacks. By 1844, he was on the brink of realizing his dream, when his own shortcomings cost him a chance at a fortune. He would have to settle for immortality.

Born in 1800, his father operated a mill in Naugatuck, Connecticut, making buttons. One of Amasa Goodyear's first great contracts was with the US Army, supplying fasteners for the uniforms that soldiers—possibly including William Miller and Andrew Jackson—wore into battle in the War of 1812. When Charles Goodyear struck out on his own, with wife Clarissa at his side, he opened a hardware store in Philadelphia in 1826, selling goods made by themselves and members of the family. He did well, but overextended and eventually lost the business. He ended up, not for the last time, in debtors' prison.

When he got out, he decided to put his skills to a different use: he would become an inventor. Goodyear first encountered the substance that would become his life's obsession in 1834, on a life preserver in the New York City store of the Roxbury India Rubber Company, the most successful of the handful of rubber producers that emerged in the 1830s. He thought he could make a better valve for the preserver. The proprietor told him not to bother. Rubber had no future, he explained to Goodyear, as he showed him stacks of disfigured life preservers that had melted from the heat of the New York summer. "Forget your valve. The one invention that could save the rubber industry and earn a fortune for the inventor would be a method of preventing rubber from . . . this," the salesman said as he waved at the pile of sludge.

And so, Goodyear's star was set. People used rubber, mostly for clothes and shoes. They liked the waterproof quality. And it was new, like America, so Americans wanted it to be part of their lives. By the late 1820s it was a bit of a fashion statement. Something of a rubber bubble formed by the early 1830s, and like every bubble, this one burst. Rubber was simply not dependable in the extremes of summer and winter. The bottom fell out of the business, providing Goodyear with both opportunity and raw material—the rubber crash flooded the market and drove down the price. Goodyear, who earned some money as a blacksmith, bought all he could.

Years of torment would follow. Goodyear was a dedicated experimenter, but he was a terrible businessman. He had to go begging, hat in hand, dozens of times. Evicted repeatedly, the family moved from place to place. Goodyear and his wife lost four children. His own health was persistently bad. His ideas were pilfered by competitor Horace Day, albeit without much success. (Day's lack of mastery would later become dangerously apparent far away from the manufacturing cities of the Northeast.)

Despite these difficulties, Goodyear proceeded on. He saw good results from treating rubber with nitric acid. This earned him a fresh dose of financing, and a patent, in 1837. Goodyear thought he saw the light at the end of the rubber hose. He provided samples to President Andrew Jackson and got an encouraging note in return. Henry Clay and John C. Calhoun were also impressed enough to encourage Goodyear in writing. But the good fortune didn't last. Nitric acid was not the answer, and the Panic of 1837 wiped out Goodyear's benefactors and what little retail business he had scared up for the nitric acid–treated hats, aprons, and life preservers he had produced.

While Charles Goodyear was toiling in obscurity in America, Thomas Hancock was making a going concern of rubber production in Britain. Hancock hadn't figured out the secret to making rubber impervious to temperature either, but he was less bothered by that than was Goodyear. He was happy to sell mediocre rubber. He also had a better head for business, and more reliable partners. And soon the paths of the two would cross.

With an assist from a fellow inventor, Nathaniel Hayward, Goodyear developed a method of adding sulfur and white lead to the rubber, which yielded positive results. Hayward patented the sulfur method, and Goodyear purchased the patent. He wasn't quite there yet, but he was confident enough now to solicit the business of the US government. In 1839 he won a contract with the Post Office to supply mailbags. He treated the bags with his new sulfur solution and the older nitric acid process, and it seemed to work. When the job was done, Goodyear took some time off to spend with his family, feeling like success was at hand. When he returned to work, the rubber bags had turned to useless slop.

He had to move again. He was back to going door-to-door looking for investors. But God had chosen him for this work. He was "the instrument in the hands of his Maker." Who was he to stop?

And, indeed, the moment had come. Many tales are told of how Charles Goodyear came to realize that what his sulfur-treated rubber needed was heat. But, like Colt's submarine battery, the truth is shrouded in mystery. No one was there. And Goodyear's haphazard record-keeping and incomplete recollections offer few clues. What is known for sure is that some rubber ended up on a stove, and when Goodyear discovered it, the stuff—which he called "fire proof gum"—was elastic and stood up to extremes of both heat and cold.

There was still a lot of work to do, and he was broke again. He began wandering the streets of Woburn, Massachusetts, where he now lived, in effect borrowing the fire of millers and smiths and small manufacturers to conduct his experiments. Workers in these facilities complained that Goodyear was getting in their way. They also made fun of him. "We used to laugh and think it was a trifling thing," one remembered. Eventually, says a biographer, "Goodyear's industrial world had shrunk to the confines of Clarissa's kitchen." She might have wanted him to return to blacksmithing, but she never lost faith in her husband's vision.

Later, Goodyear's patent would be defended in court by Daniel Webster in his last major case, for which he would earn the lordly sum of $15,000. Of Clarissa Goodyear, the great man would say, "In all his distress, in all his trials, she was willing to participate in his sufferings, and endure everything, and hope everything; she was willing to be poor; she was willing to go to prison, if it was necessary, when he went to prison; she was willing to share with him everything, and that was his only solace."

After a year of working with sulfur, Goodyear still hadn't figured out how to repeat the process. Months of traveling and begging ensued, to little effect. His father, brother, sister-in-law, and niece died of malaria in Florida in the summer of 1841. And still, Goodyear proceeded on. During a trip to New York, he met brothers William and Emory Rider, who agreed to set up a factory for Goodyear in Springfield, Massachusetts. More fatefully, they introduced him to Englishman Stephen Moulton.

And still, by the summer of 1842, despite urgings from the Rider brothers, Hayward, Moulton, and others, Goodyear had not applied for either an American or British patent for the sulfur/heat process. The reasons seem clear: Goodyear had become cautious. The failure of the postal bags and other disappointments had instilled in him a deep desire to get the process right before he sprang any more rubber surprises on the world. Instead of applying for even a provisional patent, Goodyear decided to have Moulton carry some samples to England, to search for investors. He trusted Moulton. And, besides, Moulton was no scientist. He had no real understanding of the process that he could reveal to anyone.

Unfortunately for Goodyear, not everyone in England was as trustworthy or uninformed as Moulton, who left samples of the product with an associate of Thomas Hancock. Hancock seized the opportunity to begin experimenting on them. What he was doing was not illegal. Goodyear had no patent. Hancock was perfectly within his legal rights—ethics were another, though irrelevant, question—to explore the mysteries of fireproof gum and see what he could come up with. For a year he worked at it, and finally unlocked the secret, more or less, receiving a provisional patent on November 21, 1843. That gave him six months to finalize the process and receive a full patent. In January 1844, Goodyear finally got around to filing for British, American, and French patents. He was too late.

Hancock got his British patent—by far the more valuable—in May. A month later, on June 15, 1844, Goodyear's US patent was approved, No. 3633, for "Metallic Gum Elastic Composition." He would eventually enjoy a comfortable living off the flat-fee sale of his rights. But, considering the impact of vulcanized rubber—the modern world is inconceivable without it—Goodyear deserved a better fate. He was robbed even of the value of his French patent by a quirk in French law that rendered the patent useless because Goodyear had once sold some rubber shoes in that country. The English got to name the process—vulcanization, which admittedly has a better ring to it than fireproof gum or metallic gum. And Goodyear would spend years in court, defending his claim to discovery.

The funny thing was, Goodyear didn't seem to mind. He got to keep experimenting. He didn't have to fret over ledgers or worry about meeting a payroll. The man who had often compared his trials to those of Job had accomplished the task that he believed God had set him on earth to accomplish. That was enough. "The history of inventions as well as authors, with few exceptions," he wrote, "proves that whoever attempts by inventions to improve the conditions of others, usually impairs his own, except so far as he may add to his happiness, from the satisfaction of having done good to others."

"We Will Surely All Perish"

Unfortunately for John C. Frémont, the rubber from which his boat was made was not up to Goodyear's standards. Having the year before courted disaster, he now—a year older but apparently no wiser—rowed his "miserable rubber boat" out toward an island in the middle of the Great Salt Lake. It was a pleasant day, but the swells on the lake still tossed the small craft about and all could see a storm brewing well off in the distance. Halfway to their destination, Horace Day's inferior boat began leaking. A bellows

Frémont had brought along probably saved their lives, allowing each man to take a turn pumping air into the inflatable craft while the others rowed as rapidly as they could. "Frémont directed us to pull for our lives," Carson recalled, "if we do not arrive on shore before the storm commenced we will surely all perish." They managed to keep the contraption afloat long enough to reach the island about midday. "We done our best and arrived in time to save ourselves," Carson noted. The trip was hardly worth the effort or the risk. Frémont dubbed the spot, devoid of life and offering little in the way of interesting terrain to explore, Disappointment Island (it was later renamed Frémont Island). After climbing a few hills and taking some readings, the party returned to the beach, built a campfire, and settled in for the night in makeshift lodges built from driftwood.

The next morning, battling headwinds and even choppier water in the hazardous boat, Frémont's men returned to the base camp, packed up, took their leave of the lake, and headed back toward the Oregon Trail. Worn out and hungry, they killed a horse to eat, although Frémont and Preuss skipped the meal. "Mr. Preuss and myself could not yet overcome some remains of civilized prejudices, and preferred to starve a little longer," Frémont wrote. Preuss, preferring not to starve or eat horseflesh, "purchased antelope meat from a roving Indian."

The others didn't seem to mind. Mountain man Basil Lajeunesse was "singing and laughing this morning" having "filled his belly" with horse-meat. Carson went ahead of the main group to ensure they would have supplies available at Fort Hall, a British fur trading station on the Snake River in what is now Idaho. "If the emigrants get ahead of us, we shall not find much there," Preuss noted.

Luckily for Frémont's wife, Jessie, she was spared the details of the party's culinary endeavors. She was already worried enough for her husband. About the time they reached Fort Hall at the confluence of the Snake and Port Neuf rivers, she received a letter he had written shortly after moving out on the trail in June. At that point, he told her that he expected to be home by the new year. She dutifully passed along this bit of good news to a friend, Adelaide Talbot, the widowed mother of teenage voyageur Theodore Talbot, writing her that "by the middle or end of December they expect to be in this place."

If Frémont actually believed that in June, he had other plans in mind by fall, and Preuss noted that "this side trip to the Salt Lake costs us so much time that he [Frémont] himself has probably given up the idea of reaching the Pacific Ocean and still be home this winter." Frémont's simple orders from Abert had charged the explorer with noting areas along the trail that would be of use to emigrants, including watering holes and pasture land. Frémont knew that Benton and his fellow expansionists were just as interested in finding sites for military outposts. His former mentor, Joel Poinsett, was another who had strongly supported the building of a line of forts during his time as secretary of war. Others, including Kearny, who had supplied Frémont's howitzer, thought occasional marches up the trail would cost less and work just as well. But Frémont was here to do the bidding of Benton's Military Affairs Committee, which was trying to get the Senate to consider fort-building legislation.

"A military post, and a civilized settlement, would be of great value here," he wrote of the area between the Bear and Snake rivers, "and cattle and horses would do well where grass and salt so much abound." The head of the scientific expedition was also taking careful notes in his role as the missionary of Manifest Destiny.

As Frémont plotted his next moves, the weather turned. On September 19 and 20 it snowed all day and night, with the temperatures dipping into the low twenties. The rivers froze over. Supplies were low, and Frémont knew it would likely get worse. Some discontent—beyond the usual from Preuss—began to emerge in the ranks, so Frémont decided to send ten of the worst grumblers back to St. Louis, led by the horse-fed Lajeunesse. He entrusted them with letters, including some intended for Jessie, but they would lose them in a river crossing. On September 23 the rest of the men left Fort Hall and headed for Oregon, following the Snake River.

One of the mileposts along the way for Frémont, like other westbound travelers, was the Whitman Mission, off the Oregon Trail about twenty-five miles east of the Hudson's Bay Company's fur trading post at Fort Walla Walla in what is now southeastern Washington. Dr. Marcus Whitman and his wife, Narcissa, had come to the region in 1836 as Presbyterian missionaries trying to convert the Cayuse Indians to Christianity. They enjoyed few successes on that score, but the mission had grown into something of a successful commercial enterprise and soon became a way station for tired and hungry pioneers on their way to Oregon's Willamette Valley, three hundred miles or so further west. When Frémont arrived at the mission on October 24, Whitman was away, but a "fine-looking large family of emigrants, men, women and children, in robust health" were benefitting from Narcissa's hospitality.

Frémont and his men would too. There was no corn meal or flour to be had, but they scooped up a supply of potatoes, "which are produced here of remarkably good quality" and "furnished a grateful substitute for bread," and other items. Frémont sent a bill to Abert for $182.31, payable to Whitman, for "supplies furnished to the Exploring party under my command."

From there, it was a relatively easy passage west along the southern bank of the Columbia. Frémont, with Preuss and two others, went ahead to visit Fort Vancouver, headquarters of the Hudson's Bay Company and the center of British influence in Oregon. The man in charge there, John McLoughlin, was well known as a benefactor of emigrants, much to the chagrin of his masters in London, who would have preferred fewer Americans pouring into the territory.

Human kindness was one thing, but McLoughlin went above and beyond. It had long been the British position that their claim to Oregon was stronger than the American claim because, among other things, it was impossible for enough Americans to complete the overland trek and make settlement worthwhile. McLoughlin's generosity, Hudson's Bay officials feared, was not serving company or national interests. By 1844, McLoughlin had provided more than $31,000 in company credit to about four hundred overlanders, to say nothing of the uncounted thousands of dollars of his own money he had spent saving lives. The fields around the fort were rich with grain, fruit trees, and vegetables, which McLoughlin shared generously. He may have irritated his bosses, but he played a role in easing anti-British hostility in Oregon. "They say that one can get everything here that one's heart desires," Preuss noted. "God knows we need quite a few things."

Fort Vancouver was officially the end of the line for the expedition. With his assigned mission completed, it was now time for Frémont to turn around and head home. He wouldn't make it by Christmas, as he had assured his wife and as she had fondly hoped, but he might make it by spring. That

offered little satisfaction to Preuss. "In December my old girl will be surprised to receive only a letter instead of me," he complained. But instead
of turning homeward, Frémont turned southward, toward California, with
twenty-five men.

About a month after Frémont's decision to follow his sense of adventure
rather than his orders, Lajeunesse's party was in St. Louis, without the lost
letters but relaying "many details of the Summer's campaign" to Jessie and
reporting "perfect success in all their undertakings." They spared her the
details about being so hungry they had to kill a horse to avoid starvation.
And they were entirely ignorant of Frémont's decision to continue exploring
rather than returning home.

"On the Summit of the Pass"

When Frémont left St. Louis, he probably did expect to be home by Christmas
1843. Instead, he spent the holiday in northern Nevada, on the western rim
of the Great Basin, staring up at the snow-capped peaks of the Sierra Nevada.
But, home or not, it was still Christmas. "We were roused, on Christmas
morning, by a discharge from the small arms and howitzer, with which our
people saluted the day. . . . Always, on days of religious or national commemo-
ration, our voyageurs expect some unusual allowance; and, having nothing
else, I gave them each a little brandy . . . with some coffee and sugar, which
here, where every eatable was a luxury, was sufficient to make them a feast."

Soon even the ever-optimistic Frémont started to lose heart. Having
spent the night in a dry basin with bad grass, "our new year's eve was rather a
gloomy one. The result of our journey began to be very uncertain." Here, no
doubt, were the "discomforts" that Longfellow had ruefully noted accompanied the adventure. As they moved along the rim of the basin, Frémont
reported that "with every stream I now expected to see the great Buenaven-
tura," the mythical river that so many Western explorers had assumed—
incorrectly—connected the great river systems of the inter-mountain region
to the Pacific. Frémont didn't find it because it didn't exist. On January 19
he stopped looking and turned westward toward the Sierra Nevada.

As they approached the "somewhat rough-looking mountain," rock faced
and snow covered, a wall of ice and stone blocking their progress, Preuss noted

that "we still do not know where we really are." They received a few pointers from local Indians, who suggested Frémont move southward, indicating that drifts in the mountains could be as much as forty feet deep. Soon enough, Frémont found out this was not much of an exaggeration. As the party plodded up through the drifts, it became clear that the beloved howitzer, which Frémont and his wife had gone to such trouble to procure, would have to be left behind. On January 29 "that ridiculous thing," in Preuss's phrase, was abandoned, having never been fired at anyone, except a few buffalo.

Jessie might have appreciated the irony. Just a few days after the howitzer was left to rust in the snow, a member of the corps who had returned east with Basil Lajeunesse stopped by the house in St. Louis to trace on a map what he believed was Frémont's progress to date. The voyager "satisfied me that he would be here in February." It was already a month later than she expected his return, and Jessie was getting anxious—"from the moment I open my eyes in the morning until I am asleep again I look for him."

He wouldn't arrive anytime soon. Still heading west, on February 2 the group—strung out across a long line—covered only sixteen miles. The next day they managed less than half that. Floundering in deep snow, a large number of their horses and mules fell by the wayside. There was no grass available for the animals to eat. Those that didn't quit altogether began eating the saddles, the bridles, and each other's tails. Some of the men, copying a design they had seen on Indians, rigged rough pairs of snowshoes that helped a bit. Materials at hand—tree limbs, saddlebags, and such—were used to build sledges to aid the movement of equipment. They pounded the snow with shovels, mallets, and their feet to smooth out a path. Often, though, the howling wind quickly blew drifts back over their handiwork.

On February 10 Frémont established a base camp, in sight of a pass that Carson was sure he remembered from a previous trip to California fourteen years earlier. Over the next few days, all the men who had been strung out behind the lead group caught up, although the supply train was running behind, which led to another four-footed casualty being claimed on February 13.

> The meat train did not arrive this evening, and I gave Godey leave to
> kill our little dog (Tlamath), which he prepared in Indian fashion;

scorching off the hair, and washing the skin with soap and snow, and then cutting it up into pieces, which were laid on the snow. Shortly afterwards, the sleigh arrived with a supply of horse meat; and we had to-night an extraordinary dinner—pea soup, mule, and dog.

Preuss again demurred, as he had with the horse in Idaho, and soothed his hunger pangs by reading a copy of Byron's *Don Juan* he had brought along. But the feast helped fortify the rest of the troop against the bitter cold. Some nights it was "too cold to sleep" as snow fell and gale force winds blew. On sunny days, the glare of the sun off the snow was blinding, and some of the men wore black silk handkerchiefs as veils to protect their eyes. Frémont led a small group up a nearby peak from which they spotted a large mountain lake off in the distance, becoming perhaps the first white men to see Lake Tahoe.

After a month of struggle, Frémont finally crossed the summit at elevation 9,338 feet. "On the 19th, the people were occupied in making a road and bringing up the baggage; and, on the afternoon of the next day, February 20, 1844, we encamped with the animals and all the materiel of the camp, on the summit of the Pass in the dividing ridge." It was a moment worthy of celebration, and "the people, who had not yet been to this point, climbed the neighboring peak to enjoy a look at the valley." Frémont had come through the Sierra in winter, a brave, foolhardy venture that was outside the purview of his orders and would delay his return home by eight months. But he had shown that it could be done, and the feat would soon be repeated by emigrants much less well equipped than Frémont and his men.

Still, it was not quite literally all downhill from there. The weather turned warmer, proving a hindrance in making progress through the snow, which no longer had a sturdy crust on top. On February 27 Carson found a "hill side sprinkled with grass enough for the night," and on the twenty-eighth—the day of the explosion aboard the *Princeton*—they rested the animals in a narrow ravine and sent parties back up the mountain to hurry along stragglers who had fallen behind.

Preuss got lost, giving him something real to complain about for a change. "A fine mess," he called it. "I sit here alone and cannot find the others." A day later he recorded drily in his journal that "this is beginning to get serious." Preuss made it back to camp after being lost for three days, but Baptiste Derosier, who had been sent to look for him, disappeared without a trace. (Amazingly, he turned up two years later, alive and well, in St. Louis.)

From the summit, the party took two weeks to reach the safety of Sutter's Fort. Traveling through "surpassingly beautiful country," the remaining horses and mules were strengthened by plentiful grass, but the men passed up chances to shoot game in their haste to reach civilization. They got a little something to eat in an Indian village, then pressed on to another, where they encountered "a well dressed Indian" who greeted them in "very well spoken Spanish" and informed Frémont that he was an employee of John Sutter. The date was March 6. They had lost nearly half of the seventy or so horses and mules they'd started up the mountain with. They were tired, hungry, and, in Carson's words, "in as poor a condition as men possibly could be." But they had reached the promised land.

"Thin as a Shadow"

John Augustus Sutter was a Swiss émigré who arrived in California in 1839, befriended local Mexican officials, and in short order established a "colony," which he christened New Helvetia, on a forty-eight-thousand-acre land grant at the confluence of the American and Sacramento rivers. He ruled over the estate like a baron of old, employing Indians and Mexicans and producing grain, timber, fruit, wine, and other necessities of life. As pioneers began trickling into California, Sutter's Fort—like John McLoughlin at Fort Vancouver in Oregon—became a lifeline for the bedraggled masses.

Frémont's party spent two and a half weeks enjoying Sutter's hospitality at the fort. While they recuperated, gold was discovered—then lost—elsewhere on the property.

John Bidwell, one of the leaders of the first group of emigrants to California, who had crossed the Sierra Nevada in 1841 after leaving their wagons behind, now worked for Sutter as superintendent of a farm on the Feather River. While Frémont was in residence at the fort, one of Bidwell's employees, Pablo Gutierrez, had hiked up into the mountains looking for his wife, who had gone missing. He didn't find her, but he did stumble across "clear signs of gold," as Bidwell recounted the story years later, along the Bear

River. When he returned to work, Gutierrez informed Bidwell of his find. Intrigued, Bidwell and Gutierrez sojourned up to the Bear River a few days later, to the spot where the Mexican was sure a gold vein was located.

But they couldn't find it. Gutierrez, who knew something about rudimentary gold exploration, told Bidwell they needed a *batea*, which he had seen Mexican miners use, but there were none to be found in Alta California Territory. He would have to take leave from work to travel to northern Mexico to get the proper equipment. Bidwell thought this an extreme measure. But he didn't even know what a *batea* was—the Spanish word for the simple shallow bowl used in panning for gold.

Bidwell, after the adventure of his trip west three years before, must have been itching for another. He suggested that instead of Gutierrez leaving for Mexico, the two of them save up enough money to travel back east, where "ingenious Yankees" could make them the best *batea* money could buy. The idea must have baffled Gutierrez, but as little more than a serf under Sutter and Bidwell, he was in no position to argue. They left the matter there, and swore each other to secrecy.

Bidwell and Gutierrez never bought a *batea*, either Mexican or Yankee, and never went back to the Bear River together to look for gold. Less than four years later, another Sutter employee, James Marshall, found what Gutierrez had first seen in 1844, a few flakes of gold swimming down a mill race near the site of their earlier expedition, giving birth to the California Gold Rush.

While Frémont rested and gold was being undiscovered in California, two thousand miles away in Missouri Jessie continued her optimistic vigil. Assuming, based on reports filtering back to St. Louis from mountain men and other travelers, that her husband had spent the winter holed up at Fort Hall, in British-occupied Oregon, Jessie guessed in early March that "he cannot be here until the middle of April," which she amended to "the last of April as the earliest date" a few weeks later.

When late April arrived without her husband, she moved the goalposts once more. Again assuming, from what experienced mountain men had told her, that Frémont wintered in Oregon or camped at the foot of the mountains, she guessed that "he will not be here until the middle of May." The notion that she would be waiting longer still brought out the poet in her. "The advancing season cannot fail to bring them," she rhapsodized.

"The locust trees by my windows are covered with white blossoms. They look as if they had come forth to meet a bridegroom."

While Jessie waited amid the spring flowers, Frémont's mountain men embarked on the last great adventure of the expedition. On April 24, an old Mexican man named Andreas Fuentes and a young boy, Pablo Hernandez, came into the camp, looking nearly as bedraggled as had Frémont's men when they stumbled out of the Sierra Nevada seven weeks earlier. They told Frémont they were the only survivors of a Paiute raid that had separated them from the other members of their group, which had been traveling with about thirty horses along the Old Spanish Trail. Frémont offered them the hospitality of the camp, which was set up near a water hole on the mostly arid Mojave River, but that was all. He had no interest in slowing his progress to come to the aid of strangers along the trail.

After breaking camp the next morning, however, a little further along the trail they came upon signs of the Paiute raiding party, at which point the mountain man honor code kicked in for Kit Carson and Alexis Godey. Both volunteered to help the two refugees recover their lost property, and Carson fully expected some of the others to join in. When they didn't, the two mountain men rode off together, with Fuentes tagging along on a borrowed horse. Fuentes soon dropped out and returned to camp. The two mountain men pressed on. They tracked by moonlight until the rocky ground became too difficult to traverse, then made a fireless camp to await the dawn.

At first light they were back in the saddle, and soon spotted the purloined horses, collected on high ground above an encampment of four Paiute lodges. Creeping up silently, Carson and Godey got within about forty yards of their prey when some stirring among the horses alerted the Indians to their presence. In a flash they were rushing the lodges on foot, whooping Indian-style as they raced through the camp, dodging arrows along the way. One projectile pierced Godey's shirt collar. Frémont's men returned the fire with rifles, and two Paiutes were quickly dispatched. Seeing this, the others raced away to safety. Godey, angered by his brush with death, went to scalp the two casualties while Carson stood guard over their lone prisoner, a slow-footed youth who failed to escape with the rest.

Much to Godey's surprise, one of the shooting victims was not quite ready to surrender his scalp. The man, who had been shot twice, "sprung to his feet, the blood streaming from his skinned head and uttering a hideous howl," in Frémont's retelling. Adding a lachrymose note to the squalid scene, "an old squaw, possibly his mother, stopped and looked back from the mountain side she was climbing, threatening and lamenting." The wailing did nothing to deter Godey. He finished claiming the scalp, then "did what humanity required and quickly terminated the agonies of the gory savage."

By the next afternoon, Carson and Godey were riding back into Frémont's column, Fuentes's horses in tow, raising a "war whoop . . . such as Indians make when returning from a victorious enterprise." At the end of Godey's long gun hung the scalps, dripping blood.

From there, it was relatively smooth going. The corps continued on northeast, revisiting the Great Salt Lake, then turning eastward across northern Colorado. On June 8, the day of the Texas treaty vote, while Jessie suffered bad headaches and baby Lily the whooping cough, Frémont halted the corps "at a little spring of bad water" where

> we had not even the shelter of [cedar trees] from the hot rays of the sun. At night we encamped in a fine grove of cottonwood trees, on the banks of the Elk Head river, the principal fork of the Yampah river, commonly called by the trappers the Bear river. We made here a very strong corral and fort, and formed the camp into vigilant guards. The country we were now entering is constantly infested by war parties of the Sioux and other Indians, and is considered among the most dangerous war grounds in the Rocky mountains; parties of whites having been repeatedly defeated on this river.

But they encountered no more hostile Indians and continued making good time. Not good enough for Jessie, though. Just after the annexation vote, she wrote that she would "look for their being here the first of July." Having written many letters over the past year trying to buck up the spirits of Adelaide Talbot, and knowing she would find out about Theodore's return before Mrs. Talbot would, Jessie sympathized that "I wish I had Morse's telegraph" with which to send on the news. "It would surely be a better use than disappointing Presidential candidates, and bothering the country about the Texas Treaty," she wrote.

Without a telegraph, the news came slowly. Occasional letters from the West had found their way into Eastern newspapers, allowing the public to follow some of Frémont's adventures. One from Thomas Larkin, the US consul at Monterey, appeared in the *New York Tribune* on June 21 reporting on the expedition's arrival at Sutter's Fort, "The starvation and fatigue they had endured rendered them truly deplorable objects."

The first of July found Frémont still 750 miles west of St. Louis, at Bent's Fort, where William Bent's son, George, fired "repeated discharges from the guns" to greet the weary travelers. Preuss complained that he "enjoyed nothing but mosquitoes," but the party spent four days at the trading post, resting and recovering and knowing that, finally, "all the dangers and difficulties of the road being considered past," they were almost home.

Finally, late in the evening of August 6, John C. Frémont arrived in St. Louis. He went immediately to the Benton home, but finding it dark decided not to barge in. Instead, like a schoolboy, he tossed a handful of gravel at the window of the sleeping quarters of the family coachman. It was open. The pebbles flew into the room, waking up the servant, who saw Frémont, "thin as a shadow," in the moonlight. Sleepily, he told Frémont that Jessie was spending the night at the home of a cousin whose husband was sick. Frémont rushed over to the cousin's house but, seeing it dark also, decided to wait until morning rather than wake everyone. He wandered into town and found a spot on a bench in front of Barnum's Hotel, where he determined to while away the night.

But it paid to be famous, even in 1844. A clerk recognized Frémont and offered him a room, which he happily accepted. He hadn't slept in a proper bed in more than a year. The morning of the seventh, a messenger arrived at the home of Jessie's cousin, delivering the news that Frémont had been seen in town. Soon after, he came through the door. He swept Jessie up in his arms, covered her with kisses, and asked after baby Lily and the family. The house quickly filled up with family and friends, robbing the couple of privacy for a time as John graciously greeted each well-wisher before finally stealing away with his bride.

His expedition, planned to last eight months, had lasted fourteen. In that time he had traveled farther than Lewis and Clark had gone in almost twice the time. Much had happened in his absence. His father-in-law had narrowly escaped death aboard the *Princeton*. Expansionist James K. Polk had been chosen as Democratic candidate for president. Texas annexation had been defeated, for the moment. And hundreds more emigrants, like those Frémont had seen at the beginning of his journey, had come through St. Louis on their way to mustering points in western Missouri and Iowa, headed for Oregon and California.

As daring as some of Frémont's exploits had been, they would pale in comparison to what awaited the emigrant parties of 1844.

{ 6 }

To Oregon and California

Seventeen-year-old Moses Schallenberger was eager to get started. Yet he had to wait. He had come to Council Bluffs, Iowa, with his sister, brother-in-law, and a host of other overland emigrants who had camped since March near the Nishnabotna River in northwestern Missouri, about fifty miles from Council Bluffs. But since their arrival, rain had pelted the canvas-covered wagon that Moses now called home. He could stare out across the swollen waters of the Missouri River and imagine the West he was about to enter, but that was all he could do. The river was too high and too swift to risk a crossing.

So Moses waited with the rest of his family and a growing band of overlanders who were joining together to travel to Oregon and California. His sister, Elizabeth Louise, was married to Dr. John Townsend, one of the leaders of the party. Mrs. Townsend was "very delicate," and hoped to regain her health in the West. The family wagon was outfitted with a feather bed for her comfort.

Traveling with the Townsend-Schallenberger party were the Murphys, an Irish family that had emigrated to Canada in 1820 before moving on to the Missouri frontier in 1840. While Polk, Benton, and others dreamed of an American empire stretching from ocean to ocean, one motivation for the Murphy clan's emigration was that California was a Roman Catholic country, a possession of Mexico, where they hoped they "would find themselves under more sympathetic conditions than obtained in the United States."

Everyone who encamped at Council Bluffs and down the river near Independence, another favorite embarkation point, had their reasons for emigrating. The drive to Oregon had been fueled by Frémont's reports (and Jessie's mellifluous prose), but it predated his journeys by decades. John Jacob Astor had staked an American claim to the territory with his fur trading business shortly after the turn of the nineteenth century, and American trappers and traders poured into the area in search of furry riches in the years following. An 1818 treaty established the joint occupancy of Britain and America that was still in place in 1844, but the English had done little beyond commercial ventures to embellish their claim.

Americans were voting with their feet. The writings of Washington Irving and James Fenimore Cooper had created a romantic notion of the frontier in the minds of many. Missionaries led by Jason Lee had come in the 1830s. A steady trickle of emigrants followed, and the trickle turned into a swift current in the early 1840s. By the summer of 1844, nearly fifteen hundred more were on their way, including a band of more than fifty that would turn toward California.

Emigrant parties in 1841 and 1843 had made the left turn that took them to California, but none had yet made it over the Sierra Nevada with their wagons. These were not, as is often supposed, the great freight-hauling Conestoga wagons of legend. Rather, they were usually simple farm wagons, perhaps ten feet by four feet, with sides two feet high and topped by a canvas cover held in place by curved bows made of hickory. Ideally, a man could stand upright in the center, but not always. The cover would be waterproofed, at least by the standards of the day, with paint or linseed oil. Wagon wheels were wood of a hard variety—maple, poplar, hickory, ash, beech, elm, or oak—wrapped in iron tires.

The design of the wagon and what went into it were a constant balancing act between being prepared, being hardy, and being light enough not to wear out the oxen who were pulling the wagon load (this included people, who more often than they might have supposed ended up walking much of the distance to spare the animals the extra weight).

Recommendations about what to take on the voyage varied, but there were a few staples. An 1843 traveler, one of the thousand or so who had joined the Great Migration the year before, laid out in a letter to a Missouri newspaper the standard provisions for those who might be following in 1844: "150 lbs. of flour, and 60 lbs. of bacon to each person will be ample. You may add sugar, coffee, tea, rice, dried fruit, peas, corn meal, corn and other things in such proportions as you may see proper. . . . It would certainly be advisable to bring a few beef cattle to slaughter on the road, as you will need fresh meat. One of the most necessary things on the road is milch cows. . . . Bring as many cows and heifers as you can." The writer also noted that emigrants could trade "two poor oxen for one fat one" at Fort Hall.

Emigrants would liquidate their assets to fund the trip—an echo of the Millerites' liquidations ahead of the spring disappointment—and those who were farmers would often bring along what stock they kept. Others worked in cash. Overlanders were not, for the most part, from the economic lower classes, but relatively well-off, prosperous enough at least to fund the trip west. Items they didn't bring with them could often be bought at or near their departure point. St. Louis was a major provisioning stop, and items tended to get scarcer—and more expensive—the farther west one pushed into Missouri.

Frontier towns would come to appreciate the business brought by those passing through on their way to the west coast, but in the early years of the Great Emigration townspeople were more likely to resent the "ignorant, deluded men" who would rather risk the voyage than settle in Missouri. It was a parochial complaint, but this kind of talk influenced some borderline cases. Baptist preacher Ezra Fisher was all set to go on the 1844 trail, but canceled his plans after reading and hearing about the hardships his young family would be subjected to.

For Fisher, it was a temporary delay. He and his family headed west one year later. Others contemplated the trip but never pulled the trigger. Some, comfortable where they were, never even considered it. But for those who did, the attractions were many. Land was first among them, and some cited for their inspiration legislative efforts by Benton and his Missouri colleague, Lewis Linn, to solidify US control over Oregon by making federal land grants. But it was far from the only reason.

In some respects, the motivations of emigrants and Millerites coincided. The Panic of 1837 and the ensuing years-long depression were a spur to individuals inclined toward one or the other. Either the hard times were a sign of the end times, or they were a sign that it was time to set out for the territories. Broadly defined, overlanders were seeking opportunity—away from the more established societies of the east, or the quickly filling-up towns of the Missouri frontier. Most were born in—or were the children of parents born in—the upper South. The young and the old went, men and women, from every occupation imaginable—carpenters, coopers, blacksmiths, gunsmiths, millwrights, lawyers, ministers, weavers, tailors, shopkeepers. If Frémont was the missionary of Manifest Destiny, they were the congregation.

THE GREAT PLATTE RIVER ROAD

When the signal to move out was finally given on May 18, the humans and wagons of the Stevens-Townsend-Murphy party had little trouble getting across the wide Missouri on a crude flat boat owned by a local Potawatomi chief. They supposed they could persuade the cattle to swim across.

But the cows had other ideas, refusing to enter the water or, worse, getting stuck in the mud along the bank. Some of these were easily rescued with a spade and shovel. Others were stuck too deeply to extract. Despite their value they were deemed less valuable than the time that would be lost digging them out, so they were abandoned. The others were guided across the river by an ingenious method that had two men crossing the river by canoe with a line attached to the horns of a dependable ox. The ox was trundled into the river until he was forced to swim, at which point the men with the line could guide him, and the other cattle were more easily persuaded to follow. By the twenty-fifth, all the cattle were on the west bank.

Once across the river, a necessary rite of passage was observed when the gathered travelers chose their leaders and made their rules for the trip. Elisha Stevens, a veteran of the Rocky Mountain fur trade, was named captain. Caleb Greenwood, a wizened mountain man who claimed to be eighty but was probably closer to sixty, was named guide, a move that met with resistance from Jacob Hammer, a stubborn and independent Indiana Quaker who had joined the party on May 13 south of Council Bluffs. Hammer complained that "Greenwood is nearly blind," and also objected to a levy on each traveler that would pay Greenwood's salary, declaring that "I will not pay anything."

Nevertheless, so organized, the troop began moving westward in fits and starts. "In camp today because it is raining," Hammer reported on the twenty-eighth and twenty-ninth. Perhaps those already disgruntled by the rain blamed Stevens for the weather; they agitated for another vote for captain. The revote was held, and Stevens was duly reelected. The rain was inconvenient, but the biggest problem it posed was not immediate. Certainly travel would have been more pleasant if this hadn't been the wettest season on the plains that anybody could remember, but the real difficulty was that travel days lost in May and June could not be made up in October as the emigrants approached the snow-capped Sierras in California or Blue Mountains in Oregon. Crossing every swollen river or creek required extra physical exertion, while adding anxiety that the time lost was gone forever.

This was the first wagon train to use what would come to be known as the Council Bluffs Road (and later the Mormon Trail) that ran north of the Platte River, blazed by Astor and others heading eastward in 1813. Those traveling on the north side had it easier than the travelers on the better-worn south side, where the rains were heavier and the obstacles greater. But everyone had their share of problems. The first came on May 30 when they reached the Elkhorn River in Nebraska, not a waterway that would rival the Missouri in breadth but "a river about the size of the Wabash at Terre Haute," just wide enough at flood stage to cause a problem. One wagon, perched without support atop a flat boat, tipped over and floated a good way downstream before it was recovered. That incident sparked a change in tactics, and it took three days to get forty wagons across the Elkhorn by way of a ferry system of flat boats hauled by rawhide ropes strung across the river and tied to trees on either side.

The emigrants couldn't cross the next major river, the swift and several-hundred-yard-wide Loup, because the soft sand along its banks would capture the wagons. So they traveled westerly along the river's line, leading them to their first encounter with Indians at a Pawnee village. The Pawnees had lately been raided by Sioux, and those who remained were friendly to the travelers, whom they perhaps saw, correctly or not, as insurance against further Sioux depredations. Schallenberger reported that, since the Sioux had come and gone, the white travelers felt more secure about putting their cattle out to graze. The Pawnee shared a seven-pound mammoth tooth found thereabouts, another wonder to the travelers only late of civilization.

As the party left the Loup and headed for the Platte, the rain did not relent. In some spots the bottomlands were under twelve feet of water. Hammer, a devout Quaker, was convinced Noah-like that the torrent was a holy judgment on "those that are doing wrong willfully." In the first two months of travel, the 1844 emigrants had only eight days without rain. But within a few days of Hammer's observation about divine judgment the rain slackened and then stopped, and the train moved fully into the valley of the Platte, where further wonders awaited.

The way leading to the Great Platte River Road traversed some of the richest farmland anywhere in North America, but the overlanders—eyes fixed firmly on Oregon and California—barely paused to take notice. Now, as they moved westward, the soil changed along with the landscape to a sandier, rougher, drier terrain. Finding wood was getting to be a problem. Trees were scarce, and the camp cooks quickly adopted the practice of using buffalo dung for cooking fires. Antelope and buffalo were seen often, and the party spent most of a day parading through a giant prairie dog town, replete with a scattering of bleached buffalo bones. They crossed paths with a group of traders coming down the river, who agreed to carry letters back east.

They also began to see the toll such a trip can take. One traveler, Thomas Vance, fell ill with a fever. Although the party paused for a day to let him rest, they were back on the road the next day, and his condition worsened. On June 28, he died at sunset. Because of the scarcity of wood, he was buried without a coffin, wrapped in a quilt, with a bed of grass and sod placed atop "so that it might not be noticed by the savages, though no danger of being robbed that we know of by them," Hammer recorded.

Vance's death represented the grim reality of the journey. But for Moses Schallenberger, seventeen and on the edge of invincible manhood, such incidents must have been a momentary distraction from the adventure. Along with young John Murphy, Moses was chosen as a corporal of the guard, a more or less honorary title that nevertheless conveyed on him an air of responsibility for camp security. Moses was an excellent shot and possessed a "reckless bravery born of frontier life."

As they marched on, the travelers began to see the west unfold before them. The north side of the Platte afforded more distant views of the road's premier geological attractions—Ash Hollow, Court House Rock, Chimney Rock, and Scott's Bluff, all more easily accessible from the Southern Road. On July 4 "we come in sight of the chimnies," Hammer wrote. Mapmaker Charles Preuss, traveling with Frémont in 1842, was the second person known to draw the outcropping (after Alfred Jacob Miller), but he was the first to call it Chimney Rock. The feature, previously referred to most often simply as the Chimney, was the most noticed and described landmark on the trail, perhaps because it was the first stark example for the pioneers that they were entering a world completely different from the green and soggy one they were leaving behind.

The Stevens-Townsend-Murphy party had come out of the rain and was now moving at a steady rate of better than twenty miles a day, although their arrival at the great rock formations of Nebraska in the first week of July was testament to how much time they had lost because of the early bad weather. Ideally, the goal was to be at Independence Rock in Wyoming by the Fourth of July. Well ahead of some of their fellow northside travelers, the Stevens-Townsend-Murphy party was still several hundred miles from the rock on July 4, 1844.

But they seemed for the most part unconcerned. Weddings were held and babies were born. Occasionally—though not as often as one might think in such a religious age—church services were conducted. The group was moving briskly and buffalo were plentiful. Sometimes hunters would go off and not be seen for days, but their fellows evinced little concern, assuming they would find their way back, which they almost always did. Moses Schallenberger took part in several hunts that yielded "an abundance of meat from younger buffaloes, which is generally conceded to be superior to that from any other animal." Some in the party took time to enjoy the scenery and catalog the flora and fauna, much of which was brand new to the travelers. As they continued up the Platte, the northern and southern roads came together and grew more crowded, and the land and their fortunes were about to change again.

THE SOUTHSIDERS

Henry Sager was, in the words of his daughter Catherine, "one of the restless ones who are not content to remain in one place long at a time." A descendant of eighteenth century German immigrants, a farmer and blacksmith, the Loudon County, Virginia, native had brought his wife, Naomi, and their four children to Missouri from Ohio in 1838. In Missouri they first settled in the eastern part of the state, but after a season moved farther west, to Platte County, between Independence and St. Joseph, near where the Mormons had recently been chased from the state.

In 1844 the Sagers had six children and a seventh on the way. He thought for a while about going to Texas. But inspired by tales of the Oregon country he heard during Marcus Whitman's 1843 visit east and swayed by his wife's preference for the healthier climate, Henry Sager decided on Oregon. He sold his farm in the fall of 1843. In April 1844 he and his wife, a former schoolteacher and the daughter of a Baptist minister, packed up the family and headed for St. Joseph.

Cornelius Gilliam, a veteran of the Black Hawk and Seminole wars, an ordained minister and former sheriff and state legislator, was the first captain of the wagon train leaving St. Joe, a new embarkation point for emigrants. One of his lieutenants was James Marshall, who in 1848 would find the gold on John Sutter's ranch that John Bidwell had failed to find in March 1844. Gilliam, his family, and a few others crossed the river March 2 and set up camp on Sac and Fox Indian land to await the arrival of more overlanders. As the spring rains continued, overlanders began arriving at the camp, which Gilliam had advertised in the late summer of 1843. By the first week of May, more than three hundred people with seventy wagons and seven hundred cattle had arrived. This group started west on May 9.

Friends came to say their final goodbyes to the Sagers and on May 14, a "bright spring morning," they headed west, appending themselves to the back of the Gilliam train, which now totaled about five hundred men, women, and children.

"The first encampments were a great pleasure to us children," remembered the oldest girl, Catherine, who was nine at the time. She was joined by her brothers, John, the oldest at thirteen, and Frank, eleven or twelve that year; and sisters Elizabeth, seven; Matilda, five; and Louisa, three. On May 31, about two and a half weeks after they left civilization, Rosanna was born in the family's wagon, arriving soon after they crossed the Missouri.

The early road was rough, requiring the crossing of limestone outcrops that jostled the wagon. Naomi was weakened by the birth of her seventh child—the train gave her only two days to recover before moving on—and soon the entire family was feeling the ill effects of travel. Conditions were made worse by the necessity of having to keep the canvas drawn tight over the wagon to keep out the rain, the family cramped uncomfortably together among their belongings, in clothes that stayed wet with little chance to dry them. The rocking of the wagon gave the children motion sickness— although it was useful in other ways. Families would strap a bucket of cream to the back of their wagons in the morning; by the time they stopped for the evening, they had freshly churned butter.

Like those who had left from Council Bluffs, the Sagers had trouble with their cattle. Early on, the confused cows returned to the spot on the east bank of the Missouri where Gilliam had established his camp. Henry had to round them up, then endure a forced march to catch up to the train, an effort made more difficult by his lack of experience driving oxen. Earlier emigrants learned quickly that oxen were the right animal for overland travel—they were hardier than horses, stronger than mules, and cheaper than both—but it took time to learn how to manage them. Sager had persistent trouble until he got a useful piece of advice from the captain of their band of wagons, Gilliam's brother-in-law, William Shaw, who advised him to pelt the beasts with rocks until they did what he wanted. Shaw was known to have fought with Andrew Jackson in the War of 1812, so Sager thought his advice trustworthy and tried the method, which seemed to work. The new technique and daily experience eased the way, though they soon encountered more trouble when some of the cattle were driven off by Indians who had tagged along with the train. After all the sweat to recover them, these number were never seen again.

Even worse than those on the northside road, the southsiders were slowed by heavy rains. They had to build canoes and a flat boat to ferry the party across even some of the smaller creeks that had spilled over their banks. At the Black Vermillion River in northeastern Kansas, the party waited seventeen days, then again had to employ a jerry-rigged flotilla to get wagons and material across the raging waters.

"It rained on them incessantly for the first two months of their trip, and nearly every water course they passed was swimming," eastbound travelers reported to newspapers back in civilization.

While they were stalled at the flooded river, many of the younger men seized the opportunity to do some hunting. "The passenger pigeons were flying in flocks southward," wrote John Minto, a twenty-one-year-old Pennsylvania coal miner who had hired himself to the family of Robert Morrison, one of the "company commanders" in the military-styled organization of the Gilliam train. "It was the last time I ever saw that wonderful sight." Minto and one of his mates bagged "many" of the pigeons, still plentiful at the time.

From the Black Vermillion, the train moved on to the Blue River, taking several days to cross using pontoons made of canoes lashed together with rawhide. They followed the river northwest to its junction with the Platte. On the Fourth of July they paused for a day of rest and washing and an evening wedding, then reached Grand Island, Nebraska, about July 7, running within a few days of the group on the other side of the river.

Along the way they picked up a party that included mountain man James Clyman, who had started out from Lone Elm, Kansas, five days behind the Gilliam train and who kept in close contact once both trains were traveling along the south side of the Platte.

Eventually the torrential rains gave way to foggy mornings, pleasant prairie days, and warm evenings filled with mosquitoes. As the troop gathered knowledge in the ways of travel through open country, the journey grew more enjoyable. A routine was developed. The day began at about 4 AM, when those on guard duty would discharge their rifles to wake the camp. Fires would be started or stoked and herders would spread out to make sure none of the cattle had wandered away during the night. Breakfast—bacon, maybe bread—would be eaten, wagons squared away, and by seven o'clock they would be on their way.

Everyone always wanted to get as far to the front as possible, to stay out of the dust of the wagons. This became something of a game for some trains, and the emigrants of 1844 reported several instances of passing each other along the road. On July 6, Clyman complained that his troop had been passed and was "now in the rear of all the different parties traveling over the western prairies." On the morning of the seventeenth they passed the Gilliam company, only to be passed by them later in the day. On the twentieth Clyman reported passing the Gilliam company again, and a month later he noted they had been repassed. All told, the combined companies were strung out over two miles of the road as they jockeyed for position. Hunters fanned out as the train began to move, searching for buffalo, antelope, or whatever they might come across. A halt would be called at noon to rest and graze the animals, but by 1 PM the train was moving again.

Travelers quickly learned that it was easier on their oxen if they walked instead of riding in the wagons—and often easier on themselves, since the wagons were not supplied with springs. Somewhere on either side of sunset, camp would be made, fires set, dinner cooked—more bacon, maybe bread with butter from the churn bucket tied to the wagon, dried fruit, buffalo if the hunters were successful (although they left a lot of meat to rot on the prairie for want of a way to carry it all back to camp). Sometimes women

JAMES CLYMAN. *Library of Congress*

joined in the chase. In the evening the camp transformed into a small neighborhood, with residents visiting one another, singing, sitting and talking, their children playing, until the darkness and the weariness sent all to their wagons for a good night's sleep.

Henry Sager was a skilled hunter who often went out in search of buffalo, leaving a hired man to tend to his team while he was gone. He kept the family well fed with both buffalo and antelope. Settled in for the night, the Sagers would listen as "several musical instruments . . . sounded clearly on the evening air," and "merry talk and laughter resounded from almost every camp-fire." With the skies clear and the weather fine, travel to Oregon appeared to be not much more difficult than riding the wagon into town for church on Sunday. But their good fortune was about to come to an end.

On July 18, a cool and windy day, the Sagers' wagon rode up on a ledge, causing it to tip over on a steep hill as the party prepared to ford the South Platte. The children riding inside were unhurt, but Naomi was knocked unconscious. The accident forced her into convalescence in the back of the wagon. That meant one less pair of hands to do the work, and more weight for the oxen to pull.

Two weeks later, another near-tragedy struck the family. The children had become quite adept at leaping into and out of the moving wagon, which plodded along at the oxen-pace of about two miles per hour. On August 1, the Sagers "nooned in a beautiful grove on the north side of the Platte" on a "dry clear warm day." When they resumed the trek, Catherine took her accustomed seat at the front of the wagon. After riding for a bit, she decided to walk beside the oxen. So, as she had done countless times, she leapt out of the moving wagon. This time, though, her dress caught on an axe handle protruding from under the canvas top "and I was thrown under the wagon wheel, which passed over and badly crushed my limb before father could stop the team. He picked me up and saw the extent of the injury when the injured limb hung dangling in the air."

"My dear child, your leg is broken all to pieces!" Henry Sager wailed. Quickly the word went out and the train was halted. Sager tended to his daughter while friends raced to find a German doctor, Theophilus Degen, who was traveling with the train. Henry insisted on setting the leg himself, but Degen came and checked on his work and tended to Catherine. She seemed to be doing fine, so the whips cracked and the oxen pulled out. They pushed on that night to Fort Laramie, arriving just after darkness fell. Catherine's injury would keep her confined to the wagon, lying beside her mother. And, although the Sager children would hardly have believed it after seeing their mother stricken and their sister disabled, these misfortunes were as nothing compared with what awaited them further down the road.

A Death in the Family

Fort Laramie was about one-third of the two thousand mile journey from the Missouri River to California and Oregon. Built in 1834 as a trading post near the confluence of the Platte and Laramie rivers in southwestern Wyoming and originally called Fort William, its whitewashed adobe walls were a welcome sight for tired, dusty travelers coming up the Platte.

Supplies could be had, but were sometimes hard to come by and often out of the emigrants' price range. Sugar could cost $1.50 a pound (about $40.00 in today's money), and a pound of flour could go as high as a $1.00. And the proprietors insisted on cash. On the other hand, many of the travelers had what they believed to be a surplus of bacon and looked to trade, but could get only 5¢ a pound for it at the fort. James Clyman, guiding one of the southside trains, paid $2.50 for a dressed deerskin. "No dried buffalo meat could be had at any price," he noted. Less than a mile away was Fort Platte, which competed, not too successfully, with Laramie. It was best known as a place to buy whiskey, which sold for $4.00 a pint.

More than anything, though, Fort Laramie was a place to take stock, rest up, and enjoy a rare moment of repose before returning to the trail. "We had a beautiful camp on the bank of the Laramie, and both weather and scene were delightful," one emigrant wrote. "The moon, I think, must have been near the full . . . we leveled off a space and one man played the fiddle and we danced into the night."

The travelers might have learned along the trail that Henry Clay and James K. Polk had won their parties' presidential nominations—Clyman reported hearing the news on June 22—which likely gave rise to some good-natured political debates around the fire. "Just Whigs enough in camp to take the curse off," wrote Clyman, whose long face bore a striking resemblance to that of President John Tyler.

For many, Fort Laramie afforded the first real chance to see more than a handful of Indians at a time. As the Schallenberger train halted, something like four thousand Sioux resided in the surrounding area. Encamped with their families, they presented not a threat to the travelers, but an opportunity to trade for sturdy Sioux ponies and moccasins to replace their worn-down animals, shoes, and boots. Others swapped tobacco, powder, and shot for a plains delicacy: buffalo meat fried in the beast's marrow.

There was, naturally, a bit of curiosity on both sides, coupled with perhaps a hint of paranoia. Emigrant William Case recalled that some of the Sioux were overheard "plotting mischief." Joseph Bissonette, an experienced mountain man working as a trader at Fort Laramie, brought the supposed plotters together and told them smallpox had struck the emigrant train. Remembering how smallpox had devastated their tribe and others in the past, the Sioux were quickly on the move away from the incoming emigrants. Or so Case recounted, though he may have invented the story; there was no smallpox and the emigrants and Indians got along quite well at Fort Laramie in 1844, the last year in which not a single death of Indian or overlander would be attributable to either side on the Oregon-California Trail.

After leaving the fort, the trail pushed on along the North Platte. Eventually, though, travelers had to leave their watery companion and head out across a dusty, fifty-mile wide plain populated by little more than sagebrush and alkali lakes on the way to the Sweetwater River. There was little or no grass, and what water remained in the summer was too alkaline to drink; this didn't stop the oxen from trying, often resulting in death—a precursor to what awaited both oxen and people farther down the road.

Along the Sweetwater, the pioneers entered the final stretch of buffalo country. So Moses Schallenberger and his friend John Murphy decided they would seize this final opportunity for a grand buffalo hunt. They started out early one morning and tracked several bands for most of the day, but never got close enough to get a shot off. Each time they approached, bulls on the outer edges of the herds would sense the danger and hustle their cows off to safety. In frustration, the young men began a desultory journey back toward the trail, empty handed.

As luck would have it, while the buffalo scattered Schallenberger and Murphy began to encounter herds of antelope. They decided antelope meat was better than no meat at all, and Murphy took aim and dropped one of the beasts. Quickly they began the laborious process of butchering the animal, and over friendly banter soon lost track of time. They also lost track of their horses, which had wandered off a hundred or so yards back toward the direction of the train. Murphy continued cutting up the antelope while Moses, armed with pistols and powder horn, took off to gather up their mounts. In no time he had a handle on both, but noticed that Murphy's blanket was missing from his horse. Scouring the landscape, he saw no blanket. When he got back to where Murphy was carving up the antelope, he left the guns and the two of them went off again in search of the missing blanket. They recovered it, but when they returned to the spot where they'd left their game and guns, they found nothing.

A trip that had started out with such promise of fun—and with considerable boasting about how much buffalo meat they would bring in—was now turning into farce. Darkness was falling. They were unarmed and alone. But they felt more embarrassed than endangered. As they discussed their predicament, they began to concoct a story about being accosted by Indians who had stolen their guns and meat. They realized no one would believe them, so they marked the spot where their goods had lately been and trudged back to camp, dreading the ridicule they knew would come. All had a good laugh at the boys' expense. But when they returned to the spot the next day with four other men, they still couldn't find either the guns or any trace of the antelope.

On July 16, some of the party that had been traveling with Hammer's group moved up the train to join the Stevens-Townsend-Murphy party, which was pulling away from the larger Oregon-bound group behind them. Aside from the hunting failure of Schallenberger and young Murphy, others had been successful in their hunts and a few days later the boys would be too. The party stopped to dry the meat for the long road still in front of them. They paused at Independence Rock, a hunk of granite 1,900 feet long and 700 feet wide that stood 128 feet high at its peak and was 2.6 billion years old, half as old as the earth.

Jacob Hammer carved his name on the gray monolith "near a small spring in the side of the rock," affixing his signature to a monument that

already had many such names—including John C. Frémont's—carved or
written on it.

For mountain men like Clyman and the aged Greenwood, Independence Rock must have seemed like an old school yearbook, with names and
dates from their previous lives etched in granite instead of on paper. One
was William Sublette, a famous trapper credited with naming the rock after
camping there one Fourth of July.

As July turned to August the travelers came "in sight of the everlasting
snows on the Rock mountains." The trail grew less obliging, requiring multiple crossings of the Sweetwater as the wagons splashed back and forth to
avoid forcing the oxen over rocky outcroppings.

Up the gentle slope they went, reaching the continental divide at South
Pass on August 8. "Here is about as good road as any that we have yet
traveled on," Hammer recorded in his journal. Clyman called it "a plasant
assent," seconding Frémont's comparison of the incline to walking up Capitol Hill in Washington. From South Pass, at a height of 7,550 feet, it was still
almost a thousand miles to the end of their journey.

Pacific Springs, a hundred yards or so beyond the crest of the pass, gave
overlanders the first tangible sign that they were in the Oregon Country,
and most rushed to take a drink from the first waters of the West.

Emerging from South Pass, emigrants entered a different world than the
one they had traveled for the past two and a half months. Up to this point,
rivers had for the most part been their friends. The Platte and the Sweetwater flowed easterly and provided a relatively flat road and easy passage for
their wagons. West of the divide, rivers tended to run north-south, creating
ridges and canyons that had to be crossed (and sometimes recrossed). River
valleys turned from roadways to impediments.

Days after reaching South Pass, the parties that had been together on
the same road since the forks of the Platte began to diverge. Most turned
southwest, down the beaten path toward Fort Bridger, on Black's Fork at
the foot of the Uinta Mountains. Here, as at Laramie but on a smaller scale,
travelers could do a little trading for fresh ponies or oxen. One of the Gilliam party traded a lame ox for a new hat and many emigrants handed off
letters to eastbound travelers. Founded by mountain man Jim Bridger, the
fort was the first trading post west of the Mississippi built for the express

purpose of serving overlanders, more than a thousand miles west of the jumping off points. Civilization was already coming to the trail.

Some emigrants followed the road less traveled, rather than the beaten path. Throughout the emigration period, overlanders were constantly in search of short cuts that would speed them on their way. This process began in earnest in 1844 when the Stevens-Townsend-Murphy party took the advice of Isaac Hitchcock, an old trapper and mountaineer who had been to California as far back as 1830, and who said he knew a better way. Instead of taking the road down to Fort Bridger, Hitchcock said, head due west from the Little Sandy, about twenty miles west of South Pass. This gives you a straight line across to the Green and Bear rivers, about thirty miles, according to Hitchcock, versus eighty miles for the V-shaped trip down to Bridger and back up the Bear River Valley. Who were these flatland greenhorns to question him?

Ten miles beyond the Little Sandy was the Big Sandy, a stream about ten feet wide and a foot deep that provided the last water the travelers would see until they reached the Green River, forty-five miles—not Hitchcock's estimated thirty miles—to the west. That extra fifteen miles mattered. With no water on the cutoff, the extra distance meant there would be at least one dry camp, with virtually no grass for the herds. And because Hitchcock was mistaken about the distance, the travelers did not lay in a supply of water for themselves or the animals.

They started out at daylight across rocky, uneven terrain. The trail, such as it was, descended into a deep ravine, then ascended a steep, boulder-strewn hill that required oxen teams to be doubled to get the wagons up and over. A flat stretch provided a bit of relief, but with no water or grass the burden on the animals was barely lessened. They pushed on into the darkness in hopes of reaching the Green River, but finally had to stop near sunrise to rest the oxen. If anyone sought out Hitchcock and asked him what the hell they were doing there, no one wrote about it.

After a brief break, they proceeded on. A few hours later, a light westerly breeze blew up. The oxen got a scent of the river ahead and began hauling the wagons forward at what passes for a brisk clip for oxen. All the wagon drivers managed to get their yokes undone and let the thirsty animals run free. They successfully negotiated the four-hundred-foot-high bluffs above the swift-running river, and soon thereafter the humans caught up and found their beasts of burden basking belly-deep in the cool, sparkling waters of the Green.

Unfortunately, after slaking their thirsts, a few confused oxen headed back toward the camp on Big Sandy. With five others, Moses Schallenberger was detailed to recover them. Soon after their departure back across the wasteland of the cutoff, the six began arguing about which way the cattle had gone. So they split up, with Schallenberger and two others trekking toward the Big Sandy. The other three headed south, down the Green.

Schallenberger's group found Indians before they found oxen. Ascending the walls of a small canyon, they tied up their horses and crawled across the rocky ground to get a better look at the mounted men they spotted off in the distance. They saw a party of about a hundred Sioux, slowly making their way toward the canyon. The three white men lay as still as they could, concealed among the rocks, while the Sioux rode past, close enough for their conversations to be overheard, if not understood. Once the Sioux rode out of sight, the men remounted and rode on to the Big Sandy, where they found all the missing cattle peacefully sipping from the river. It was late, so they made a cold camp, lighting no fires so as not to alert the Sioux to their presence.

The next morning, shortly after they began herding the animals back toward the Green River, they again spotted Indians. First two, then four, and suddenly, almost without warning, dozens more, and they were quickly confronted by a band on horseback almost as large as the one they had seen pass the previous day. This time there was no chance to hide. Both parties had seen the other, so the three men rode up slowly, all the while discussing how each man would kill as many as he could before succumbing, and saying what they were sure were their last goodbyes. But the natives turned out to be a friendly party of Snake Indians out pursuing the Sioux the emigrants had seen the day before. The Indians helped drive the oxen back to the Green River camp, which they reached at about 9 PM.

The shortcut the Stevens-Townsend-Murphy party used was known for a time as Greenwood's Cutoff, on the mistaken assumption that old Caleb Greenwood had guided the travelers to and through it. Later the name Sublette Pass would be affixed. But Hitchcock's Cutoff, as it should properly be known, was such a dry, desolate crossing that perhaps no one would want to have his name attached to it.

The California-bound party left the Green River and headed northwest through the Bear River Valley, once the epicenter of the Rocky Mountain fur trapping business, toward Fort Hall, a wood-framed structure encased in adobe bricks. The fort was built in 1834 by American trader Nathaniel Wyeth, who went belly-up and had to sell out to the Hudson's Bay Company in 1837. A plump Scotsman, Richard Grant, was the chief factor, and much like John McLoughlin at Fort Vancouver, he sold goods to American emigrants, all the while trying to persuade them to head for Mexican California rather than Oregon. Schallenberger and his cohorts felt they had enough dried buffalo meat to last, but stocked up on flour, for which they paid a dollar a pound. But they needed no exhortations from the self-interested Brit on where they should head next, and after a few days' rest they were back on the trail.

Two days later, they reached the Raft River in what is now southern Idaho. Before the proliferation of cutoffs that would move the Oregon-California split further to the east, this was the original parting of the ways. Here the travelers bound for California took their leave of the Oregon-bound emigrants at the rear of their train. Eleven wagons turned southwest into unknown country.

Meanwhile, in the Oregon-bound group, Henry Sager fell ill with typhoid after leaving Fort Laramie. He was only the latest to fall victim to what was commonly called "camp fever." Just days after leaving Fort Laramie, a woman named Mrs. Susan Seabren took ill and died quickly. Little more than a week later, a Mrs. Frost died. Three days later, a little girl passed away of the same ailment.

The German doctor who had tended to young Catherine's leg back in Nebraska came to look after Sager and volunteered his services to assist the family, but was not much of a hand at driving oxen. So the other children, some of whom were also feeling poorly, pitched in, taking turns to help guide the team across streams and rocky patches. In his weakened condition Sager should have remained bedridden beside his wife and daughter in the family wagon. Instead, in late August he rode after four buffalo that caused a stir by tramping between his wagon and the one behind it. "Though fee-ble," Catherine remembered, "father seized his gun and gave chase."

It was a fatal mistake. When he returned from the buffalo pursuit, Sager was weaker than ever. Naomi Sager, still feeling the ill effects of the injuries she had suffered a month earlier, was in no condition to nurse her husband, although she tried. The wife of William Shaw, the company's captain, asked John Minto to sit up with the fading Sager the night of August 26 to provide a respite for Naomi. Minto spent the night doling out what little medicine there was—probably laudanum—and trying to reassure Sager.

> The sick man was either wholly or partly unconscious from high fever, and did not during the night ask for anything. On the two or three times I awakened her, his wife responded each time as though she was in fear that he was dead. She would call him by name and he would receive the medicine, yet seemed hardly conscious. There was no one to relieve me, and I kept vigil all night, suffering from inability to help this life, which seemed to be burning away.

The next evening the party crossed the Green, described by one of the travelers as "one of the prettiest little rivers I ever saw." Turning to his crip-pled daughter beside him, a weeping Henry wondered aloud, "Poor child! What will become of you?" When Shaw came by to check on the family, a weeping Sager unburdened himself, begging Shaw to watch over his family and deliver them to their destination. Holding back tears of his own, the rugged captain promised he would.

Henry Sager, age thirty-eight, died the next morning, just east of Fort Bridger, amid the wild sage and prairie thorn. It was a hot, dry, dusty day, and some men from the train worked up a sweat digging a coffin out of a fallen tree trunk. Sager was buried in a shallow grave on the west bank of the crystal clear Green River. The children must have been terrified of what lay before them. They had almost a thousand difficult miles yet to traverse. Their father was dead, their mother was sick, and they had witnessed two other women in the party die in the past three weeks. But as soon as the brief burial ceremony was concluded, the Sagers and the rest of the company bundled back into their wagons and resumed the trek.

Bound for Texas

Overlanders headed for California and Oregon were not the only emigrants on the move in 1844. At the very moment that the Texas annexation debate was heating up in Congress, a prince was crossing the Atlantic Ocean with ideas of planting a German colony in the Lone Star Republic. If Thomas Hart Benton had known about Prince Carl of Solms-Braunfels, a nephew of Queen Victoria and a college friend of Prince Albert, he might have enlisted the German blue blood.

Prince Carl was a leader in the Mainzer Verein, the Society for the Protection of German Immigrants to Texas, founded in Germany in 1842 for the purpose of buying land in and providing transportation to the Lone Star Republic. Neither Prince Carl nor the other nobles involved in the venture were interested in becoming Americans, and they loudly opposed annexation.

Inspired by tales of the land of plenty sent home by earlier German immigrants such as Moses Schallenberger's late parents and the ancestors of Henry Sager, the Adelsverein (noble association), so called because it was made up of twenty-one noblemen, began raising money and recruiting would-be emigrants, who were promised a cut-rate voyage by ship from Europe to Texas, wagons to take them to their land grants, a prebuilt house, seed and farm implements, schools, and churches. With such inducements, the German states, in the early throes of the unrest that would eventually lead to revolution in 1848, were a target-rich market. Hundreds of recruits were signed up.

As is often the case, things were not quite as shiny as the marketing department portrayed. The first contract the Adelsverein made for a land purchase expired before any emigrants arrived, so a new plot had to be found and purchased. That land, more than a hundred miles from civilization and not particularly fertile, happened to be occupied by Comanches. Construction of housing, schools, and churches lagged. So two leaders of the organization—Prince Carl and Alexander Bourgeois d'Orvanne, a land speculator and the group's colonial director, whom the prince would come to dislike—were selected to travel to Texas ahead of the first wave of emigrants to speed affairs along.

On May 19, as the Oregon- and California-bound overlanders were pushing away from the Missouri River, the two men departed Liverpool aboard the steamer *Caledonia*. "The weather was beautiful," Prince Carl wrote in his diary, but he quickly developed a bad case of seasickness and suffered from one malady or another for most of the voyage. Once they struck land, in Boston, on June 1, their mode of transportation changed to rail, but the complaints continued. "Had a terrible night," he wrote on June 14, "the heat, mosquitoes, roaches." They traveled through New York, Philadelphia, and Baltimore. They were less than a hundred miles from the Capitol on the day the Senate voted down annexation, but their train turned westward and took them on to Pittsburgh, then turned south to Cincinnati and finally reached New Orleans on June 19.

Ten days' rest and recuperation in Henry Clay's favorite vacation spot did not improve Prince Carl's disposition or lessen his disdain for his French companion. They boarded another steamship, the *New York*, on June 29, bound for Galveston. "Unbelievable heat, poor food, very crowded; poor company, as always," he moaned. "Spent the night in the open, slept on top of beer and whiskey kegs. Bearable, spent the whole day there also."

The port of Galveston came into view on July 1, a "low coast line with dunes." Once ashore, the prince began the work of organizing a home for the 392 settlers who would soon be arriving at this same port. First it was another trip by steamboat for Houston, then overland on horseback to the settlement of Washington-on-the-Brazos. "A night without comparison," the prince noted, "mosquitoes, fleas, lice." But he seemed to enjoy life in the saddle, riding across the open prairie, and had a grudging admiration for the stark landscape.

He also appreciated the difficulty the greenhorn emigrants would have carrying their belongings across it. Once a new land claim was arranged, the prince began making plans to stock way stations along the route from the gulf to the settlement, which would be christened New Braunfels. Those emigrants would include a doctor, a surveyor, an engineer, carpenters, masons, millers, bakers, mechanics, and soldiers. When they arrived just before Christmas, they were the vanguard of a movement that would eventually bring almost ten thousand people to Texas, the single largest immigration of Germans to the United States.

In 1844, though, they were coming not to the United States but to Texas, an independent republic. "The so-called American nation," Prince Carl wrote in a report to his relative, Queen Victoria, "is composed of the worst elements of all European nations, from the north to the south, from Sweden to Russia, down to Sicily, Spain and Portugal." Americans, he reported, were "cold and calculating," and, he charged (incorrectly), Texas had to be dragged kicking and screaming into annexation.

Texans, whose nation was populated and led by Americans, were considerably more welcoming of the prince's emigrants than he was of American interest in Texas. "All were pleased with my arrival in this country," he wrote in one of his regular reports to the directors of the Adelsverein, "which they considered to be an indication of considerable German immigration." He was also confident of support from the republic's leaders, Sam Houston and Anson Jones, who gave him "written assurances of their best wishes and zeal for the Verein's cause."

John Tyler would have done almost anything for that kind of endorsement for his Texas policy. Almost anything is what he was about to try.

{ 7 }

SUMMER OF DISCONTENT

Two days after the Senate rejected the Texas annexation treaty, John Tyler sent a message to the House of Representatives, asking that body to consider whether Texas should enter the union as a state. The House, the president argued, was just as competent to decide the question as the Senate, and though he preferred to act through treaty, that was not the only way Texas could be annexed to the United States. Cave Johnson had made the same argument as far back as May, before the Senate vote. Article IV, Section III of the Constitution empowered Congress—both chambers—to admit new states, by simple majority vote. Tyler also pointed out to lawmakers that Texas was an independent republic, freed from Mexico by its own exertions and "settled mostly by emigrants from the United States, who would bring back with them in the act of reassociation an unconquerable love of freedom and an ardent attachment to our free institutions."

Along with the message, Tyler sent the House all the documents he had previously handed over to the Whig-controlled Senate, which had been selective in choosing which papers to make public—only those they believed would help them make the anti-annexation case to voters. Now the House made them all public, including the letter in which Andrew Jackson had voiced his support for immediate annexation. This was a public relations coup for Tyler, who knew that Old Hickory's words still carried great weight.

In one stroke, the president had altered the terms of the debate, kept alive his faltering hopes for reelection, and annoyed the hell out of James K. Polk and his supporters, who hoped to ride the question of Texas annexation to victory in November. But mostly he had, once again, inflamed the wrath of Thomas Hart Benton.

After the Senate rejected the treaty, Benton introduced a bill calling for new negotiations with Texas, to include Mexico, and to set a boundary for Texas, a detail the annexation treaty had neglected to address. South Carolina's George McDuffie assailed Benton's legislation and suggested that the Missourian simply didn't understand the realities of the world.

McDuffie, in a "violent and rancorous" harangue, charged that "the speech of the honorable senator is not less calculated to excite Mexico to make war against the United States, than to excite unfriendly feelings towards us in the government of Great Britain. He has exhausted his full magazine of epithets in portraying the faithless outrage which he alleges this government would perpetrate upon Mexico by the ratification of this treaty." Echoing Tyler, McDuffie said Benton was missing the point entirely. The United States had every right to annex Texas if Texas chose to be annexed, and Mexico had nothing to say about it. Texas was a republic, its independence certain, earned by the blood of Texans and Americans alike, including a former member of Congress. And everybody knew it, except, apparently, Thomas Hart Benton. "The whole world regard the dominion of Mexico over Texas as irrevocably lost," McDuffie told the Senate.

McDuffie also defended Tyler's right to turn to the House. "I am utterly at a loss to conceive what view the senator from Missouri takes of the relations which exist between the President of the United States and the Senate," McDuffie huffed. "The Senate has adjudged the case, and presented its decision; and upon this the honorable senator conceives himself entitled as representing the power and dignity of the Senate to stand up and say 'I am sir Oracle; when I open my mouth let no dog bark.' The President must be silent! The popular branch of the legislature must be silent!"

Benton replied immediately, and in kind, charging McDuffie with fomenting disunion. "The treaty was made, not to get Texas into the Union, but to get the South out of it," Benton bellowed. He walked over to McDuffie and slammed his fist into the South Carolinian's desk. Other lawmakers held their breaths, waiting to see if pistols would be drawn—every man in the chamber knew Benton's history. But McDuffie didn't flinch and Benton backed away to continue his speech, never missing a beat in his two-hour diatribe as McDuffie sat listening. "Nothing but bodily fear could have withheld the hand of McDuffie from a challenge," observed John Quincy Adams.

Citing his authority as "the oldest advocate for the recovery of Texas," Benton accused the "criminal politicians"—Calhoun and Tyler—"who prostituted the question of its recovery to their own base purposes, and delayed its success by degrading and disgracing it. . . . A western man, and coming from a State more than any other interested in the recovery of this country so unaccountably thrown away by the treaty of 1819, I must be allowed to feel indignant at seeing Atlantic politicians seizing upon it, and making it a sectional question, for the purposes of ambition and disunion."

On the question of Tyler's use of military force, Benton was apoplectic. By moving to the defense of Texas before it was part of the union, Benton asserted, Calhoun had in effect "annexed the United States to Texas, instead of annexing Texas to the United States." Moving troops and ships into place in case of violence and in case the treaty was ratified was "a reversal of the power of the Senate, and a reading backwards of the Constitution," boomed Benton. "It assumes Texas to be in the Union, and protected by our constitution from invasion or insurrection, like any part of the existing States or Territories; and to remain so till the Senate puts her out by rejecting the treaty!"

For all the thunder, there would be no lightning for the time being. Polk's supporters feared Benton's antics might widen the existing seams in the party. Andrew Jackson was ever more convinced his old friend's brain had been addled by the *Princeton* explosion. Cave Johnson moaned that "I do not see any good that can arise from it." Some Southern fire-eaters were threatening to hold a pro-Texas gathering in Nashville, forty-five miles from Polk's home in Columbia. It was a notion that Polk warned "must not for a moment be entertained." Pro-annexation resolutions were adopted at meetings in three South Carolina counties, and the word "disunion" was bandied about. But Polk and Johnson, with an assist from Jackson, were able to squelch that idea. Polk, at least, understood how important it was to keep Benton and his allies inside the tent. "It would be worse than madness to make war upon them," Polk insisted. Instead, he assigned Johnson to organize a national—non-sectional—party gathering for the state capital on August 15, which "passed off admirably" in Polk's estimation. Others called it a "monster gathering" that was a "glorious time."

They might have been overly worried, at least so far as the potential for legislative mischief. In Washington, Tyler had launched a new debate on the Texas question just as Congress was preparing to adjourn, ending what Adams called "the first session of the most perverse and worthless Congress that ever disgraced this Confederacy." Lawmakers would leave town to return to their states and districts for the coming election with no other action being taken on the issue, and the president's fancy turned to other matters.

PRESIDENT AND MRS. TYLER

John Tyler's first wife, Letitia Christian Tyler, suffered a stroke in 1838 and never really recovered. She died at age fifty-one on September 10, 1842. By early 1844, the fifty-four-year-old Tyler was courting Julia Gardiner, the daughter of David Gardiner, a prominent landowner and former state legislator in New York. She was thirty years his junior; her own mother was younger than Tyler. She was beautiful and vivacious, and her family could trace its American roots back to 1635, which also probably appealed to the patrician Tyler. When David Gardiner died in the explosion aboard the *Princeton*, Julia had fainted into the president's arms. The trauma of the disaster seemed to have cemented their budding relationship, which had begun only a few months after Letitia Tyler's death.

On June 26, the couple married in a secret ceremony in the Episcopal Church of the Ascension on Fifth Avenue in New York City. Tyler had insisted on keeping the public in the dark about the wedding. One man who did know about it was Robert Stockton, commander of the *Princeton*, who had accompanied Tyler on the trip from Washington to New York. Two days later, the Tylers were back in the capital hosting a reception in the White House.

Tyler was the first president to wed while in office. That fact, and the disparate ages of the couple, inspired considerable curiosity among the populace and no shortage of rude commentary about a president who was none too popular to begin with. Among the critics was Jessie Benton Frémont, who noted that Julia's "dress and demeanor were much commented on by the elders who had seen other Presidents' wives take their new state more easily." John Quincy Adams called the couple "the laughing-stock of the city," and referred to their marriage as a "revolting indecency."

One of the victims of Tyler's continuous feuding with Congress was the White House itself. The legislative branch had steadfastly refused to provide sufficient funding for the mansion's upkeep, with the result that Julia Tyler moved into a new home that was not kept even in a "minimum state of cleanliness." But the Tylers were a happy couple and seemed immune to the criticism. They left Washington in early July for a month-long beach honeymoon at Hampton Roads, near the president's James River plantation. When they returned, they resumed the expected social life of a president and first lady, hosting White House soirees and serving as the center of the capital city's social life. Julia hired a *New York Herald* correspondent to serve as a public relations person for her parties, "to sound Julia's praises far and wide," in the words of her sister. Tyler frowned on such practices, but indulged his new bride in her desire to win favor.

She seemed to be just as smitten. "Papa was the only handsome man (except the President) I have ever seen," she commented. They were an affectionate couple, so much so that Julia drew rebukes from her mother and sister for too often touching the president while in public. Properly chastened, Julia promised to watch herself. "I very well know every eye is upon me, my dear mother, and I will behave accordingly," she wrote.

Tyler's love life was faring better than his political fortunes. While on his honeymoon, Mississippi senator Robert Walker visited, to perform the "most disagreeable duty" of asking Tyler to withdraw from the presidential contest in favor of Polk, so as not to split the pro-expansionist vote and hand the election to Clay. Others were delivering the same message without benefit of a personal audience. Writing in the *Richmond Enquirer*, Thomas Ritchie all but begged Tyler to get out of the race and thus "render our common victory and triumph certain and complete." Democrats down the ticket were also growing worried about plans cooked up by Tyler supporters in the crucial states of Pennsylvania and New York to field a full ticket of congressional, state, and local candidates, which could sweep the Democrats from office all across the country.

Tyler knew the impossibility of his situation, but wasn't going to get out of the way without receiving something in return. Tyler's forces were, for the most part, nominal Whigs who had become Democrats of convenience because he had found them government jobs. Tyler wanted assurances that his hirelings would be welcomed back into the Democratic fold "as brethren and equals"—in other words, if Polk won, they'd get to keep their jobs. It seemed a small enough request to Walker, who urged Polk to write a private letter to Tyler offering some assurances along these lines. Walker also thought it might be a good idea if Polk could prevail upon Jackson to write a letter saying nice things about Tyler, an idea Jackson—invoking the supposed "corrupt bargain" between Clay and Adams in 1824—summarily rejected. Polk was also reluctant to get personally involved in any kind of deal.

Tyler also wanted the Democratic newspapers to ease up on their criticism of him, arguing that they had been so unrelenting that even were he to withdraw, his friends might not flock to the Democratic banner. On this count Jackson was more obliging. He wrote to his old friend Francis Blair, asking that the *Washington Globe* go easy on Tyler. The cantankerous Blair had run the newspaper since 1830, when Jackson asked him to move from Kentucky to Washington to edit the Jacksonian house organ, and the editor was not likely to deny any wish to his patron. "Support the cause of Polk and Dallas and let Tyler alone," Jackson told Blair. So it was done, and other Democratic papers fell into line. Jackson was also willing to write to former allies in the Tyler administration, who could let it be known to the incumbent that Jackson thought it would serve Tyler better in public opinion and history if he exited gracefully.

Jackson was an infinitely more skilled politician than Tyler, who probably knew that he had no broad constituency but, like politicians of all epochs, hated to let go. The *Westfield News Letter*, a Whig newspaper in western Massachusetts, used Millerism to make the political point that was obvious to all but Tyler: "one delusion worse than Millerism: that of thinking of John Tyler as a great public benefactor."

Having squeezed all he thought he could out of the Democrats, and realizing the hopelessness of his political position, Tyler prepared to announce his withdrawal. But he did not go quietly. First he wrote to Jackson to let him know that he was taking himself out of the race. Two days later, on August 20, his official withdrawal letter was published in the *Madisonian*, addressed "To My Friends throughout the Union." It was plaintive with a touch of resentment, highlighted by regrets about what Tyler termed others' bitterness toward him and their "most unrelenting spirit of opposition." He defended his administration's record and appealed to the Democrats-cum-Whigs to return to their party, protect the currency, increase trade, block the bank, and ensure the success of the expansionist agenda. "Eight years ago we recognized Texas as independent," he wrote, still beating the annexation drum, "and surely our right to negotiate with her implied no worse faith than in 1827, to negotiate with Mexico for Texas, without consulting Spain." Tyler could at least take pride in this signal accomplishment: Democrats had adopted Texas as their own; it was now at the center of the political discussion and it would stay there for the remainder of the campaign.

The Death of the Prophet

Joseph Smith's presidential campaign was in full swing by summer. Missionary/campaigners had been sent out to every state, with some of the highest church leaders converging on Boston at the end of June for a state convention that would elect delegates to send to Baltimore in July, the only such state gathering beyond Nauvoo.

As was the case at virtually every stop, the campaigners first held church services. In this instance, the religious sessions ran over the last two days of June, with half the members of the Quorum of the Twelve Apostles in attendance, including Brigham Young. On July 1, they got down to political business. The convention site was the Melodeon, an ornate theater and one-time mechanics institute that was a popular venue for lectures, concerts, and conferences in downtown Boston. Young was selected as presiding officer, and other speakers included Orson Hyde, Orson Pratt, and Lyman Wight. "The convention was addressed with much animation and zeal," reported

Wilford Woodruff, another of the Twelve Apostles in attendance. Local newspapers provided full coverage.

Not all the zeal displayed was on the part of Smith supporters. "A large number of rowdies" crowded the hall, including Abby Folsom, an abolitionist and women's rights activist already gaining a reputation for disrupting political meetings by insisting on the right of women to speak. And speak she did, interrupting an evening oration by Young. She was soon joined by a young man who began yelling insulting remarks at the church leader, egged on by a number of those seated around him. When several saints attempted to shout them down, the protesters yelled even louder, leading to physical attempts to restore order. When that failed, someone dashed out to fetch the police. Boston's finest responded quickly, but the mob assaulted the officers as they attempted to establish order and get the troublemakers out of the hall. After considerable struggle and some bloodletting, the galleries were cleared and the convention resumed. "This proves that the voice of the people rules," Young declared ruefully. "That is, the voice of the rabble." He had no idea how right he was.

The convention nominated Smith for president and elected two delegates—Heber C. Kimball and S. B. Wallace—to attend the Baltimore convention. But there would be no national convention. Joseph Smith was already dead.

The campaign contingent first read rumors of Smith's murder on July 9. "Sometimes the Mormons are all killed; sometimes they are half killed, and sometimes the blood is knee deep in Nauvoo," Young wrote in a letter to Elder Willard Richards, Smith's secretary back in Nauvoo. "Sometimes old Joe, as they call him is taken by the mob and carried to Missouri, sometimes he is gone to Washington, sometimes he has runaway, given up to the authorities, etc. etc. One might suppose him to be a sectarian God, without body, parts or passions—his center everywhere and his circumference no where."

The delegates lingered in various cities in New England for another week, hoping that the rumors proved false, until letters arrived confirming the prophet's death. Young, who had been in Peterborough, New Hampshire, arrived back in Boston on July 17. The next day, the grief-stricken Young, Kimball, Hyde, Pratt, and Woodruff made plans to return to Nauvoo.

Joseph Smith, along with his brother Hyrum, had been murdered by a mob while being held in jail in Carthage, the seat of Hancock County, about a day's ride from Nauvoo. According to the lawyerly historians of the murder case, the killings were "not a spontaneous, impulsive act by a few personal enemies of the Mormon leaders, but a deliberate political assassination, committed or condoned by some of the leading citizens in Hancock County."

As had happened in New York, Ohio, and Missouri, religiopolitical violence stalked the Mormons in Illinois. The pot had been boiling almost from the day of the saints' arrival. But from the moment Smith had escaped Missouri's attempt at extradition in 1843, according to Illinois governor Thomas Ford, a union of Whigs and Democrats, acting not on religious or even economic grounds but from political motives, "determined upon driving Mormons out of the State; and everything connected with the Mormons became political."

For Mormon critics, Smith's creation in March 1844 of a legislative/executive body known as the Council of Fifty simply confirmed what they already suspected: that the prophet was building the governing framework of a theocracy. While Smith—a presidential candidate whose brother was running for the state legislature—was a participant in American democracy and demanded that American institutions protect his people's rights, in Nauvoo he had been building a base of power that was anything but democratic. The accumulated authority of the head of the church, the mayor of the city, presiding judge of the local court, and commander of the Nauvoo Legion inspired legitimate consternation among the locals. Their response was anything but legitimate.

The mob had many fathers, but its main mouthpiece was Thomas Sharp, anti-Mormon editor of the *Warsaw Signal* in the town neighboring Nauvoo. Sharp had spent three years agitating against Smith, raising reasonable questions about the reach of Smith's civil powers but damning his own cause by resorting again and again to calls for violence. By the spring of 1844, Sharp had been joined in an unholy alliance that united anti-Mormon locals and dissenters from within the church who were voicing many of the same concerns about Smith. Their criticisms were not rooted in the same core belief. The locals hated Smith and the Mormons. The dissidents believed not that he was evil, but that he was a fallen prophet, and they hoped to redeem their church from the theocratic polygamists who they believed were destroying it.

They started by demanding that the church-friendly Nauvoo Charter be repealed. In this they had firm allies among the locals, who feared more than anything the growing political power of Smith and his followers. Then two locals tried to have Smith arrested for failing to respond to a civil lawsuit. The Nauvoo court (of which he was chief judge) released him on a writ of habeas corpus. Sharp cried that "Joe Smith is above the law."

Turning to the county courts, Smith's foes won an indictment against him for perjury and adultery. Smith wanted the case to be tried immediately. That would not have served the agitators' purposes, and the case was held over. While Smith was arguing his case at the county courthouse in Carthage, Sharp leveled another not-so-veiled threat: "We would not be surprised to hear of his death by violent means in a short time."

The final act began on Friday, June 7, when the church dissenters published the first—and, as it turned out, only—issue of the *Nauvoo Expositor*, a newspaper that included seven stories aimed both at locals and potential dissidents. One essay, designed to inflame non-Mormons, accused Smith of preaching and practicing polygamy. Another piece, with a tone more in sorrow than in anger, "sought a reformation in the church." A thousand copies were printed and distributed throughout Nauvoo and the surrounding area. The most overtly political article took dead aim at Smith's presidential candidacy, telling Mormons they were "voting for a man who contends all governments are to be put down and the one established upon its ruins."

The appearance of the *Expositor* threw the civil machinery of Nauvoo into action. At a city council meeting the next day, Smith charged that the paper was "calculated to destroy the peace of the city." He would, he declared in the spirit of Henry II bemoaning that troublesome priest Becket, "rather die tomorrow and have the thing smashed, than live and have it go on."

Debate resumed on Monday. One councilman suggested a fine for each dishonest article—the dishonesty to be decided by Smith and the council—but Smith was determined to be rid of the troublesome newspaper. At 6:30 PM the council passed an ordinance declaring the *Expositor* a public nuisance. By eight o'clock, the press that had printed it was smashed to bits by loyal Mormons.

Sharp and other newspaper editors went berserk. Echoing Missouri's Lillburn Boggs, the *Warsaw Signal* declared its readiness "to exterminate, utterly exterminate, the wicked and abominable Mormon leaders," and called for an attack on Nauvoo. Smith was charged with inciting to riot, but again won a writ of habeas corpus from the Nauvoo court when county law enforcement officials came to arrest him.

Smith's critics saw this as proof of their contention that justice could never be done within the legal system of Nauvoo. So they ramped up their extralegal preparations, raising money to buy guns and ammunition and sending out recruiting notices for armed men to mount an attack on the saintly stronghold. Smith saw this as proof of his contention that his people were threatened by mobocracy, and he declared martial law.

The clear declaration by both sides that they were ready to resort to armed conflict brought the governor into the picture. Thomas Ford had been something of a friend to the saints and, as much as any non-Mormon politician could, he enjoyed the trust of Joseph Smith. Ford told Smith he should surrender himself to civil authorities in Carthage to answer for the destruction of the *Expositor* press. Smith, citing the inflammatory writing of Sharp and others, responded that his life would be forfeit if he set foot in Carthage. So, instead of turning himself in, Smith, with brother Hyrum in tow, fled the jurisdiction. The brothers crossed the Mississippi River into Iowa. They would present themselves for arrest, Smith wrote to Ford, if he would "disperse the mob, and secure to us our constitutional privileges, that our lives may not be endangered when on trial."

Fleeing like a thief in the night did not add to the luster of Smith's reputation, even among the most faithful, and he took to heart the criticism he was hearing secondhand. Just a day after they left, it was Hyrum who told his brother, the prophet, that "we had better go back and die like men." On June 23 they returned across the river; the next day they traveled to Carthage, "as a lamb to the slaughter."

They were first held in the same hotel where Governor Ford was staying. But a mob began gathering quickly once word spread that the Smiths were holed up in the Hamilton House, and the Carthage Greys, the local militia that was supposed to be responsible for security, had not yet fully mustered. The Greys were also not fully reliable—many of the unit's officers and men were among the most vociferous critics of the Mormon leaders. Ford knew this, but after the Smiths were taken into custody and transferred to the Carthage jail, he nevertheless sent the Greys to protect the jail from the encroaching mob.

In court that day, the Smiths made bail on the inciting to riot charge, only to be immediately rearrested on charges of treason, resulting from the declaration of martial law in Nauvoo. Ford refused to intervene on their behalf, and they were ordered held without bail until June 29 pending the arrival of a witness, Mormon dissenter Francis Higbee.

They would not live to see June 29. Hancock County militia troops from hostile Warsaw were already marching toward Nauvoo with the intent to spark an incident that would justify an invasion. Ford got wind of this and ordered a halt, sending a messenger to the marchers to disband. Most did. But a few hundred did an about-face and began marching back toward Carthage at midday on June 27.

In the little two-story jail, Smith wrote a letter to his wife, Emma, in which he told her that they were being well treated and tried to reassure her that there was no immediate threat to their lives. "There is no danger of any extermination order," he wrote. "Should there be a mutiny among the troops (which we do not anticipate, excitement is abating) a part will remain loyal and stand for the defense of the state and our rights." It's not at all clear why Smith thought this, or if he really did. Perhaps he retained a latent faith in Ford, or maybe it was just his native optimism bubbling to the surface, or a simple desire to reassure his wife. At any rate, in this case Joseph Smith proved not to be a prophet, and he might not have believed his own words anyway. When visitors were allowed in to see the Smiths, they were able to get a Colt revolver and a single-shot pistol into Joseph's pockets. He passed the single-shot on to Hyrum, who took it reluctantly. "I hate to use such things or see them used," Hyrum told his brother.

"So do I," Joseph said, "but we may have to defend ourselves." He knew that only seven men from the Carthage Greys were stationed outside the jail as a first line of defense.

At about four in the afternoon, a large mob was sighted making its way toward the jail. The rest of the Carthage Greys were in formation on the far corner of the village square, about as far away from the jail as they could be and still be in town. When they got word that the mob was approaching, officers ordered the men to prepare to march. But the men responded slowly, and the officers did nothing to hurry them along. One man, Tom Marsh, shouted that they should get a move on and to hell with the formation. "Come on you cowards," he yelled at his fellows, "those boys will all be killed." But Marsh was referring to the seven Greys standing guard, not the Smiths. Without waiting for any of the others to join him, Marsh started at a sprint toward the jail. Most of the mob was already there, their faces smudged with dirt to hide their identities.

In a scene that would be replayed within days in Philadelphia, the reluctant militia unit fired directly into the onrushing mob. No one was hit, and the angry throng quickly overwhelmed the defenders. Inside, the Smiths were upstairs with visitors Willard Richards and John Taylor, having earlier refused a suggestion by the jailer that they remove to the cell for their own protection. Now they heard gunshots outside. Richards rushed to the window and saw the mob encircling the jail. He shouted back to the Smiths, who were poised to shoot. Richards and Taylor used their bodies to bar the door as they heard the loud clomping of men running up the wooden stairs. As they braced themselves against the door, a hail of gunfire blasted through it. Miraculously neither Richards nor Taylor was hit, but Hyrum was shot in the face.

"I am a dead man," Hyrum said, turning to Joseph, and was then hit in rapid succession by three more shots.

"Oh, my dear brother Hyrum," Joseph wailed. Then, with an unsaintly wrath, he charged to the door, opened it enough to reach his hand out, and fired the Colt into the stairwell. One man made it to the door and Joseph punched him in the face. Behind him, Taylor tried to leap out of the window but was felled by several shots. The wounded men's blood drenched the floor, and gunshots spattered more across the walls and windows.

Joseph dropped his empty gun and made for the window. As he stepped over Taylor he was hit by two shots from the doorway and one from outside. "Oh Lord, my God," he screamed, and tumbled through the window, landing with a thud on the ground. Some witnesses said Smith's body was not further harmed. Others said a militia officer ordered four men to raise Smith up so he could be shot again, and that after they fired, Smith fell forward, dead.

The violence in Illinois was over. More was about to erupt in Pennsylvania.

"A Disturbance of the Public Peace"

As the summer's events unfolded, Whigs were increasingly uneasy. The high spirits of spring, when the Democrats had shunted aside Van Buren and nominated Polk, were giving way to anxiety as Tyler removed himself and support for expansion seemed solid. Some Whigs saw an opportunity to bounce back through a potential alliance with nativists, who were successfully organizing in the northeast in the wake of the May riots in Philadelphia.

As was so often the case during the 1844 campaign, Clay tried to split the difference. He told nativists that their motivations were sound, but could produce positive results only "if conducted with discretion and prudence." Mostly, though, as with Texas, he simply wished the issue would go away. He felt confident that the Whig program, by itself, was enough to win the election, especially against a nonentity such as Polk. Let us not, he told a Philadelphia nativist who had inquired about his views on immigration, "throw any new issues into the Presidential canvas." It was the same answer he had given in April on Texas. Let's talk about what I want to talk about, he was telling voters, instead of what you want to talk about.

Back in the Midwest, Abraham Lincoln, who had idolized and campaigned for Clay, also tried to find a middle ground. At a June 12 public meeting in Springfield, Illinois, he came out in favor of residence in the country for some period of time before citizenship—though he wouldn't specify how much time—while arguing that Whigs should not endeavor to make naturalization "less convenient, less cheap, or less expeditious."

Former New York governor William Seward saw nothing but trouble in the issue. His state was home to tens of thousands of recent Catholic immigrants, and he predicted disaster if the Whigs aligned publicly with nativist parties. But he was equally sure that no one was listening to him on this issue, having "asserted my opinions concerning the Philadelphia riots in a way that will for long put me out of favor with a portion of my countrymen."

Following the May riots, a grand jury had convened to hear evidence against a number of those involved in the violence. On June 17, the jury's final report was published. It vindicated the nativist American Republican Party, whose members included two in the jury pool. There were no Irish names on the jury list.

The riots were a result of the "efforts of a portion of the community to exclude the Bible from the Public schools," the jury found, an insidious plot that "in some measure gave rise to the formation of a new party, which called and held . . . meetings in the district of Kensington." Those meetings were "the peaceful exercise of the sacred rights and privileges guaranteed to every citizen by the constitution and laws of our state and country." These peaceable meetings, the jury ruled, were violently disrupted "by bands of irresponsible men, some of whom resided in this country only a short period." Catholics protested the nonsensical conclusions of the grand jury, but there was little recourse for them.

Having been given a pass by the grand jury, the American Republican Party planned a major parade and rally for the Fourth of July in Philadelphia. Sheriff Morton McMichael feared the worst. "In the present excited state of popular feeling," he wrote to other local authorities on June 28, "it is possible that some accidental cause may produce disturbance on the approaching Anniversary of our National Independence." He called on the police and militia to be ready, but also suggested that "it is desirable that the citizens themselves should be prepared to assist the constituted authorities, in any efforts they may be called upon to make, in maintaining the supremacy of the law," having apparently learned nothing about the actions of mobs during the May riots. He asked each alderman to assign additional policemen to each ward. Major General Robert Patterson, commander of the Pennsylvania militia, who like McMichael had suffered criticism for being late on the scene at the May riots, also put his troops on alert for the holiday.

As it turned out, the parade went off without a hitch and no violence broke out. And what a parade it was. Five thousand people participated and ten thousand watched. But while so many Philadelphians enjoyed the summer festival, others were prepping for war. After the violence that had destroyed the Catholic churches of St. Michael's and St. Augustine's, William Dunn, brother of the pastor at St. Philip de Neri's church, had been given permission by the governor to form a company of militia to defend church property. The troops were kept busy drilling on July 3, then took the holiday off to enjoy the parade with the rest of the city. On the fifth, a wagonload of muskets arrived at the church from the state arsenal to replace the broomsticks Dunn's band of Catholic militia had been using for drill. Rejecting the notion that secrecy was needed, Dunn and his men unloaded the guns in broad daylight, in front of plenty of passersby, not all of whom were friendly. Word of the delivery quickly spread around town: the Catholics were arming themselves and turning St. Philip's into a fortress.

Early the next day, McMichael was again sending out warnings. "Information has been conveyed to me, that there is some reason to apprehend a disturbance of the public peace this afternoon and evening," the sheriff wrote on July 6, requesting again that local authorities, the citizens, and the militia prepare for trouble in the working-class Southwark neighborhood on the city's southern edge.

Nativists responded by organizing, and that evening a thousand people were gathered in front of St. Philip's. Dunn had every right to the state-supplied weapons, having received the governor's go-ahead to form a defense unit. But he took the sheriff into the church, then confessed that they had more guns hidden away than those that had arrived the day before.

McMichael, desperate to avoid a confrontation, decided to split the difference.

"I have . . . been into the Church, and have taken possession of all the arms we were able to find," McMichael fibbed to the masses. He had taken the July 5 guns, but left behind the ones Dunn had procured earlier. "A number of your own citizens, selected by your own Aldermen, are here to prevent any more arms from being taken in, as well as to protect the Church from injury. I therefore beg of you all, as good citizens, to disperse, and retire to your homes. Further measures will be taken tomorrow to allay the excitement and to preserve the peace." He then ostentatiously handed the twenty or so new guns over to the deputies he had posted at the church entrances, and used ramrods to show that they were unloaded.

His demonstration did not settle the crowd of nativists and his pleas to disperse went unheeded. So seventeen men were chosen to enter St. Philip's and search further. By now it was midnight. The men left the darkness of the close, crowded street for the cooler, candlelit confines of the church. Dunn was waiting for them, pistols strapped to both hips, but he fired no shots. The searchers spread out, opening doors, peeking under pews, pushing through dusty closets, looking for a cache of arms. Eventually they found the guns, along with "several armed individuals" who were quickly shorn of their weapons. McMichael got Patterson to send over a unit of City Guards, who cleared the street without further incident. It had been a close call, but Friday ended without violence.

On Saturday, Philadelphia would not be so lucky. By the middle of the morning, a crowd of a thousand or so had again assembled in the streets surrounding the church, facing a line of well-armed militia. This tense standoff persisted until mid-afternoon, when General George Cadwalader, commander of the City Division of the First Brigade of the Pennsylvania Militia, arrived, reminded the throng of nativists that the governor had given the church officials permission to arm themselves, and ordered the mob to disperse. When they didn't, a red-faced Cadwalader stormed off. A few minutes later, McMichael arrived along with 150 "deputized" citizens, armed with clubs, but no guns. The deputies formed a line across Queen Street and began marching and swinging, driving the crowd up the street and away from the front of the church. Once the thoroughfare was emptied, McMichael posted guards at each intersection to keep the rabble out. Soon after, more militia arrived. It appeared St. Philip's was now impregnable.

But Cadwalader went a step further and began breaking up clusters of people who had gathered together outside the restricted area. Then he brought in artillery, three small cannons, posting the guns at strategic points along the barricades. And he introduced the first visible small arms of the encounter, placing men with bayonets at Second and Third Streets, on either side of St. Philip's.

Sight of the cannon and the guns caused a rumble in the crowd. They began jeering the troops, then throwing rocks. McMichael's posse arrested several, which naturally brought on more jeers and more rock throwing. Soldiers were hit; some were injured. Cadwalader stepped in front of his troops.

If the rock throwing didn't cease immediately, he shouted, he would open fire. People began moving out of the middle of the street, looking for a place to flee or something to hide behind. The rock throwing slowed, but didn't stop. Cadwalader shouted the order to take aim, by platoon (which would slow the pace somewhat by requiring one group of soldiers to wait until the first group had fired).

Simultaneously with the order to aim, but before the order to fire had been given, Charles Naylor, a former Whig member of Congress who was serving in the sheriff's posse, raced in front of the guns, risking his own life, shouting "My God, don't shoot! Don't shoot!" and telling Cadwalader that he would have to kill him first if he wanted to kill anybody else. Naylor, a lawyer, had no military training at this point. (Later, during the Mexican War, he raised his own company of volunteers and served as captain.)

Unimpressed with the show of valor, Cadwalader ordered Naylor arrested for inciting mutiny. Someone pointed out to the commander that Naylor was a member of the posse. "All the more important to make an example of him!" shouted Cadwalader in response. Naylor was hauled away. The nativists, sensing that they had narrowly escaped a massacre, scattered.

That seemed to be the end of it. No more mobs gathered that evening in the neighborhood, and officials felt secure enough by Sunday morning, July 7, to send the sheriff's posse home. Cadwalader left two militia units in place to guard the church. But the authorities had been too optimistic. By late morning, a crowd of about two thousand had reassembled, this time with a fresh cause: release Naylor, they demanded. If he were not freed, they would do what was necessary to free him themselves.

After some back-and-forth, the head of the Markle Rifles, one of the two militia units left to safeguard the church (the other was the aptly named Hibernia Greens) agreed to release Naylor, a wise tactical retreat considering how outnumbered his men were. Naylor soon appeared from inside the church, where he had been held, and exhorted the cheering masses "to do as he intended to do, to retire to their homes."

About half of them did. But hundreds remained, and they were becoming unruly. Some boys had brought a four-pounder cannon up from a ship docked in the Delaware and positioned it in a vacant lot behind the church. It wasn't clear if any of them knew how to use it, and they had no solid shot.

But they filled it with nails, scrap iron, broken glass, even hard walnut shells, "every kind of missile that chance and haste could furnish." When they fired at the rear windows of the church they missed, but knocked a few bricks off the corner of the building and gave a start to everyone in the street.

Things were quickly getting out of hand. Neither Cadwalader nor Patterson sent any help to the two militia units, now surrounded by a mob. Instead, representatives of the American Republican Party showed up, urging calm. They had been exonerated by the grand jury, but the court of public opinion had not been so forgiving. Lewis Levin climbed atop the cannon and proposed what sounded like a compromise: the militia would depart if the crowd stopped attacking the church. American Republican Party members would protect the church, he promised. While Levin was talking, a gang had made a run at the church on the other side, smashing in one of the doors. The militia commander ordered his troops to fire, and the marauding gang backed off, but no militiamen fired, and one yelled "Don't shoot!"

True to Levin's word, some party members interposed themselves between the mob and the church. The crowd again demanded that the Hibernia Rifles, a Catholic militia unit, be sent away, to be escorted by the Markle Rifles. Sensing that it was his only option, the unit commander, Captain Colahan, acquiesced. But getting away was not that simple. As they marched down the street, locals threw rocks and bricks at them, and the Irish unit first broke into a trot, then, at Colahan's order, stopped, loaded, and fired.

Instead of scaring away the assault, the firing enraged the mob, which rushed the militia. One soldier was caught and beaten to death. Still, the American Republicans stood by their promise to guard the church—no easy task. And eventually, at about four in the afternoon, some "ruffians and sailors"—the description was made by militia colonel Charles J. Jack, the man who had inspired a similar group to march on Kensington in May—used a battering ram to knock a hole in the concrete wall in front of the church. Hundreds of "ruffians" poured in. They stole some articles from the church, but the American Republicans quickly recovered them. A few small fires were started, but again party members were there to douse them. After a couple hours of relatively harmless hooliganism, they were able to clear the church of troublemakers. Again, it appeared, serious violence had been averted.

Then Cadwalader arrived. Trailed by militia and armed sheriff's deputies, he ordered the American Republicans out of the church. He would take
over security, he told them. The party members who had kept the peace had
little choice but to accede to his demand. Here, "the affair had reached its
turning point—from riot to civil war," said a contemporary account.

Cadwalader decided to clear the street and ordered a Captain Hill to
charge the crowd outside the church. Some in the crowd pleaded with the
soldiers, to no avail. "I have received my orders and I will certainly obey
them," Hill informed the protesters. "Obey and be damned!" came the
shouted reply. Someone grabbed Hill's sword and pulled him to the ground.
Cadwalader ordered the militia to prime their muskets. It was a repeat of
the previous encounter, only Naylor wasn't there to calm things down. If
these people didn't disperse immediately, Cadwalader warned an alderman,
he would order his men to fire. City Guard Lieutenant Thomas Dougherty
made the same threat. And in a flash, both did, at almost the exact same
moment. Several people were hit—two would die. A few armed nativists
began firing back sporadically, and units were sent into surrounding houses
to disarm whoever was doing the shooting.

Many of the party members fled, reassembling in a meeting hall a
few blocks away to discuss their options. Some, though, headed for the
docks to get more firepower. They wheeled two artillery pieces back to the
church, where about fifty people were gathered, and began firing. They
knocked out the nearby street lights, then fired into the mass of militia,
killing two troops from Germantown. The unit had artillery, too, and fired
back, wounding three of the nativists. An artillery duel had broken out on
the streets of Philadelphia. People screamed and scattered. The nativists
moved their guns—their muffled wheels hard to hear above the din—
keeping the militia guessing as to their whereabouts. They used scrap for
ammunition, whatever they could find—rocks, glass, nails. Cannon and
musket fire continued for hours; dozens of people were injured and two
more were killed.

Cadwalader eventually sent for cavalry help. The horsemen arrived
about midnight and couldn't see much of anything. So they waited patiently
for a gun to be fired. When one was, they charged the flash, only to be
tripped up by a rope the nativists had strung across the street in front of the

gun. But the nativists couldn't get off another shot, and when the troopers remounted, they quickly captured the gun, scattered the gunners, and killed a couple of the resisters. By 2 AM, all the guns, large and small, had fallen silent. Twelve people were dead, four dozen wounded.

Within days, two thousand soldiers were patrolling the streets. Normalcy, of a kind, returned. There was no more talk, for now, about Bibles in the schools. The Whig press was quick to blame "a few drunken rowdies" and to acquit both nativists and the militia. "Cadwalader may have been hasty and mistaken," wrote one reporter, "but the mob had no business there, and ought to have dispersed long before any blood was shed." The Democratic press gave the American Republicans grudging credit for their defense of the church, while excoriating the nativist rabble-rousers more generally. "The sooner they are shot down, the better it will be for the peace, safety and honor of the community," was one writer's opinion.

Among those arrested was Lewis Levin, charged with using his *Daily Sun* to incite to riot and treason. He was held in jail only briefly, and never went to trial. Instead, Levin was elected to Congress, an indication that there was political hay to be made in courting the nativist vote, at least in some quarters. "The deplorable tumults in Philadelphia, are likely to work in our favor, in political results," predicted Richard Rush, who had served as attorney general under James Madison and minister to Great Britain under James Monroe; he had run for vice president with John Quincy Adams in 1828, then defected to the Democrats. "The Whigs are rather in danger of being caught in a snare they had themselves set." Just so, as Henry Clay would learn to his regret.

THE NEXT PROPHET

Almost six weeks after the assassination of Joseph Smith, the community of Nauvoo was still in turmoil. Half the church leadership that had served under Smith—the Quorum of the Twelve Apostles—had been out on the campaign trail and had still not returned. The rudderless crew was looking for someone to step forward and take the helm. Many feared the movement that Smith had built could not survive his death. There were also concerns that the locals, having shed Mormon blood, might develop a taste for it.

Into the vacuum stepped Sidney Rigdon. He seemed like a logical choice. One of the early fathers of the church, he had been at Smith's side as long as anyone. Smith had chosen him to be his running mate in the presidential contest. Rigdon was a marvelous preacher, a rare combination of spellbinding speaker and learned intellectual. He, too, had been out of town for weeks, since the middle of June. He had gone to campaign in Pittsburgh, where he arrived one day after Smith's murder. It took another week for an edition of the *Nauvoo Neighbor* to find its way into his hands, confirming the vague rumors that he, like Young and the others, had begun to hear.

At first, Rigdon wanted all the Apostles to gather in Pittsburgh, where he and another of the Twelve, John Page, had been campaigning and preaching. But a letter soon arrived from Young urging that all return to Nauvoo as fast as possible. There, they could "sit down together and hold a council on the very ground where sleeps the ashes of our deceased friends." Acknowledging that this was the proper course, or at least that he was outnumbered, Rigdon packed his bags and hurried back to Nauvoo.

With a 575-mile head start, Rigdon got there before Young. He arrived August 3, and on hand to greet him were four of the Quorum of Twelve: John Taylor and Willard Richards, who had been wounded at Carthage, and Orson Pratt's brother, Parley, and George A. Smith, who had been campaigning nearby when they heard news of the murder and had rushed home immediately. Ignoring the fact that he had hoped to stay in Pittsburgh and bring the Twelve to him, Rigdon told them that he had a revelation telling him to come home, and that it had been delivered in the voice of Joseph Smith. Rigdon had begun making his play to succeed the martyred prophet.

Pratt organized a meeting of the five men for the next day, a Sunday, at Taylor's home. Still recovering from the gunshot wounds he had suffered in Carthage, Taylor had difficulty getting around. But when the four met at Taylor's bedside on August 4, Rigdon was a no-show. After waiting a bit—Rigdon had after all traveled hundreds of miles over the past several days; perhaps he was overtired from the journey—Pratt went looking for him.

He found Rigdon on a street corner, talking with a man Pratt didn't know. When Pratt urged Rigdon to come along to the meeting at Taylor's house, Rigdon demurred, continuing a meandering conversation that sounded rather pointless to Pratt. Finally Rigdon was ready. "Well, well! Brother Pratt," he said, "I must go with you now without delay." But delay he did. Passing a gathering of saints headed for worship, Rigdon felt the spirit move in him and told Pratt he had to preach to the throng that was congregating on an open meeting ground atop the hill east of where the Nauvoo temple was being built.

Word spread quickly and Rigdon's reputation as a preacher drew thousands to the spot. They also knew he had been out campaigning and were eager to hear any news from the outside world about the murder of Smith. On that count Rigdon disappointed. His message was not about the dead prophet, but the next prophet. Rigdon described a vision that had been delivered to him in his Pittsburgh boarding room, and told the crowd he "was the identical man that the ancient Prophets had sung about, wrote and rejoiced over, and that he was sent to do the identical work that had been the theme of all the Prophets in every preceding generation." Shouting to the assembled mass, he announced that he would now be the "guardian" of the church, the successor to Joseph Smith.

There is no record of how the crowd responded, but it is fair to assume it was with a mixture of hopefulness and anxiety. They wanted certainty and security and felt neither. A quick settlement of the question of succession, many believed, would be best for the church and the saints. But not everyone was convinced it should be Rigdon. Within days, Wilford Woodruff, another of the Twelve, would call Rigdon's revelation a "second-class vision." Others shared his doubt. So when Rigdon called for a general meeting of the saints, to be held August 8, four days hence, he was hoping to bypass the leadership and appeal directly to the people—and, not incidentally, settle the question before Young and the others returned to bolster Pratt, Richards, and those who were counseling patience.

On Tuesday the sixth, Rigdon preached to a smaller congregation than the one that had gathered on Sunday, warning the flock about the possibility of a mob descending on the leaderless citizens. It was not a subtle approach, but it struck a nerve considering the recent violence and the history of persecution many of those in attendance had endured. But his window was closing.

Just a few hours after the sermon, Brigham Young, Willard Woodruff, and three other apostles came chugging down the Mississippi aboard the

steamboat *St. Croix*, the final 120-mile leg of an arduous 1,200-mile journey by train, boat, and wagon across New York and the upper Midwest.
"When we landed in the City," Woodruff wrote in his diary, "there was a
deep gloom [that] seemed to rest over the City of Nauvoo which we never
experi[en]ced before." The people, he noted, "felt like a sheep without a shepherd." The gloom was real, but the assertion that the saints had no shepherd
was not. They had two who aspired to the post, and one would have to go.

Ten members of the Quorum of the Twelve Apostles were now present
in Nauvoo, including the president, Young. They met twice—in the morning and early afternoon—at Taylor's house. No one kept a record or wrote
in any detail later about the proceedings. But subsequent events would indicate that the group reached a consensus that Young was the man to lead the
church and that Rigdon needed to be stopped before momentum carried the
saints with him. Part of the meeting was also likely spent in simply bringing those who had been absent up to speed on the fast-moving events of the
summer. In any case, when the second conclave ended, Young, acting in
his capacity as president of the Twelve, called a broader meeting to be held
later that day that would include the Apostles, the leadership of the Nauvoo Stake (a group of congregations), and the priesthood. The larger group
could not be accommodated at Taylor's home, so the venue was set for the
not-quite-finished Seventies Hall, a red-brick building named after the missionaries who had carried the Mormon gospel to the Gentiles.

It was about 4 PM when the meeting came to order. The Seventies Hall
was usable, but the detritus of construction could still be seen lying around,
and there was a scent of fresh brick and mortar to accompany the August
humidity. Rigdon spoke first, at the invitation of Young. He declared himself "a spokesman for Joseph Smith," and wanted nothing more than to see
that the foundation laid by the prophet did not crumble from the lack of
being "governed in a proper manner."

Young responded that he had little interest in who led the church—it
could be Shaker founder Ann Lee for all he cared—"but one thing I must
know, and that is what God says about it." And God, Young asserted, spoke
through him, as president of the Twelve. "I have the keys and the means of
obtaining the mind of God on the subject." Rigdon was basing his claim on

an appeal to the authority of Joseph Smith, which he said ran through him. Young was appealing to a higher power.

On the eighth, the assembly Rigdon had called for before the return of Young was held as scheduled, at 10 AM. Five thousand people turned out. The morning was so breezy that Rigdon abandoned the stand erected for the purpose, which was downwind from the crowd, and climbed atop a wagon at the other end of the field so he could be better heard. The saints, seated on the ground or on small benches, obligingly turned around to face into the wind.

Rigdon, perhaps sensing that the tide was running against him, was not his usual mellifluous self. He spoke for an hour and a half, a rambling discourse on the life of Jesus, Queen Victoria, and several other topics that seemed to have little bearing on the question at hand. It was so bad that Young, a hard judge of men, would later say that he felt sorry for the saints who had endured Rigdon's meanderings.

He certainly felt no sympathy for Rigdon. As he was closing, Rigdon began to call for a vote on the question of who should lead the church. Dramatically, Young, whom most of those in the crowd hadn't seen for months, leapt up onto the makeshift stand. "I will manage this voting for Elder Rigdon," Young said. "He does not preside here. This child will manage this flock for a season."

Many of those in attendance would later swear that when Young spoke they heard the sound of Joseph Smith's voice. "As soon as he spoke I jumped upon my feet, for in every possible degree it was Joseph's voice, and his person, in look, attitude, dress, and appearance," one witness said. "I knew in a moment the spirit and mantle of Joseph was upon him." Another said "it seemed in the eyes of the people as though it was the very person of Joseph which stood before them." Wilford Woodruff would later say, "If I had not seen him with my own eyes, there is no one that could have convinced me that it was not Joseph Smith."

Young himself never made any claim of transubstantiation. The beleaguered saints, yearning for a lost prophet and disappointed in Rigdon's utterances, needed to believe. Young's dynamic presence afforded them the opportunity.

After a break, the meeting reconvened and Young dominated it. He spoke for two hours, but summed up the message in two sentences. "You cannot appoint a prophet," he reminded the saints, "but if you let the Twelve remain and act in their place, the keys of the kingdom are with them and they can manage the affairs of the church and direct all things aright." Left unsaid was the fact that, as president of the Twelve, while they were directing things aright, he would be directing them. And then he put it to the people. "Do you want Brother Rigdon to stand forward as your leader, your guide, your spokesman?" he asked. Rigdon, who had been silent up to this point, chimed in, asking Young to seek a vote not on him, but on the Twelve. "Does the church want, and is it their only desire to sustain the Twelve as the First Presidency of this people? All those in favor, raise your right arm." And so they did, virtually unanimously. "If there are any of the contrary mind, every man and every woman who does not want the Twelve to preside, lift up your hands in like manner." No hands went up.

"The church," Young confided to his diary that night, "was of one hart and one mind."

CAMPAIGN SEASON

Henry Clay had shown during his Southern sojourn in the spring that he was, like Young, an effective campaigner and a man ahead of his time in relating personally to voters. But even Clay was restricted by the etiquette of the day during the electioneering season. Instead of pleading for votes from the stump, he retired to Ashland, his Lexington estate, to correspond, greet visitors, and direct his operatives.

Polk did the same, setting up shop at home in Columbia, Tennessee. And he established the parameters of the debate by taking two of the Whigs' favorite issues off the table right at the outset. As he prepared to write a letter of acceptance of the party's nomination, Polk was buffeted by advice on the question of whether he should declare himself a one-term president. Aaron V. Brown, a former Tennessee congressman and advisor to Polk, pushed him to make such a pronouncement. "In your acceptance, you must some way or other express yourself in favor of the one-term system," Brown wrote to Polk. "This is important. I might say all important and you will know exactly how it will be highly useful. I need not say who and how many of our friends expect it."

Brown was not concerned with neutralizing Whig complaints about executive authority. He was referring to potential Democratic presidential candidates in 1848—Cass, Benton, Woodbury, Wright, Buchanan, even Calhoun—"our friends" who would be much more likely to enthusiastically support Polk if they knew a space would be open for them in four years.

Polk was hearing arguments on both sides of the question, but the alacrity with which he made his announcement indicated that he had probably already made up his mind. Writing on June 12, he told his party and the electorate "that if the nomination made by the convention shall be confirmed by the people and result in my election, I shall enter upon the discharge of the high and solemn duties of the office, with the settled purpose of not being a candidate for re-election." In one sentence, Polk enlisted the aid of every senior Democrat in the campaign and squelched the usual Whig complaints about "King Andrew" and the Democrats' abuses of executive power.

Polk took only a few more sentences to deal with another crucial issue: the tariff. As a Southerner, Polk had long supported a revenue-only tariff—levies high enough to pay the costs of a limited government but not so high as to afford any special protection for domestic industry, which was mostly found in the North. Now, as a national candidate in need of votes in New York and Pennsylvania, Polk made an adjustment in his rhetoric and emphasis, if not entirely in his position. If a revenue tariff turned out to provide some protection without that being its sole intent, then that was agreeable to Polk: "making revenue the object, protection the incident," as Andrew Jackson Donelson, namesake and nephew of the former president, put it. The details would be settled when the president and Congress came together to set the rates. Mississippi senator Robert Walker urged Polk to "go as far as your principles will permit for incidental protection," and that is exactly what Polk did. Writing to Democrat John K. Kane of Pennsylvania, Polk borrowed Walker's words and promised "discriminating duties as would produce the amount of revenue needed, and at the same time afford reasonable incidental protection to our home industry."

Whigs howled about Democratic duplicity. Clay prodded his allies to punch back on the tariff, but their responses were largely ineffective. Polk had taken another step toward securing Northern Democrats behind his candidacy. He had already made a small accommodation in the language of the Democratic platform that hedged ever so slightly on Texas, with its commitment to "the reoccupation of Oregon and the reannexation of Texas, at the earliest practicable period."

As Democrats campaigned around the country, though, they found plenty of support for bringing Texas into the union, even in places where conventional wisdom suggested it was not a popular position. During Senate debate on the annexation treaty, petitions poured into Congress from all over. While many from the North opposed the treaty, not all did. On May 30, sectionalism was set aside for a brief moment when a pair of pro-annexation petitions from the Northeast were presented, one from Middleton, Connecticut, and another that was "very well written, from German adopted citizens of New York, in favor of the annexation of Texas." Silas Wright, while professing support and warm regards for Polk, warned that the machinations of the Calhoun "clique" had created a situation in which "our Union was never so much in danger as at this moment." But his seemed to be a minority opinion.

The British lent a hand to the expansionist cause when they sent the sloop-of-war *Modesta* up the Columbia River in July to anchor off Fort Vancouver, a pointless show of force in the Oregon country that stoked the ire even of non-expansionists and gave Clay just one more thing to worry about.

For their part, Northern Whigs employed the emotional issue of war, warning mothers and fathers that annexation of Texas meant their sons would be sent off to fight against Mexico to defend the slave power. In the South, they tended to ignore the issue. "Clays letter has had no influence on Southern whigs," Cave Johnson reported to Polk. At a giant June rally in Memphis, Texas never came up. In July in Lexington, speakers took the Clay position—that Texas was a distraction from the real issues of the campaign.

But Southern Whigs were not as opposed to annexation as Clay and some others believed. The foremost historian of the Whig party, Michael F. Holt, argues that Clay got the wrong impression during his spring trip across the South because he spent all of his time with upper-class Whigs, Southerners who had the most to gain from the national Whig economic program and the most to lose if Texas joined the union and siphoned off slaves and markets. Working-class Southerners wanted Texas because of the opportunity it afforded them, which was not readily available in their hierarchical home states.

Beyond the substantive issues of the campaign, the parties slashed at each other in highly personal attacks that would make many a modern political consultant blush.

One widely circulated abolitionist handbill accused Clay of being a "notorious Sabbath-breaker, Profane Swearer, Gambler, Common Drunkard, Perjurer, Duellist, Thief, Robber, Adulterer, Man-stealer, Slave-holder, and Murderer." Another charged that the history of Clay's "debaucheries and midnight revelries in Washington is too shocking, too disgusting to appear in public print." Some of that was true, of course, which helped make the charges stick and made it tougher for Whigs to respond. Even John Quincy Adams had reflected that "in politics, as in private life, Clay is essentially a gamester." Democrats were not above using the legislative process to make a similar point. One lawmaker proposed including a prohibition on wine purchases in an appropriations bill for the White House should Clay take up residence.

At the same time, Whig newspapers accused Polk of being a duelist, while others attacked from the opposite extreme, calling him a coward for supposedly dodging a challenge. An abolitionist newspaper in New York accused Polk of using a branding iron to mark his slaves, an utter falsehood but one that played on Northern voters' knowledge that Polk was a slaveholder. Unfortunately for Whigs battling for votes in New York with the Liberty Party, it also helped remind the same voters that Clay was, too.

Clay had to deal with charges—again, true—that he was not affiliated with any organized religion. Apparently his selection of the saintly Theodore Frelinghuysen as his running mate had not provided as much insulation against such attacks as he had hoped, so Clay felt duty bound to respond. Acknowledging that he was "not a member of any Christian Church," he nevertheless possessed "a profound sense of the inappreciable value of our Religion." Frelinghuysen spent some time during the campaign trying—in effect—to bring Clay to Jesus. Shortly after their nomination, the running mate had written to the party leader that "our names have been brought together, here, by the voice of our fellow men. My prayer for you and my own soul shall be fervent, that, through the rich grace of our Saviour, they may be found written in the Book of Life of the Lamb that was slain for our sins."

While Clay was defending himself against charges of irreligion, Frelinghuysen came under attack for being "much too mixed up with these Bible societies." Again, the charge was true, and one Frelinghuysen likely embraced as praise rather than criticism. But the swipe at Frelinghuysen had a deeper meaning. As mayor of Newark, New Jersey, in the late 1830s, Frelinghuysen was on the receiving end of the early rush of Irish and German Catholic immigration. As the new arrivals spilled out of a crowded New York City and into his jurisdiction, the mayor had at first petitioned authorities in New York and New Jersey to do more to deal with the influx. When they didn't, he suggested making the masters of the vessels that carried the immigrants financially liable for their charges. That certainly would have alleviated the economic distress caused by the arrival of thousands of penniless immigrants on Newark's streets. But it also would have brought the carrying trade to a screeching halt—no ship master would run such a financial risk—and immigration would have ground to a halt.

Catholic and Democratic politicians in the Northeast remembered Frelinghuysen's stand. Frelinghuysen never uttered an anti-Catholic sentiment. But he was associated with people who did, and he sensed that his prominent position as a leader in the Benevolent Empire could encourage unscrupulous opponents to imply a sympathy of views that did not exist. "I have never spoken but in decided condemnation of the mob scenes of violence and blood in Philadelphia," he said, and cloaked himself in the protection of "the principles of our Constitution, which allow full freedom of conscience and so forbid all religious [discrimination]."

Nevertheless, some Catholic associations were highly critical of Frelinghuysen, particularly his leadership roles in the American Bible Society and the American Board of Commissioners for Foreign Missions, in which, they alleged, he was "countenancing the slanders of a gross set of Presbyterian bigots. . . . Can he be ignorant of the plots and machinations of the fanatics against our government? We think this sufficient to alarm every friend of civil and religious liberty." Frelinghuysen's defenders said the Catholics had it backward. "We never supposed it possible that the intolerant spirit of Romanism would have openly arrayed itself in this republican country in opposition to a candidate for office on the ground of his advocacy of the universal spread of the Scriptures and his active and pious efforts for the advancement of the religion of the Redeemer throughout the world."

Clay tried to address the situation by appealing to a higher power—in this case the Catholic prelate of New York, Bishop John Hughes. He enlisted former congressman John Lee of Maryland to inquire of Hughes whether Democrats were actively trying to organize Catholics against Whig candidates. Hughes was moderately reassuring, telling Lee to relay to Clay that he clearly saw the difference between the esteemed Henry Clay and "the sentiments & conduct of the intolerant Whigs." But Hughes's recognition that there were indeed intolerant Whigs afoot could not be reassuring to Clay, nor could the archbishop's assessment that "his brethren would be divided on the Presidential vote." And, unknown to Hughes, at the same moment Clay was seeking his support, the candidate was writing a letter—not intended for publication—in which he backed the changes in immigration law favored by the nativists.

The twin issues of immigration and abolition continued to hound the Whigs. Liberty Party candidate James G. Birney was highly critical of Clay, much more so than of Polk, on the assumption that it was antislavery Whig voters who were persuadable while Democrats were lost to his cause. Birney personally wrote a pamphlet, "Headlands in the Life of Henry Clay," that detailed Clay's lifetime of support for slavery, despite the Kentuckian's frequent rhetorical flourishes against the practice.

Birney brought a controversy on himself by agreeing to run for the Michigan legislature as a Democrat. Whigs pounced, making the argument that Birney was nothing more than a tool of the Democracy designed not to win elections or even promote the antislavery cause, but simply to deprive the Whigs of their just deserts. "No man has labored so hard or effectively to secure the electoral vote of Michigan to Mr. Polk," the *New York Tribune* accused Birney. "It was right therefore that he should receive from them this mark of their confidence and gratitude." Complaints from the Whig press were effective in stirring up indignation against the Liberty Party, but Birney's action was more naïveté than corrupt bargain. Poet John Greenleaf Whittier, a party member, called it "more than a crime—it was a blunder." Later in the campaign, a forged letter imputing just such anti-Clay motives to Birney and in which he supposedly promised not to agitate on slavery was circulated. The fraud was quickly exposed, but considering Birney's known animus toward Clay, some people might have believed it.

Adams saw a correlation between the two movements, which should have been working for a Whig victory instead of against it. "The Native Americans are falling into the blunders of the abolition societies," he wrote. "They have an excellent cause, which they will ruin by mismanagement."

But the most damaging broadsides against Clay were the work not of lying Democrats or radical abolitionists, but of Clay's own overactive pen and muddled thinking about Texas. If his Raleigh Letter was a self-inflicted wound that festered, his attempts to clarify it were bad medicine applied to the sore.

On July 1, the *Tuscaloosa Monitor* in Alabama printed a letter from Clay—who was now clearly worried about Southern reaction to the Raleigh Letter—in which he wrote that "Personally I could have no objection to the annexation of Texas, but I certainly would be unwilling to see the existing Union dissolved or seriously jeoparded for the sake of acquiring Texas." To a deep thinker like Clay, this was a mere clarification, an expounding on a point that he believed had been clearly addressed before but that some might need more fully explained to them. It may well have been little more than a change in tone or emphasis, but the effect was to confuse voters who had heard clearly less than two months earlier that Clay was opposed to Texas annexation. As Clay now explained it, he could support annexation if not for those disunionists—centered in South Carolina—who were using the annexation issue to plot the South's separation.

This First Alabama Letter, as it came to be known, did not serve the purpose that Clay had hoped it would. It annoyed Southerners, who resented being cast as disunionists for supporting an expansion of the union and who saw in Clay's criticism a sop to abolitionists. Worse, it confirmed for anti-slavery Northerners every doubt they had ever harbored about Henry Clay. When push came to shove, he was against them, not with them.

Having tried to assuage both sides and doing the opposite, a lesser man might have backed away. Not Clay. After penning two letters on Texas that satisfied almost no one, he then sat down and proceeded to write a third, also sent to an Alabama paper. Feeling sanguine about holding onto anti-annexation Northerners whom he felt sure would not defect to Polk in any case, he addressed this Second Alabama Letter—written July 27 and published in the *Tuscumbia North Alabamian* on August 16—to the concerns of Southern supporters of annexation. Certainly, Clay explained, his position on Texas was a matter of not wanting a war with Mexico, and had nothing to do with trying to please those pesky abolitionists. Slavery, he was sure, was going to disappear eventually, so Northerners had no standing to argue against the acquisition of Texas, "which will exist as long as the globe remains, on account of a temporary institution" like slavery.

Clay, who consistently during 1844 violated the first law of politics— talk about what the voters want to talk about, not what you want to talk about—was now violating the first law of holes: when you're in one, stop digging. The Second Alabama Letter reverberated across the North. In New York, Whig fixer Thurlow Weed judged that "things look blue." His ally William Seward said he "met that letter" on every campaign trip and that it "jeopards, perhaps loses this state." Seward was a cynic who claimed to have no convictions beyond his own ambition, which was considerable. Abolitionists mistrusted him because he would not abandon the Whigs, and pro-slavery men despised him. But he was an effective campaigner and had an instinctive feel for the state's voters. If he was worried, Clay needed to be worried, too.

After Clay's bungled attempt to extricate himself from a Texas prison of his own making, the campaign season took more twists, some of which buoyed Whiggish spirits and one that boded ill for the party.

Whigs won control of the Louisiana state legislature in July, along with one of two congressional seats being contested. They also won the governorship and state legislative elections in North Carolina the following month, along with making healthy gains in the Missouri and Kentucky state legislatures. Whigs believed these local victories were good omens as they looked ahead to November.

But, after demurring for most of the summer, Silas Wright finally consented to becoming the Democratic candidate for governor of New York.
Having rejected the party's overtures to join the national ticket as the vice
presidential candidate, Wright expressed a strong desire to remain in the
Senate. He had earlier declined Tyler's offer to move to the US Supreme
Court after Van Buren had turned down a similar proposal from the president. The Senate had its problems, but the thought of dealing with the
acrimony and internecine fighting in Albany between the Hunkers, the
Whig-light faction that favored internal improvements, and Van Buren's
orthodox-Jacksonian Barnburners was nearly enough to sour Wright, a true
statesman, on the idea of politics altogether.

But former governor William Marcy told Polk that New York was
in danger of being lost to the Whigs because of a weak statewide ticket.
Polk and Wright liked each other personally, and Wright was quick to
assure the candidate that his refusal to join the ticket as vice president
was in no way a reflection on his feelings for Polk. For his part, Polk
desperately wanted Wright to run for governor to help secure the state for
the Democrats, but respected Wright enough not to push, all the while
hoping the soft-sell would be more effective. "It will be most unfortunate,
if the domestic difficulties in the state shall have the effect to weaken our
cause, as I think there is some reason to fear they may," Polk told Andrew
Jackson. "It is a matter however in which neither I, nor my friends, *out of
the state*, can interfere."

A man of duty, Wright eventually saw where his lay, and in the first week
of September the Democratic state convention nominated him for governor,
displacing the incumbent, William C. Bouck, a longtime party operative
and canal commissioner who had lost a race for governor in 1840 before
winning the seat in 1842. "The selection of Silas Wright . . . is received with
the liveliest exhibitions of joy by the people," a friendly newspaper reported.
Wright's foes understood the reaction. "He is the hardest man for us to
beat," one New York Whig said of Wright. "He gives them that which they
lacked—strength and union." Wright's candidacy, the growing anti-Whig
sentiment among urban Catholic immigrants, and Clay's Alabama letters
had dramatically altered the landscape in the Empire State, just two months
before voters would go to the polls.

"The Hopes of a Better Inheritance"

The presidential campaign was of little consequence to William Miller. Disappointed but not deterred after Christ failed to appear as predicted in March, Miller spent much of the next few months resting at home in Low Hampton, although he did put in an appearance at the Annual Conference of Adventists in Boston during the last week of May. There he confessed his error about the exact timing, but reiterated his belief "in the speedy coming of our Saviour."

His faith in the message as strong as ever, Miller began making plans for a trip across upstate New York and into the Ohio Valley for later in the summer.

With his son, George, and Himes in tow, Miller left Low Hampton on July 21, headed west. The first stop was Rochester, the beating heart of the burned-over district. He preached several times in a meadow in the nearby village of Scottsville, where he "was listened to with unusual interest." From there the three moved on to Lockport and Buffalo, crossed into Canada and preached in Toronto. Then Miller moved on to Cleveland, and a hundred or so supporters from Akron came up on a canal boat to hear him speak. Afterward, he and Himes traveled back to Akron with them on the boat, with Miller delivering a water-borne sermon that led to a festive spirit of hymn-singing and prayer. Time was running out, they were all certain, so they made the most of whatever opportunity presented itself for fellowship.

They moved southwest across Ohio, making quick stops in small towns along the way. Reaching Cincinnati on August 19, Miller attracted four thousand listeners to his first appearance, and spent a week preaching in the Queen City. The group had planned to push on, but Miller was growing weary and they heard reports of flooding further to the west. So, reversing course, they started back up the Ohio River by steamship, giving Miller a chance to recharge his batteries. He was recovered enough to give five lectures in McConnelsville, then take another boat down the Muskingum to its confluence with the Ohio at the town of Marietta, perched on bluffs above the river.

On the thirty-five-mile journey back to the Ohio, Miller encountered three dozen Methodist ministers traveling together to a conference in

Marietta. Certain that they were going to confront him once they learned he was aboard, Miller retired to a quiet spot to read. Soon enough, a nattily clad man of the cloth approached, then walked past, then returned, and repeated this charade several more times. Finally he stopped and asked, "Is your name Miller?"

Without looking up from his book, Miller replied, "Yes."

"The one who had prophesied the end of the world?"

"I do not prophesy," Miller retorted, then told the minister that he was most likely the man he was looking for.

"I do not believe we can know when the world is to end," the Methodist challenged Miller.

Miller didn't reply, so the minister continued. "God has not revealed the time," he said.

At this Miller sat up a little, looked at the man, and told him that he could "prove by the Bible that God had revealed it." Let me ask you a few questions about the Bible, Miller suggested, and I will show you.

Intrigued, the minister begged leave to retrieve his Bible. When he returned, he had not only the good book, but about twenty of his comrades, for moral and intellectual support. Beginning in the plodding, plain way he had begun thousands of sermons, Miller asked the Methodist to read the first three verses of the twelfth chapter of Daniel.

> And at that time shall Michael stand up, the great prince which standeth for the children of thy people: and there shall be a time of trouble, such as never was since there was a nation even to that same time: and at that time thy people shall be delivered, every one that shall be found written in the book.
>
> And many of them that sleep in the dust of the earth shall awake, some to everlasting life, and some to shame and everlasting contempt.
>
> And they that be wise shall shine as the brightness of the firmament; and they that turn many to righteousness as the stars for ever and ever.

"Is the resurrection brought to view in those verses?" Miller asked.

The minister stood silent for some time, then replied that he was not sure that was the case.

Well, then, Miller asked, what did the verses mean? When the minister responded that he chose not to answer, Miller said, "Oh, very well, we have nothing more to say together; for I did not agree to convince you, if you would not answer a few questions."

At that, an elderly minister who had taken a seat on one of the capstans asked his fellow Methodist why he would not answer Miller's question. When the obstinate man still refused to answer, the elderly man turned to Miller. "It does refer to the resurrection," he said.

"Well, father," Miller said, "I perceive you are an honest man. I will, if you please, ask you a few questions."

The first minister piped in. "Don't answer. He will make a Millerite of you."

But the older minister was unafraid, and he and Miller bantered back and forth for some time, in each instance agreeing on the interpretation of the scripture they were considering. At one point the Methodist exclaimed that "I never saw this in this light before." After an hour of Q&A, several others confessed that they had never considered Millerism to be as logical as Miller had just presented it to be.

Miller had seen the effect before. When you're portrayed as a lunatic but then present as a sane, rational person, the surprise in the face of listeners can be easily understood. Still, it must have been reassuring to Miller that even in the wake of the spring disappointment, some at least were still willing to listen.

As Miller and Himes were reviving the spirits of the faithful in Ohio and helping skeptics see things in a new light, the movement was being pulled in another direction in New Hampshire. At a camp meeting in Exeter, not far from where the first Adventist camp meeting had taken place just a few years before, a listless congregation was listening to speaker after speaker with little enthusiasm. Then Samuel Snow rose and began preaching the message he had first revealed back in February, a new interpretation of Daniel's prophecy that called into question not Miller's thesis, but his timekeeping. March had not been the end of the process, Snow told a now attentive crowd. Christ did not come then, he explained—as he had in his February 22 article in the *Midnight Cry*, before the spring disappointment—because the twenty-three hundred day/year prophecy ended not in

1843, but in 1844. The Lord would return, Snow assured the flock, on the tenth day of the seventh month of the Jewish calendar, the Day of Atonement. In 1844, that was October 22. Snow's vision moved the camp meeting to a "crusading zeal" and reinvigorated the Millerite movement, pushing it beyond the grasp of Miller and Himes.

"When that meeting closed, the granite hills of New Hampshire were ringing with the mighty cry, 'Behold the bridegroom cometh; go ye out to meet him,'" remembered Joseph Bates. "As the loaded wagons, stages, and railroad cars rolled away through the different states, cities, and villages of New England, the cry was still resounding, 'Behold the bridegroom cometh!' Christ, our blessed Lord, is coming on the tenth day of the seventh month! Get ready! Get ready!" Now, the man who had founded the movement and the man who had spread its message across the country would have to decide whether they would bask in the light or be left behind in the darkness.

The masses were quick to answer the call once again. On September 4, the same day Silas Wright was nominated for governor, a New York Customs House officer tendered his resignation. His concern, though, was related not to the political year, but to eternity. It was time, said the official, to get his worldly house in order, because the end was nigh. "Dear Sir," the Millerite wrote to his boss, "Inclosed is my warrant which I resign into your hands. . . . And may the Lord, by his spirit, convince you of the truth, and prepare you to meet him with yours, in the hopes of a better inheritance."

Two weeks later, Miller was in New York City, almost home from his journey to the west. He spoke in earnest about his mistakes, but assured all listeners that Christ was indeed coming. He had more invitations to speak, but once again feeling worn out by his travels, he demurred and headed for Low Hampton.

{ 8 }

THE GREAT
DISAPPOINTMENT

Back home in Low Hampton, an exhausted Miller turned his attention to the "seventh-month movement" that had swept through the
Adventist ranks in the weeks following the spring disappointment. Miller
had resisted the setting of a new date even more strongly than he had the
setting of the first one. But he had given in to Himes and others then, and
now he was faced with another decision, which he hardly felt up to making.

"I am once more at home, worn down with the fatigue of my journey,
my strength so exhausted and my bodily infirmities so great, that I am
about concluding I shall never be able again to labor in the vineyard as
heretofore," he wrote.

Much had changed while he was away. In addition to the fervent expectations associated with the new date, Millerites had begun to drift away—in
some cases they were driven away—from their churches in much greater
numbers. This was a severe disappointment to Miller, who had always urged
his followers to remain within their denominations. "I found on my arrival
here that my brethren had relinquished the meeting house to a small minority of our church, who separated from us last spring, because the second
coming of Christ was there preached—though they claim to be looking for

Him," he observed. "Rather than contend with them, our brethren have peaceably relinquished the chapel to them, and will build, if time continues."

Miller spent several days buried in study. Snow and the other proponents of the October 22 date had never suggested that Miller's underlying conclusion was wrong, only that the timing was off by seven months. As Miller reviewed their case, he began to hedge. Finally, on October 6, he wrote to Himes that "I see a glory in the seventh month which I never saw before."

Himes, who had canceled a planned trip to Europe because of the excitement surrounding the new date, was not yet totally on board, although he had written to Miller that "this thing has gone over the country like lightning" and seemed to be recruiting his mentor to the seventh-month movement. Putting the finishing touches on the October 2 issue of the *Advent Herald*, he attached a disclaimer—as he had back in February—to an article by Snow promoting October 22 as the appointed day. "While there is much evidence clustering around that day, sufficient to induce all who love the Lord's appearing, to hope He will then come, yet if the evidence may fail of making it a demonstration," Himes opined, "why should any who are waiting for His appearing, feel to oppose the idea that the Lord may then come?"

Just one week later, in receipt of Miller's letter lending his endorsement to October 22, Himes crossed over. "We are shut up to this faith, and shall, by the grace of God, look for the event, and act accordingly," he wrote. With that, other leaders in the movement quickly got on board, although one, Charles Fitch, would not live to see the day. Persuaded to the new date as he lay sick in bed in Buffalo—he had taken ill after baptizing a group of converts in a chilly river—he died on October 14.

George Storrs was to Snow for the seventh-month movement what Himes was to Miller. A fervent abolitionist, he had joined Miller's movement in 1841 and quickly became a prominent spokesman. Storrs had been an annihilationist, a proponent of a controversial theological movement that preached that a loving God would never condemn lost souls to eternal damnation, but instead would annihilate the souls of the damned. He published the *Bible Examiner*, a journal that spread the annihilationist message, and continued to preach the idea even after becoming a Millerite, although other leaders, including Miller and Himes, flatly rejected annihilationist teachings. Within a few weeks of Snow's February 22 article in the *Midnight Cry*, Storrs was writing in the *Bible Examiner* "with feelings such as I never before experienced. Beyond a doubt, in my mind, the tenth day of the seventh month will witness the revelation of our Lord Jesus Christ in the clouds of heaven." Others quickly took up the call.

Storrs's annihilationism was a minor distraction. All manner of theologies and creeds emerged during the Second Great Awakening; the notion that God might take mercy on the damned was hardly the most farfetched.

Plenty of Americans—not just Millerites—believed in the soon coming of Christ. But most, like Lyman Beecher, were postmillennialists, who used the idea of Christ's Kingdom to justify their reformist views: before God comes, man needs to clean up his own act. Premillennialists like Miller were largely uninterested in politics. Postmillennialists married religion and politics into a perfect union. "The evangelical movement supplied Whiggery with a conception of progress that was the collective form of redemption: like the individual, society as a whole was capable of improvement through conscious effort," explained Whig Party historian Daniel Walker Howe.

The religious ferment of the day was not restricted to Christian theology. While many mainstream Christians were questioning what they considered the outlandish views of the Millerites, others were beginning to call into question the very essence of revealed religion. Transcendentalists argued that people were not fallen but inherently good, and that it was organized religion that corrupted them.

The year 1844 also saw the first systematic examination in the Western world of Buddhism, and its introduction into the American consciousness via a translation of a Buddhist text from the French by transcendentalist Henry David Thoreau. In the Ottoman Empire, the sultan (officially, at least) barred the death penalty for Muslim apostates who converted to Christianity.

Even more revolutionary, scientists were casting doubt upon the very nature of man. The 1844 publication of Robert Chambers's "Vestiges of the Natural History of Creation" preceded Charles Darwin's theories about the origin of species by a decade and a half and sparked a popular debate over evolution. To be sure, Chambers maintained that a sort of proto-intelligent design was at work, keeping God in the equation. Over time, under pressure from even more radical ideas from Darwin and Alfred Russell Wallace, Chambers's theory would come to be seen as the protector of the religious element in human development.

"Get Ready, Friends"

Transcendentalism, Buddhism, and evolution existed in a world outside William Miller's consciousness. Mainstream denominations such as the Baptists and the Methodists were on the verge of splitting in two over slavery, but the issue was of little concern to Miller. His eye was now fixed on October 22, and so were the eyes of thousands of people who had put their faith in his teachings.

Miller did not want people quitting their jobs or ignoring their earthly responsibilities. "I have never taught a neglect of any of the duties of life, which make us good parents, children, neighbors, or citizens," he wrote. "Those who have taught the neglect of these . . . acted in opposition to my uniform teachings."

But with heaven at hand, earthly possessions seemed increasingly worthless. Farmers refused to bring in their crops, shops were shuttered, workers walked off the job. Others took a different tack, paying off debts or giving money to charity. Some took pains to explain themselves, or to offer warnings to non-believers. Clorinda S. Minor, a prominent Millerite writer and speaker, took out an ad in the *Philadelphia Public Ledger* just days before the expected advent. "Warning—I believe according to the Scriptures, that the Lord Jesus Christ, will be revealed in the clouds of Heaven, on the tenth day of the seventh month, which agrees with the 22nd inst. I therefore entreat all whom this may reach to prepare to meet their God." A tailor in the City of Brotherly Love closed his shop and hung a sign on the door reading, "This shop is closed in honor of the King of Kings, who will appear about the 22nd of October. Get ready, friends, to crown him Lord of all." A hatter in Rochester, New York, flung open the doors to his establishment and invited passersby to come in and take what they wanted.

Many struggled with the logical dilemma: if I do not dispose of my worldly goods, does that mean my faith is weak? If I do, will my neighbors consider me insane? Beyond Miller's advice, some leaders suggested disposing of "all you have which you do not actually need for the present wants of yourself and family." This was the course taken by Henry Bear of Lancaster, Pennsylvania, who "got rid of all my money except eighty dollars." One prominent Baptist minister in New York City who held no sympathy for Millerism nevertheless provided comfort to those confronted with such a Hobson's choice. "Were this doctrine of Mr. Miller established upon evidence satisfactory to my own mind, I would not rest till I had published in the streets, and proclaimed in the ears of my fellow-townsmen, and especially of my beloved flock, 'The day of the Lord is at hand! Build no more houses! Plant no more fields and gardens! Forsake your shops and farms, and all secular pursuits, and give every moment to preparation for this great event!'"

The outward manifestations garnered much of the attention, but the inner world of believers was rich with a quiet expectancy. "Those who sincerely love Jesus can appreciate the feelings of those who attached with the most intense longing for the coming of their Saviour," remembered Ellen G. White, a teenager in 1844 who would keep the Millerite banner waving by going on to cofound the Seventh Day Adventist denomination. "We approached this hour with a calm solemnity. The true believers rested in a sweet communion with God." Under a "Millerite Fanaticism" head, the *New York Tribune* reported on its front page of October 21 that "the crowd at the Juliana Street Church is still as great as ever."

For others, just as devoted but still feeling the tug of earthly attachments, the days leading up to the advent could be heartbreaking. On October 21, just one day before the appointed time, Joseph and Prudence Bates watched tearfully as fourteen-year-old Joseph Jr. sailed from the port of New Bedford, Massachusetts, on a long-planned adventure aboard a whaling ship.

The faithful had long contended with the taunts of scoffers in person and in print. As the day approached, the anti-Millerite segment began to take on an even more hostile form. "In the evening, a rabble came up from the village, and began to pelt the tent where the meeting was held, with apples from the orchard," remembered Uriah Smith. "Waxing bolder, as the meeting became more earnest, they gathered around the door and began to direct their missiles against the lanterns hanging on the center-poles in the house-shaped tent. These were soon hit and demolished, and then scattered over the floor of the tent, and all were left in total darkness. The rabble grew bolder, and seizing hold of the framework of the tent, and cutting the guy-ropes, soon leveled it to the ground. Meanwhile, the crowd had seized a large hog, brought him to the tent, lifted up the curtain and pushed him in, and there we were—women, children, and the hog—in darkness under the cover of the tent—not a very pleasant companion, and not a very agreeable situation."

October 22 dawned a bright, clear day in Rochester. Believers began gathering early in the morning at the Talman Building downtown, within view of the Erie Canal. Later a storm blew through and knocked down the city's liberty pole, which many of the gathered took as a sign. Ninety miles away in Ithaca, the building where believers gathered caught fire, another sign—in this case, one that sent the Adventists out into the streets and gave pause to nonbelievers who saw the fire and briefly considered that it was the beginning of the end of the world. Everywhere people gathered they stayed all day and into the night, praying and preaching, hailing the "last hours of time" and the "brink of a new eternity." Abolitionist and Liberty Party cofounder Gerrit Smith of Utica gloried in the appointed day. "I cast myself on his mercy like the thief on the cross," he told his wife.

But the last hour came, and nothing more happened. In Rochester, as in many other places, as the day wore on into night some slept, some pushed through. By dawn, when it became clear that Christ once again was not coming, they began to wander off, headed for home in a state of tired confusion and bitter disappointment.

In Low Hampton, Miller and Himes, who had come down from Boston, spent the day with their families at Miller's farm. Like others, they prayed and sang hymns. One story passed down through the family says they waited on a rock outcropping west of the farmhouse, but Miller never mentioned it in any of his writings. "We held meeting all day and our place of worship was crowded to overflowing with anxious souls apparently," he reported.

The anxious souls at Miller's farm, like those all around the country who had believed in him, were again disappointed. "The 22nd of October passed, making unspeakably sad the faithful and longing ones," wrote

Luther Boutelle, a Millerite lecturer, "but causing the unbelieving and wicked to rejoice."

William Lloyd Garrison's *Liberator* berated the "deplorable fantasy of the brain" that had led otherwise rational people to believe in such nonsense. Wild tales of Millerites wearing white ascension robes and gathering on hilltops to be taken up spread like wildfire; none of them bore the testimony of an eyewitness, but it helped sell papers. Himes was accused of profiteering, not for the first time. The general tone was captured by an item published about five weeks after the Great Disappointment: "The Millerite delusion, it is said, is not yet over. Their leaders are again advertising their meetings and their hearers are again willing to be deceived. An old lady, says a Providence paper, was called on the other day by a neighbor and accosted with, 'Why, marm, I am surprised to see you here. How happens it that you did not go up last night, when the world was destroyed?' Well, I did start, said the old woman; but la, mercy on me, marm, I forgot my snuff box!"

But Miller, twice disappointed, was unbroken. "My mind is perfectly calm," he wrote to Himes, "and my hope in the coming of Christ is as strong as ever." Before the month was out, publication of both the *Advent Herald* and the *Midnight Cry* had resumed.

"If You Only Knew How We Have Suffered"

After Oregon-bound Henry Sager died at the Green River in late August, his widow, Naomi, hired a young man traveling with the train to drive the wagon carrying her and her seven children. He proved to be somewhat unreliable. But Theophilus Degen, the German doctor who had tended to the family in their injuries and illnesses, was a constant comfort. And the children pitched in. They cared for their mother, devoted themselves to their chores, and made nets of the wagon covers to bring in a haul of fish once the train passed Fort Bridger in southwestern Wyoming.

At first it seemed the hired hand Naomi engaged would be a great help. He drove the wagon up the Bear River Valley. It was fairly easy terrain, moving north by northwest, but even on the smoothest road the children could not have managed by themselves, with Naomi still ill in the wagon. Her plan was to get to Fort Hall, trade her failing oxen for horses and mules, and pack the final leg of the journey into the Whitman Mission, where she hoped to be able to stay for the winter before moving on to the Willamette Valley come spring.

Soon enough, though, trouble struck again. The new driver volunteered to go hunting for the family if he could use Henry's gun. Naomi consented and he took off, never to be seen again. Degen and other men from the train pitched in to help the older boys, but this latest setback dampened Naomi's spirits even further, and her condition worsened. "The nights and mornings were very cold," Catherine remembered, "and she took cold from the exposure unavoidably." Fort Hall came and went, and Naomi Sager was too ill even to get out of the wagon to do her horse trading.

After leaving the fort, her fever worsened. She developed sores in her mouth, making it even more difficult to eat, so malnutrition was added to her list of ailments. And, as the trail turned south and west down the Snake River, the road grew rougher. Restricted to bed in the back of the wagon, constantly jostled and subjected to swirling dust, she "suffered intensely."

She "was taken delirious" and began having conversations with her dead husband, "beseeching him in piteous tones to relieve her sufferings." Mercifully, she soon fell unconscious. Again, Degen was there to help care for her and the children. Other women in the company took turns wet-nursing the baby. Adults up and down the train looked in on the children, shared what little food they had, and helped drive the wagon. "Those kind-hearted women would also come in at night and wash the dust from mother's face and otherwise make her comfortable," wrote Catherine.

As she passed in and out of consciousness, she knew the end was near. She called for Degen, who came instantly. With tears rolling down his cheeks, the doctor promised Naomi that he would see her children safely to the Whitman Mission. She won the same promise from the train's captain, William Shaw. And she seized a lucid moment to bid her children "an affectionate farewell."

On September 22, near Salmon Falls on the Snake, ten-year-old Rebecca Parrish suffered the same accident that had felled Catherine Sager back in Nebraska. On a cool, clear day on which the party traveled about ten miles, Rebecca tumbled after jumping off the wagon and a wheel rolled over her leg, crushing her thigh. The girl survived, but the travelers took it as a bad omen.

The next day they started out at seven in the morning and kept on until midnight, "without water or grass for the cattle," the cliffs of the river being too steep to descend. On the twenty-fourth they crossed the river at Three Islands. Naomi Sager's condition grew worse. For the better part of two days she moaned in agony but did not regain consciousness as they passed "through the worst mountains and over the worst road we have yet seen," as judged by mountain man James Clyman.

On the evening of the twenty-fifth, a woman from the train came by to try to soothe Naomi, speaking with her as if she could hear, but getting no response. As she wiped the dust from the dying woman's forearms, she barely felt a pulse. Then Naomi opened her eyes and said softly, as if speaking to her husband, "Oh, Henry, if you only knew how we have suffered." Then she died.

"The tent was set up, the corpse laid out, and next morning we took the last look at our mother's face," Catherine wrote. Someone cut her name into a head-board, which was stuck in the ground to mark the roadside grave. "Willow brush was laid in the bottom and covered the body, the earth filled in—then the train moved on."

Degen, Shaw, and many others adopted the orphans. Baby Rosanna was taken by a woman in the train and cared for with more stability than she'd ever had in her brief life. But that meant the family was split up, at least for the moment. The older children had a vague notion of the Whitman Mission in their future, but had no real idea what that entailed. They were simply orphans in the wilderness, being cared for by kind acquaintances. Ahead of them lay more than two hundred miles of rough country. The weather was growing colder every day. And at the end, who knew if the Whitmans would even take them in?

The trail turned northward up the Snake, toward Fort Boise, built in 1834 by the Hudson's Bay Company to compete with Fort Hall, then in the possession of American Nathaniel Wyeth. The British soon enough owned both forts. But like Fort Hall and Fort Vancouver, Boise served as a way station for Americans pouring into the Oregon country. Before leaving the

Snake, the Sager wagon collapsed and some men from the company cut it in half, converting the wagon to a cart that could more easily be pulled by the weakened oxen.

From Fort Boise, the trail left the Snake and struck out across the Blue Mountains, the last great obstacle between the pioneers and their destination. For the Sager orphans, the mountains would provide one final test of their perseverance.

They still had the tent in which Naomi's body had been laid out. At night the children crowded together in it for warmth and some protection from the elements. But twice the bitter cold nearly caused a tragic accident. A week or so after her mother's death, as Louise Sager was trying to warm up next to a blazing fire, her long dress caught the flame. Louise screamed and the ever-vigilant Degen moved swiftly to beat the fire out with his bare hands, singeing himself in the process but rescuing Louise from serious injury. A little farther on, but still in the mountains, Frank Sager tried to use gunpowder to kick-start a reluctant campfire built of wet wood. It worked, but the flame shot up the powder and the horn exploded in his hands. He bolted to a nearby creek and plunged his burned hands and face into the icy water. His face was blackened from the powder and his eyebrows and lashes were singed off, but he survived.

They came out of the mountains in the middle of October and camped in the company of some adults from the wagon train who volunteered to stay behind while others rode ahead to the mission to obtain flour and other supplies and bring them back to camp. Thus provisioned, they were ready to begin the final leg of their journey to Whitman Mission. When they reached the Umatilla River, Shaw sped ahead on a fast horse toward the Whitmans, a hard day's ride ahead, to alert the missionaries about the orphans. Back on the river, the children purchased potatoes from local Indians, "the first potatoes we had eaten since we started on our long and sad journey."

When Shaw brought his sad tale to the mission, it was not news to the Whitmans. Immigrants passing by on their way to the Willamette Valley had already alerted the missionaries, who had begun discussing between themselves whether they would take on the children. It was not an easy call.

Narcissa Whitman—like William Miller and Joseph Smith—had been raised on the rim of upstate New York's burned-over district, at the foot of the Finger Lakes, a child of the Second Great Awakening. She had longed to be a missionary, and married Dr. Marcus Whitman with the intent of joining him in his labors. Traveling west in 1836 with Henry Spalding, Narcissa and Spalding's wife, Eliza, became the first white women to cross the continental divide.

But ministering to the Cayuse was much more difficult than Narcissa had imagined back in Prattsburgh. The Indians were not especially receptive to the new religion, Narcissa was not particularly adept at proselytizing, and Marcus was frequently absent, trying to balance his religious missionary work with his favored occupation—serving as an advocate for emigration to Oregon. But the Whitmans were able to turn the mission at Waiilatpu in what is now southeastern Washington into a going concern, and it would soon become a life-saving stopping point for hungry and worn-out pioneers while still managing to convert some of the Cayuse.

Narcissa became pregnant on the way west and in early 1837 gave birth to a daughter, Alice. Already discouraged after a year of mostly futile mission work, Narcissa's spirits were revived by the baby. But on a sleepy Sunday in June 1839, while Marcus and Narcissa were reading in their house, two-year-old Alice slipped out in search of a drink of water. Narcissa, noticing the quiet, looked up, and realized Alice was not there. She sent one house servant to look for her. Then another came to say that he had found two cups along the bank of the Walla Walla River, which flowed through the mission property. Narcissa and Marcus ran the short distance down to the water, where they found a Cayuse who volunteered to dive into the river to search for Alice. He found her a short way downstream. The parents tried desperately to revive their little girl, but it was too late.

Narcissa saw God's hand in everything, but that did not make coping with her daughter's death any easier. She grieved deeply, thousands of miles from home, with little support from family or friends. Eventually, though, she would return to something of a routine existence. Then, in the autumn of 1840, the Whitmans adopted the mixed-blood daughter of a former fur trapper, and the next year they adopted another, two being "very little more trouble than one," according to Narcissa. A few months later, a mixed-blood boy joined their brood. "The Lord has taken our own dear child away so that we may care for the poor outcasts of the country and suffering children,"

Narcissa wrote of her adopted children, Helen Meek, Mary Ann Bridger, and David Malin.

If mission work was not her true calling, motherhood was. So when the opportunity to take on the Sager orphans was presented, Narcissa was ready to listen. She told Shaw they would consider it, although she was not quick to commit. Tripling the size of their family in an instant would require some careful consideration. She also worried for her busy husband, who "if he had a hundred strings tied to him pulling in every direction, could not be any worse off."

The Whitmans were always welcoming, so much so that Narcissa sometimes complained that Marcus too often gave travelers the choicest supplies and left the mission with the dregs. He charged those who could pay, but often provided food free of charge to those who said they couldn't, even if deep down he suspected they could. And, as a doctor, he treated a host of medical conditions, delivered babies, tended to injuries, all while rarely taking any payment. In the early 1840s, the mission was more or less on the pioneers' route to the Willamette Valley. By 1844, with more direct paths cut, those who headed to the mission for the most part were only the ragtag and needy—still a good proportion of the emigrants.

The Sagers certainly fit that description. Shaw returned to the camp to take the children—except baby Rosanna, who was left behind with Shaw's wife, "very sick, with doubts of its recovery"—in their cart to meet the Whitmans. Degen accompanied them. Hungry, dirty, and traumatized, the children made a "pitiful sight . . . going to find a home among strangers."

They reached the mission in the afternoon. "For weeks this place had been a subject for our talk by day and formed our dreams at night," Catherine remembered. When finally it became real in front of them, it was not at all what they had pictured in their minds' eyes. "We expected to see log houses, occupied by Indians and such people as we had seen about the forts." Instead, they saw a neat white adobe mission house, surrounded by fencing, with a garden and irrigation ditch. The house fronted a blacksmith's shop and a tidy corral, with a mill next to the river. It was an island of civilization in the wild. To the beleaguered Sagers, it must have seemed like heaven.

The cart halted near the irrigation canal. Shaw, who was already in the house talking with Narcissa, saw the family pull up and pointed at them through a window. "Your children have come," he told her, hopefully. "Will you go out and see them?"

Outside, the children tried to make themselves presentable. Bonnets were found for the older girls, Catherine and Elizabeth. Louisa and Matilda "huddled together, bareheaded and barefooted." John and Frank were both crying. All were "dirty and sunburned," looking "more like Indians than white children." Degen, already weeping, held the oxen.

As Narcissa approached, the girls ducked behind the cart. She turned to the boys. "Poor boys," she said softly, "no wonder you weep." Quickly, she shifted into organizational mode, arranging the tattered remains of the children's goods and enlisting Degen and the boys to carry them. Helen Meek, now seven, showed them where to take the things. Narcissa then helped Catherine, who was still not fully mobile, down from the cart, gently took three-year-old Louisa by the hand, and escorted them toward the house. Shaw watched the tender scene with awe.

"Do you have children of your own, Mrs. Whitman?" he asked.

"All the child I ever had sleeps yonder," she said, pointing to Alice's grave beyond the garden, at the foot of a hill. "It is a great pleasure that I can see her from the door."

The simple adobe house seemed like a "mansion" to Catherine Sager as they entered. The Whitmans' other adopted daughter, Mary Ann, was washing dishes. "Well, Mary Ann, how do you think you will like all these sisters?" Narcissa asked her cheerfully. She sat down and invited the children to gather around her, taking Louisa in her lap, and asked each their name, and about their journey and their family. They told her about the baby, still back at the camp on the Umatilla, too sick to travel with them. As the children spun their tale of woe, all the astonished Narcissa could manage in response was an occasional "poor children." Every emotion she had felt at the loss of her own daughter must have filled Narcissa with empathy for these orphans.

Marcus Whitman, who had been working in the mill, came upon this scene as he entered the house. As he took it all in from the doorway, Narcissa turned to him and said, "Come in, doctor, and see your children." But both Whitmans knew it wasn't quite as simple as that.

The dying wish of both Sager parents had been that their children remain together as a family. Shaw emphatically passed that wish on to the

Whitmans, reminding them—as if they needed reminding—"that a missionary's duty was to do good, and we certainly were objects worthy of missionary charity." Narcissa quickly determined that she would like to keep the girls, but wasn't sure about adding two rowdy boys to their family. Marcus worried about what the men who sent him to Oregon—the American Board of Commissioners for Foreign Missions, of which Theodore Frelinghuysen was a leading member—would think about him taking on a family of Christian children. The board had already tried to shut him down once—it was during his trip east to convince them otherwise that the Sagers first heard his pitch for Oregon settlement. (Whitman had also visited with John Tyler on that trip.) And, he wasn't too sure about keeping all the girls, but thought the boys could prove useful, tending the crops and animals and working in the mill. He also worried about bringing a sickly baby into the family, and how it might affect his wife, who had already lost one young child.

Practicality and duty combined, in the end. "If you are going to have the girls," Marcus told his wife, "I must have the boys." Narcissa was not immediately persuaded, but the couple told Shaw to leave the children; they would take care of the boys at least until spring, and they would send word to him then about the final disposition of John and Frank.

With that, Shaw and Degen said their goodbyes to the children they had protected and cared for across two thousand miles. "Our faithful friend, the German doctor, left us at last, safe in the motherly care of Mrs. Whitman. Well had he kept his promise to our dying mother," Catherine remembered fondly.

Baby Rosanna arrived a few days later half-starved, "in the hands of an old filthy woman, sick, emaciated, and but just alive," Narcissa said. By then the Whitmans had decided to keep all the children and had sent word up the trail to Shaw. The children, reunited, had now found a home at the mission. They also found a small token of their parents: the teen who had borrowed their father's gun and run off had apparently felt a pang of conscience and left it at the mission for them. Rosanna slowly regained her health under Narcissa's care. In a gesture that must have moved the Whitmans deeply, the children asked that her name be changed to Henrietta Naomi, to honor the parents who had died trying to make a better life for them.

"Unacquainted ... With the Climate"

After the parting of the ways at the Raft River, the twenty-six California-bound emigrants of the Stevens-Townsend-Murphy party headed toward the Humboldt River, which would guide them and their eleven wagons across Nevada. Between them and the Humboldt lay 160 miles of alternating uplands that blocked their way and valleys filled with a choking dust kicked up by the animals from the volcanic rock they were crossing. Always, in one direction or another, they could see mountains. But the air was cool and clear, and the Raft yielded a gastronomic treat the likes of which the pioneers had not seen on their journey, and maybe had never seen in their lives: crayfish, which became an instant hit.

The pioneers passed through the City of Rocks, a formation of granite monoliths in what is now Idaho. By this time the party had seen plenty of rocks and were mostly inured to the scenery, however spectacular. But the City of Rocks mattered because, as the travelers looked southwest from the pass, they were looking into another country. Across the imaginary lines, which now divide Idaho from Utah and Nevada, was Mexico.

In 1844, this was still largely uncharted territory. The Mexican hold was tenuous, at best. American and British trappers had ventured into the area over the past few decades, but it was (and still remains) largely devoid of human settlement. The emigrants of the three previous years had barely left a trace, and the way was not nearly as well marked as the road through Nebraska and Wyoming and up to Fort Hall.

The Humboldt, or Mary's River as it was known then, was not like the Sweetwater or even the Platte. Reaching the head of the "dreadful" Humboldt meant they were three-fourths of the way to their destination. And it would be indispensable as a highway and a water source as the party made its way across the wastes of Nevada. But it was not much of a river—shallow, rocky, and alkali, a friend you didn't particularly like but couldn't do without. And, at the river's end, it emptied not into another river or a bay or an ocean, but into the desert. A Gold Rush–era traveler would call it the "meanest and muddiest, filthiest stream" he had ever seen. The Humboldt section of the road ran for a "very monotonous" 350 miles. Each hot, dusty mile brought a growing uneasiness that at the end of the river they weren't quite sure where they would be going next.

Along the way, Caleb Greenwood, the aged mountain man, chatted in sign language with natives who had come up to trade with the emigrants. These "Digger" Indians, as the overlanders called them—Western Shoshone and Northern Paiute—were among the poorest people anywhere on the North American continent, subsisting on "grasshoppers, rats, roots, and grass seed." But they were friendly and caused no problems, even as the travelers descended on the camp by the dozens.

Around the first of October, the party reached the Humboldt Sink, where the "knowledge of their guides entirely ceased." The old trapper Isaac Hitchcock had been to California with legendary mountain man Joseph Walker, but not by this route. For Greenwood, this was virgin territory altogether.

At the sink, "the cattle were let out to grass, the horses unharnessed, while the men and women, too, busied themselves with repairing outfits, mending damaged vehicles, washing soiled clothing, and the younger members busied themselves in shooting game, which, in the shape of wild ducks, geese, sage hens, as well as antelopes and deer, were very abundant."

They stayed at the sink a week. The men had many discussions about what route to take next. Some wanted to bend southward and try to go around the mountains they knew were in front of them. Others favored a straight line west. None actually knew what lay before them, or exactly how to get where they were going.

But one of the Indians who had followed along with them from camp to camp told them about an east-flowing river about fifty miles to the west where they could find "forage and trees." This river, the Indian said, would lead them up to the mountains and a place where they could cross. He also volunteered to guide them to it. They couldn't make out his name; to a couple of French Canadians who had joined the party near Fort Laramie it sounded like "Truckee," so that's what they called him.

Three of the older men—John Townsend, Joseph Foster, and Elisha Stevens—went with Truckee to look for the river. They were gone three days. When they returned, they reported that they had found it, just as Truckee had said, but the route to the headwaters was a difficult one. The

Forty-Mile Desert was the name eventually given to this boiling stretch of wasteland. Not all members of the emigrant party were entirely sold on the route—they had vivid and unhappy memories of Hitchcock's "shortcut" to the Green River—but they all agreed to make the trip together. They prepared two days' rations and filled every container they possessed with water. If this did turn out to be another wasteland like the one Hitchcock had taken them across in Wyoming, at least this time they would be prepared.

Before setting off, though, young Moses Schallenberger almost got them all killed.

He had been given more and more responsibility as the journey went on, and his "conduct on the march had been conspicuous for coolness and discretion," according to the party's chief chronicler. But on the day of their departure for the river, he had mislaid his horse's halter. He looked around and finally saw it—or one that looked like it—partially tucked under a blanket worn by one of the "Digger" Indians that had followed the camp. Schallenberger told the man to hand it over, but either he didn't understand or he pretended not to. Moses then grabbed the halter and tried to pull it away. He couldn't wrest it loose, and the Indian backed away and drew his bow. Moses turned and bolted for his wagon to retrieve his rifle, which

Moses Schallenberger.
Stanford University

he aimed at the man who still had the halter. Just as he was about to pull the trigger, Martin Murphy knocked the muzzle into the air and the shot went astray. Other Diggers came rushing up to see what had happened. The whites did the same. All was confusion for several minutes, but Murphy and Townsend, with an assist from Greenwood, got things sorted out to the satisfaction of the offended Diggers, who were presented with several armfuls of presents. Outnumbered four-to-one, Murphy's quick action in response to Schallenberger's rash one may have averted a disaster for the group.

Moses was properly chastised by Townsend, his brother-in-law, but he would soon enough have an opportunity to make amends to the group.

To cross the Forty-Mile Desert, the party traveled non-stop from morning until midnight, halting only to rest and water the oxen at a hot spring, which made some of the animals sick. They then pressed on, through choking alkali dust that was knee deep in some places. The humans were in reasonably good shape, having put away barrels of water for the trip. But the animals suffered mightily. At mid-afternoon the next day they came within sight of the river that Truckee had promised was there. The oxen—just as they had done at the Green River—broke free and headed for the water. The travelers were so happy they named the river for Truckee.

They rested for two days, then proceeded on.

Having found the river and what appeared to be a usable road, the emigrants discovered that the road and the river were all too often one and the same. It took them about five weeks to travel seventy miles, and they had to cross and recross the river more than thirty times.

As late October bore down on the party, a few dustings of snow had already fallen on them along the way. The cattle suffered aching feet from spending so much time in the river. Then more snow fell, covering the grass that lined the banks, so the oxen became not only sore but hungry as well. The travelers found that rushes tall enough to stick up out of the snow sprouted periodically along the river bank. Some men would ride ahead and harvest them, leaving them to lie in the path of the oxen so they could eat a few at regular intervals along the way and not become sick from ingesting too much at once.

Truckee's directions carried them to a point where the river forked, with the main channel bearing southwest and the smaller tributary due west, up into the mountains. Open grass was available at the fork, so they paused for a few days to rest and feed the animals and to consider their options. The Sierra Nevada loomed above them, and they could see the snow at the summit.

Like Frémont had a year earlier not too many miles from this spot, they pondered which direction to take. Having no cannon to abandon, they decided they would leave behind some of the wagons, but push on with the rest up the tributary heading west, which seemed the likelier route for wagon travel. And they made a bold decision to split up. The other group—which included three of the Murphys and Elizabeth Townsend—would abandon wagons altogether and travel by pack to the southwest. The Murphys were confident that their hunting skills would keep the group fed. Remarkably the two thousand–mile trek had been a curative for Mrs. Townsend and she was feeling strong enough to strike out on her own, without husband or brother, across a snow-covered mountain. The once delicate Elizabeth now "was able to spend the whole day on horseback." Traveling fast and light, they might be able to get through to Sutter's Fort quickly enough to send back help if, God forbid, the others became stranded.

It was the middle of November. A couple feet of snow already blanketed the ground. The westbound group pushed on a few miles until they came to a bright, clear lake sitting at the foot of the mountains, perhaps twenty miles from the summit that rose another 1,160 feet into the sky in front of them. "Standing at the bottom and looking upwards at the perpendicular," a future traveler would write, "the observer, without any further knowledge on the subject, would doubt if man or beast ever made a good passage over them." They camped beside the lake, which in a few years would bear the name of the Donner party, who followed the 1844 travelers' path, and they reconnoitered the mountain for several days, walking up toward the granite face in search of a way through.

After four days of exploring, they thought they had found one. Only a handful of the remaining adults in the party insisted on trying to get their wagons over the pass; others "thought it would be impossible with their heavily laden wagons to reach their journey's end," Schallenberger remembered. So the others, including Townsend, decided to leave behind their wagons and the goods they had carried with them for use or sale in

California—books, valuable silks, hunting and farming implements, tools, ammunition—in the hope they would be able to recover them come spring. But they worried that Indians or the elements might cost them their treasure, so Moses Schallenberger, who had just turned eighteen, volunteered to stay behind with the wagons.

"There seemed little danger to me in undertaking this," Schallenberger reasoned. "Game seemed to be abundant. We had seen a number of deer, and one of our party had killed a bear, so I had no fears of starvation. The Indians in that vicinity were poorly clad, and I therefore felt no anxiety in regard to them, as they probably would stay further south as long as cold weather lasted. Knowing that we were not far from California, and being unacquainted, except in a general way, with the climate, I did not suppose that the snow would at any time be more than two feet deep, nor that it would be on the ground continually."

It was a brave, loyal, and possibly foolhardy move by the young man. Perhaps he could have been dissuaded by his sister, but she was already on her way over the mountain to the south. Townsend consented, demonstrating his growing trust in his young brother-in-law, and left two cows to help tide him over. But the others could not consent to letting Moses spend the winter alone in the wilderness of the Sierra Nevada. One of his buffalo hunting partners, Allen Montgomery, a close associate of Townsend back in the world, volunteered to stay with Moses. Then Joseph Foster, who had gone with Townsend and Truckee to find the river route to the mountains, said he too would stay behind.

That settled, the party of twelve married men with their wives, a dozen children, and five single men trundled off around the lake, five wagons in tow. The three men who had volunteered to stay behind helped them tote their goods up the mountain before returning to the lake.

ACROSS THE SIERRA

Townsend's party set up a base camp about a half mile beyond the far reach of the lake and began the seemingly impossible task of hauling the wagons and their belongings up the steep granite face.

Slogging through two feet of snow even at this relatively low altitude, they unloaded the wagons and methodically carried their contents up toward the pass. The going was slow. The temperatures were bitter and the snow grew gradually deeper as they climbed. No one wanted to leave the children at the base camp, so they came along, more cargo than carriers. Once the clothes, foodstuffs, and other goods were cached at the front of the pass, they came back down, double-teamed the oxen (possible because they had left some of the wagons behind), and headed back up. At first, it was what might be termed normal rough going. The wagons were empty and the double teams made slow but steady progress. But about halfway up they ran into a sheer rock face ten feet high, impossible for the oxen to pull the wagons over, and nearly impossible for the people to get over themselves.

They considered abandoning the wagons and strapping necessities to their backs. Before giving up, though, they spent some time poking around and finally found a small slot in the rock, large enough—maybe—for the oxen to pass through single file. If they could get the beasts to the top of the rock, they could re-yoke them and haul the wagons over the outcropping with chains. The oxen were none too happy about being gouged and prodded up the steep, slippery incline, but one by one they were pushed through the slot, then left to wait while the men went back down the rock to attach them via chains to the wagons.

Some of the men invoked the assistance of the almighty—Stevens in particular would remember praying with deep conviction and being granted a vision of success. Invoking the proverbial admonition that God helps those who help themselves, the men pushed from below while the oxen pulled from above, and after much exertion all five wagons were carried over the rock and then on up the mountain to the summit.

From there they believed it would be relatively smooth sailing down the western slope, maybe three days' march across still rough country, but at least it was downhill. Three days later, they were not out of the mountains, the sky was threatening, and the pregnant Mrs. Martin Murphy was about to deliver. So they made camp about ten miles on the California side of the summit and held council.

They stayed a week, during which time they built a cabin, Mrs. Murphy gave birth to a daughter, Elizabeth (later given the middle name Yuba, after the river next to which she was born), and another three feet of snow fell. Getting out now with a newborn baby, wagons, and tired oxen seemed like too much to ask, so they decided to leave the wagons behind, for now. They planned to slaughter most of the oxen for food, believing the meat would stay fresh in the freezing temperatures, and to leave two men to watch over the women and children while the rest pushed on toward Sutter's Fort.

Leaving people behind was risky. They now had two groups waiting for rescue, and God only knew where the team that had left on horseback was at this point. The Stevens-Townsend-Murphy party, which had remained a remarkably unified group across two thousand miles, was now spread out across hundreds of miles of the Sierra Nevada.

The men who were headed to Sutter's Fort took a few cattle and stumbled down the mountain through the snow in the first week of December. In truth, though these Midwesterners didn't know it, they had been remarkably lucky with the weather. As bad as it was, it could have been much worse. After two days they spotted bare ground in front of them and raced along with the hungry oxen to reach it. Another few days of fairly easy going brought them to Sutter's, where they found the pack team relaxing on the veranda, looking little the worse for wear.

That group had come around Lake Tahoe, moved west down the shoreline and found a moderately easy pass to cross, then made a steady descent down a tributary of the American River, which flowed through Sutter's domain. The river trail was rough, but there was no snow and plenty of game. They watched the storm that had dumped three feet of snow on their comrades from the safety of the lower elevation and arrived at the fort neither hungry nor harried after about three weeks.

All assumed they would quickly gather a rescue party and return for those left behind. Sutter had other ideas. Jose Manuel Micheltorena, the governor of Mexican California, was in the midst of suppressing a rebellion and had enlisted the aid of Sutter, who considered the newly arrived Americans to be fresh recruits. They wanted to retrieve their families, but Sutter convinced them that a wintertime rescue effort through what might now be as much as twenty feet of snow was impossible. If they had built a sturdy cabin and left plenty of food behind, he assured the emigrants, their loved ones would be safe until spring.

The war, such as it was, was of little interest to the Americans, who nonetheless realized that they were no longer in America. The native Californians resented the intrusion of Mexico City as much as they resented the trickle of emigrants from America, and rose up in arms against both. If the snow in the mountains wasn't enough to keep the newly arrived party from joining up, the threat by the Californios to drive all the foreigners back where they came from probably had some effect. Resignedly, the men accepted Sutter's judgment and marched off on New Year's Day 1845 to fight the Californios, with Townsend serving as regimental surgeon.

While the men were fighting, the women and children left at the top of the mountain had surprise visitors: Allen Montgomery and Joseph Foster appeared out of the snow. But where was Moses Schallenberger?

{ 9 }

"THE SEVEREST STRUGGLE EVER WITNESSED"

Voting for president took place over twelve days in November, beginning on the first with Pennsylvania and Ohio. Most states voted on November 4, New York on November 5, and Delaware and Vermont on November 12. The election of 1844 was the last in which states would vote for president on different days. Out of a total population of slightly more than 19 million, 2.7 million votes would be cast. The twenty-six states had 275 electoral votes, and 138 were needed to win.

After months of virulent attacks, fabrications, and outright lies, what everyone expected to be one of the closest elections in the nation's history came down to a few voters in a handful of states. New York, with the largest block of electoral votes at 36, and Pennsylvania, second at 26, were crucial; Louisiana and Polk's own Tennessee were the Southern states most in doubt. Both sides had pulled out all the stops. The Whigs had more money to spend, but the Democrats were better organized in the big cities of the Northeast, where it looked like the election would be decided. The two parties were likely guilty of some fraud, although the record would seem to indicate that the Democrats were more guilty. John Slidell, a New York native who had been elected to the House from Louisiana, helped deliver hundreds of extra votes by transporting Irish and German immigrants from New Orleans, where they'd already voted at least once, to Plaquemines Parish, where their anonymity allowed them to vote again—and again—for Polk.

Clay, who had suffered more during the summer from self-inflicted wounds than from anything the Democrats had done, tripped himself up again in the campaign's final weeks. After the debacle of the two Alabama letters, Clay supporters in the North tried to do damage control. His abolitionist kin, Kentuckian Cassius M. Clay, was invited to campaign in Ohio by Congressman Joshua Giddings. Then, in mid-August, Cassius published a letter in the *New York Tribune* asserting his distant cousin's bona fides on the crucial question of the day. "I do not mean to say that [Henry] Clay is an emancipationist," he wrote, "but I believe his feelings are with the cause. I know that those most immediately within his influence approximate to myself in sentiment on the subject of slavery."

Cave Johnson's prediction in April that Clay would "play hide & seek with the Abolitionists" had come true. Now the game was up.

Henry Clay moved quickly to repudiate Cassius's letter, writing to the *Lexington Observer* and *Kentucky Reporter* in the first week of September that "Mr. C. M. Clay's letter was written without my knowledge, without any consultation from me, and without any authority from me." The letter went on to say that not only had he not been consulted, but his cousin's contentions were far off base. "So far as he ventures to interpret my feelings, he has entirely misconceived them. I believe him to be equally mistaken as to those in the circle of my personal friends and neighbors, generally."

This letter threw Clay's Northern supporters into a state, and they warned Clay that many of their fellow antislavery men were abandoning him for James Birney of the Liberty Party. Clay being Clay, he wrote three more letters attempting to talk his antislavery supporters down off the ledge, stating in no uncertain terms that "I am decidedly opposed to the immediate annexation of Texas to the United States." He also argued that none of the letters he had written on the subject were inconsistent with one another and that he did not plan to write any more, which must have come as a considerable relief to his supporters. It certainly provided a moment of mirth for the Democrats, whose candidate had for the most part followed the wise counsel "that the less said is the easiest word."

"Clay . . . has at last determined he will write no more letters," wrote former Democratic congressman William Taylor of New York, "the wisest step he has taken since his nomination."

Just as had happened in July, the Liberty Party saw an opportunity and seized the moment. Party activists harangued their base—religious voters in the North, particularly in Massachusetts, New York, northern Ohio, and Michigan—and made good use of Clay's confusing series of letters. Seward had seen firsthand the increasing power of the Liberty Party. In the wake of its convention in Buffalo the previous year, the party had strengthened across New York, hiring seven full-time employees and organizing dozens of county-level meetings ahead of the 1843 election. Successes were also claimed in other states. Enough Liberty Party voters turned out for their gubernatorial candidate in Vermont that no candidate received a majority and the election had to be decided by the state legislature. In Chicago, the party won its first-ever, if minor, local office in March 1844.

The Cassius Clay controversy erupted at about the same time that the abolitionist press and some mainstream Whig newspapers were also devoting attention to the case of Delia Webster, a Vermont native who had been arrested in Lexington, Kentucky, for aiding in the escape of a slave family. The escape took place the last weekend of September, and the father, mother, and son were successfully spirited across the Ohio River and on into Canada. But Webster and her coconspirator, a Methodist minister from Oberlin College named Calvin Fairbank, were quickly arrested and jailed. Webster ran a girls' academy in Lexington and wanted to return, rather than continuing northward with the escapees. So Fairbank, as part of their cover story, returned with Webster to the city, hometown of Henry Clay.

"Imprisoned, ironed and manacled within sight of the shades of Ashland," as a Democratic newspaper put it, Webster made a plea for the famed attorney Henry Clay to represent her. Clay was indeed living at Ashland during the campaign, so the case had to be known to him. But there was no chance he would join such a controversial cause while trying to persuade Southerners that he was not the friend of abolitionists that Cassius Clay was making him out to be.

Democrats—including, apparently, Webster's own lawyer, who was a Polk elector—spread stories about Webster's ill-treatment to make Clay look bad in the eyes of Ohio abolitionists. Lexington's Whig paper, the *Observer and Reporter*, called the lawyer out for his duplicity. He eventually left the case, to be replaced by a Whig lawyer who was a Kentucky elector for Clay. The city's Democratic paper, the *Gazette*, painted Clay as a great friend of Webster and Fairbank, who, the *Gazette* charged, were ardent Whigs. "The great desire of their hearts may be comprised in two words: stealing Negroes and electing Clay."

Webster's case would not go to trial until mid-December, well after the election was decided. But the arrest and agitation coming during the final month of the campaign harmed Clay just when he could least afford it. "For the elevation of the great embodiment, Kentucky's favorite son, they are billing and cooing for abolition votes, upon the alleged ground that he is no enemy to the cause," reported the *Emancipator*, an abolitionist paper, "while at the same time, a fair daughter of the Green Mountain tenants a *Kentucky prison*, almost in sight of Ashland, upon a charge of being friendly to the cause. This is the sympathy of Henry Clay's friends at *home* for abolitionists. Let every true abolitionist remember this fact, when he is entreated to trifle with his vote by casting for the Whig candidate for the presidency."

"THE FATE OF THE COUNTRY"

But the abolitionists of the Liberty Party represented only one of Clay's problems in New York. While Clay was creating more confusion among his own base, Democrats were working to increase the size of theirs, naturalizing more than 60 new voters every day, rising to a crescendo on the eve of Election Day, when they registered 497 recently arrived immigrants in New York City alone. The courthouse was so crowded that the windows were flung open to allow people to enter and exit the building more quickly.

Here, Clay's muddling of the issue was less significant than his acquiescing in the selection of Theodore Frelinghuysen as his running mate. Early Clay biographer Carl Schurz, looking to deflect blame away from his hero, called the saintly Frelinghuysen a "stern anti-Catholic." That was somewhere between wildly overstating the case and just plain wrong, but Catholic voters certainly perceived Frelinghuysen—whom Bishop John Hughes of

New York referred to as "a sincere, honest, and honorable bigot"—and other Protestant luminaries of the Benevolent Empire as overweening nannies, at a minimum.

Two protestant clergymen at an 1844 meeting of the American Missionary Society, one of the many such groups of which Frelinghuysen was a member, referred to the Catholic Church as the "Whore of Babylon." For Catholic leaders, Frelinghuysen did not do enough to distance himself from such remarks. This was mostly a problem in the Northeast, but it mattered in closely contested Southern states as well, where Irish immigrants were fewer in number but just as committed to bloc voting for Democrats.

Some of the Whigs' late-season campaign tactics added to the Catholics' concerns. In early October a placard appeared in Philadelphia calling on all Protestant denominations "to unite in putting down the Catholics by voting the Whig ticket." Supreme Court Justice John Catron, a Polk ally, had absolute confidence in the Whigs' ability to deliver the immigrant vote to the Democrats. "The Catholics are with us, & the other side will keep them so, no fear of that."

Others saw a different religious hand at work. The *Boston Courier*, a Whig paper, blamed the Whigs' difficulties on Whig-inclined Millerites who failed to vote because they believed the world was coming to an end and "they did not think it worth while to vote for somebody to legislate for the country after the world is burned up." In a more serious vein, Silas Wright warned about a Whig "coalition with a small band of 'Millerites' in one town" in upstate St. Lawrence County.

Whigs were indeed doing what they could to secure votes from all corners. "They are literally bargaining right and left," noted Democratic vice presidential candidate George M. Dallas, "courting Roman Catholics and promising everything to the Natives, and even avowing that Abolitionism is a fundamental article of the Whig creed." But Dallas was not too worried. The nativists had won city elections in April, but "we have pursued a course . . . calculated to win them right again," he told Polk. And Cave Johnson assured Polk that even if the nativists and Whigs managed a combination, it would affect only state and congressional races, not the top of the ticket.

All across the country the candidates' surrogates and supporters were working feverishly as the various election days approached.

Thomas Hart Benton reported huge crowds turning out to hear him speak on Polk's behalf in Missouri. The Democrats' torchlight parade through New York City on November 1 was "magnificent beyond any description" and "struck terror into the Whigs." Polk and his allies were also laboring mightily to secure the candidate's home state of Tennessee, where he had lost the last two gubernatorial elections. No presidential candidate had ever won while losing his home state.

For the Whigs, Seward spoke in more than twenty counties in New York during the course of the campaign. At home in Auburn, he wrote to Clay in late October that he would "not undertake to give you an opinion of the probable result of the election in this state, upon which is suspended the whole question and of course the fate of the country." On this point Seward would prove a prophet. (Another prophet, Brigham Young, had built the fireplace in Seward's parlor during his years as a carpenter and builder in the burned-over district.) Seward was less accurate in predicting that "the election will not prove as close a one as many suppose, and the present setting of the current is clearly and strongly flowing rapidly enough to give us success."

Seward was generally clear-eyed and no-nonsense, but in this case he might have given in to a dose of wishful thinking. Still, others—including Clay himself—were equally sanguine, or perhaps just reacting to the inevitable rush of adrenalin that accompanies the final days of a campaign. Last-minute efforts in Pennsylvania included the disbursement of $20,000 to key precincts. Unfortunately for the Whigs, the Democrats intercepted a letter that detailed the disbursals and followed the Whig agents around the state to tell voters of the nefarious plans to buy their votes.

Pennsylvania and Ohio voted first, on November 1. Whig-aligned nativist candidates in Philadelphia won three of the four congressional seats they contested—including a victory by Lewis Levin, who had been indicted for inciting to riot stemming from his actions during the July violence. But the coalition fell apart at the presidential level, as Cave Johnson had predicted. Ohio's 23 electoral votes—the third-largest of any state—looked solid for Clay, but Pennsylvania's 26, second only to New York with 36, appeared to be swinging to Polk.

Twenty-one states voted on November 4, by which time James Buchanan was feeling confident enough that he wrote Polk to congratulate him on a "glorious victory" and to begin sucking up for a job in the next administration. "Yours is a grand mission," the craven Pennsylvanian wrote, "and I most devoutly trust and believe, that you will fulfil it with a glory to yourself and permanent advantage to the Country."

Among the states voting on the fourth was Illinois, where the Mormon "brethren all concluded to vote for Polk and Dallas," Nauvoo Chief of Police Hosea Stout reported. But the decision was a somber and joyless one. "It was with peculiar feelings that I went to the polls," wrote Stout, whose thoughts that day were with "the man we had elected as the man of our choice for president of the United States: our beloved Prophet Joseph Smith whose voice seemed yet to sound in the air, teaching this nation the way they might be saved and the means to pursue to avoid a disunion and overthrow of our government."

New York voted on November 5. It was, reported a key Democratic operative in Manhattan, "the severest struggle ever witnessed in this city." Hoping that the nativists who had swept city elections in the spring would come to their rescue, the Whigs instead had to watch as fears of nativism spurred a massive turnout by recent immigrants, almost all of whom voted Democratic. Outside the city, upstate abolitionists were abandoning Clay for Birney. Dedicated antislavery men in the burned-over district were riding ox-drawn sleighs through a foot of snow in the last days of the campaign to ensure that their vote turned out. And Silas Wright's coattails were proving as effective as Democrats had suspected they would. Beyond Wright's personal popularity, his proclaimed opposition to Texas annexation helped muddy the differences between the two parties on the issue for Empire State voters.

Early returns from the city favored Polk. As upstate votes began to be counted, it looked better for Clay. The outcome remained in doubt for three days, while most of the remaining states went to the polls. (Vermont and Delaware would not vote until November 12.) When New York's final totals were made public, Polk was the victor by 5,106 votes out of almost a half-million votes cast in in the state, winning just under 49 percent of the vote. Birney received 15,812 votes. Polk failed to win Tennessee, his home state, losing by an excruciating 123 votes.

But it didn't matter. By winning New York, holding on to Pennsylvania and Virginia, and sweeping the Deep South, Polk didn't need Tennessee.

He won just less than half the popular vote in a race that was close in virtually every state, with a national victory margin of just more than 39,000
votes, but enjoyed a 170–105 margin in the Electoral College. Polk won
fifteen states to Clay's eleven. And Polk carried a healthy Democratic majority into Congress with him—30–24 in the Senate, and a whopping 144–77
in the House—an indication that annexation and westward expansion were
broadly popular—more so than Polk, perhaps. But it was also an indication that in the presidential vote, Texas—while perhaps playing a role in
broadening or narrowing margins in some states—was not a major factor in
determining the outcome.

"I feel as though our country has been snatched as it were from the
jaws of despotism just ready to swallow her up," a jubilant Ohio Democrat
told Polk, who received confirmation of his victory on November 14, at
home in Columbia. In Nashville, celebratory cannons were fired, within
earshot of Andrew Jackson at the Hermitage. "I thank my God that the
Republic is safe, & that he had permitted me to see it, & rejoice," Jackson
wrote, "and I can say in the language of Simeon of old, 'Now let thy servant
depart in peace.' "

Jackson had indeed been a faithful servant to his protégé. Time and
again Polk turned to Jackson for advice and favors, and Jackson never disappointed. Whether it was easing Tyler out of the race, lobbying Sam Houston
to do nothing that might harm chances for annexation, reining in Calhoun
and the Southern fire-eaters, or urging Tyler not to call a special session of
Congress to speed action on Texas, Jackson always wrote the letter or provided the counsel that aided the endeavor. And the nation's love for him and
its memory of his heroism aided Polk in ways that can't be quantified.

While Jackson and the Democrats celebrated, Whigs were stunned.

"I have thought for three or four days that I would write you, but really
am unmanned," moaned losing New York gubernatorial candidate Millard
Fillmore. "I have no courage or resolution. . . . I see nothing but despair on
every countenance. . . . A cloud of gloom hangs over the future. May God
save the country; for it is evident the people will not."

New York businessman Philip Hone also despaired of the electorate.
"The result of this election has satisfied me that no such man as Henry Clay
can ever be President of the United States," he commiserated to Clay. "The

party leaders, the men who make a President, will never consent to elevate one greatly their superior."

Santa Fe trader James Josiah Webb, who profited by westward expansion but was nonetheless a Clay man, was bereft. "My Country! Oh, my Country! What are we coming to when my countrymen can make such a choice," he moaned.

Dissolve the people and elect a new one seemed to be the Whigs' post-election message. Beyond blaming ignorant voters, the losers took various aim at Catholics, nativists, abolitionists, and Frelinghuysen.

Seward upbraided not his abolitionist friends for the loss, but the nativists he opposed for driving immigrant Catholic voters to the polls in large numbers. Nativism was wrong morally, he argued, as well as politically, because it cost Whigs more votes than it gained them. The nativists "gave us one vote only for two of which they deprived us, and the result is our defeat in the state."

Fillmore, who would later lead the nativist "Know-Nothing" party, blamed "Abolitionists and foreign Catholics." He called the antislavery men "vile," and laid the loss of Catholics at the feet of Frelinghuysen.

John Quincy Adams spared no one, citing the "partial associates of Native Americans, Irish Catholics, abolition societies, liberty party, the Pope of Rome, the Democracy of the Sword, and the dotage of a ruffian," by whom he meant Andrew Jackson, for "sealing the fate of this nation, which nothing less than the interposition of Omnipotence can save."

The consensus at the time was that a combination of Frelinghuysen's close ties with bigoted anti-Catholics, the Liberty Party's strength, and Silas Wright's coattails cost the Whigs New York, which cost them the election. The reluctant Wright carried the state by 10,000 votes over Fillmore, doubling Polk's margin of victory.

Certainly, Frelinghuysen's presence on the ticket cost the Whigs some Catholic votes. But politics cannot be analyzed in such a static manner. Had Clay selected someone else for vice president who was less offensive to immigrants, he might well have saved New York. But Frelinghuysen's absence from the ticket might have cost him New Jersey, which he carried by only 823 votes. Clay wrote the Alabama letters to shore up his position in the South, but he lost the election in the North. Had he taken a firmer stand against annexation and not waffled multiple times, he might have disarmed the Liberty Party and hung onto New York, even with the massive Catholic turnout against him. On the other hand, Polk lost his home state by only 123 votes. Had Clay solidified Northern support, he likely would have surrendered Tennessee, one of only two future Confederate states he won. The other was North Carolina, although he also carried slave-holding Kentucky, Maryland, and Delaware.

In the end, responsibility for the loss fell on the candidate, as his most famous intraparty rival pointed out. Daniel Webster had campaigned hard for Clay, traveling up and down the east coast. At one campaign event he drew fifty thousand listeners and spoke for three hours. But it was all for naught, and Webster blamed Clay. "I thought his election highly probable, & he certainly came near success," Webster wrote. He might have won, "but for two causes—his Alabama letter,—& a general feeling throughout many parts of the Country, & especially in Western N.Y.—that his temper was bad—resentful, violent, & unforgiving."

Perhaps it was Clay's reputation as an ungodly man, more than Frelinghuysen's reputation as a godly one, that cost the Kentuckian the victory he had sought for so long. Frelinghuysen never made that argument, but he reached out to Clay after the election in a manner that indicated he was much more worried about Clay's soul than he was about any electoral outcome.

> But, my dear sir, leaving this painful subject, let us look away to brighter and better prospects, and surer hopes in the promises and consolations of the Gospel of our Saviour. As sinners who have rebelled against our Maker, we need a Saviour or we must perish, and this Redeemer has been provided for us. Prophecy declared him from the earliest period of our fall, in Paradise, and the Gospel makes known the faithful fulfillment. "Come unto me," cries this exalted Saviour, "come unto me, all ye that are weary and heavy laden, and I will give you rest." Let us, then, repair to Him. He will never fail us in the hour of peril and trial. Vain is the help of man, and frail and fatal all trust in the arm of flesh; but he that trusteth in the Lord shall be as Mount Zion itself, that can never be removed. I pray, my honored friend, that your heart may seek

this blessed refuge, stable as the everlasting hills, and let this be the occasion to prompt an earnest, prayerful, and the Lord grant it may be a joyful, search after truth as it is in Jesus Christ.

"Eight Years of Feeble and Ineffectual Efforts"

On December 2 Congress reconvened, and Adams immediately "gave notice that I should to-morrow move a resolution to rescind the twenty-fifth rule, which excludes the reception of abolition petitions."

As good as his word, the next day Adams submitted his resolution, and immediately asked for a vote. Jacob Thompson of Mississippi moved that the resolution be laid on the table, which would effectively kill it for the remainder of the session. Rising simultaneously, Adams and Joshua Giddings of Ohio, the old man's youthful shadow, called for the yeas and nays on the motion to table. Before Speaker of the House John Jones of Virginia could order the roll to be called, John Tyler Jr., the president's son, appeared below the presiding officer's rostrum and announced that he was there to deliver to the House the annual message of the president. He handed the address to a clerk, who handed it up to the Speaker, and Thompson rose again and expressed his deep desire to hear the president's message as soon as possible.

Adams would have none of Thompson's dilatory tactics. Surely, he asserted, the vote on Thompson's tabling motion should come first, as a matter of regular order. The Speaker concurred, and the roll call began. One by one, the members called out their votes in the chamber, where it was nearly impossible to hear anything clearly. But the emotions associated with the gag rule brought out a clarity of both purpose and voice, so no one in the House had any difficulty discerning where each man stood. When the final vote had been cast, Jones ordered the clerk to report the tally on the motion to table: the yeas were 81, the nays were 104. The House then moved immediately to a vote on Adams's resolution, and the same theatrical process played out. This time, when the clerk read the tally, the ayes had it, 108–80.

"Perseverance has crowned the 'old man eloquent' with success," the *New York Tribune* reported. Adams, recording the moment that night in his diary, claimed none of the credit for himself. "Blessed, forever blessed, be the name of God!" he wrote, employing a rare exclamation mark in his journal.

The desire of politicians to avoid talking about slavery had been institutionalized almost a decade before in the gag rule. With Texas now on the agenda, Northern Democrats and Southern Whigs who supported slavery reexamined their positions, willing to soften a stance on abolition petitions in return for consideration on the question of annexation. And, as Adams had surmised back in February, Northern Democrats who had backed the gag rule as part of an effort to preserve Southern support for Van Buren now realized their appeasement had been futile. Ironies abounded. The gag rule had been instituted under the leadership of House Speaker James K. Polk. But it took Polk's election as president—or at least his dethroning of Van Buren as Democratic nominee—to liberate Northern Democrats from their obeisance to the Southern wing of the party, at least so far as the right to petition was concerned. John C. Calhoun, it turned out, had called it exactly right.

The same day the House repealed the gag rule, presidential electors met in their state capitals and cast their votes, which would be counted by Congress on February 12. It was a formality—faithless electors were not yet a consideration—but the process involved some notable characters and strange bedfellows, including future Confederate president Jefferson Davis, a Mississippi elector for Polk, and future Confederate nemesis Benjamin Butler, a Polk elector from Massachusetts.

Charles Bent, who owned the trading post in Colorado where John C. Frémont had stopped on his way back to civilization, would soon write to Manuel Alvarez, US consul in Santa Fe, on the election of Polk and the prospect of a possible war over Texas: "I am fearful that this election will cause difficulty." He couldn't have been more right.

But before Polk could begin stirring things up over Texas, Tyler was not yet finished with the topic. After the House vote repealing the gag rule, Tyler's final annual message was read. It was a valediction, tracing what he saw as the triumphs of his administration and glossing over the tragedies.

He reviewed US relations with Latin America and China, called for expanding the navy, and proposed the construction of military posts along the Oregon Trail. But the heart of the message, as it had been the heart of his administration, was Texas.

"After eight years of feeble and ineffectual efforts to recover Texas," he wrote, "it was time that the war should have ceased." Tyler returned to the point he had made back in June—and that South Carolina's George McDuffie had berated Thomas Hart Benton over during Senate debate. "Mexico has no right to jeopardy the peace of the world by urging any longer a useless and fruitless contest." Texas had won her independence. She was finished with Mexico, which had "no just ground of displeasure against this government or people for negotiating the treaty," Tyler insisted. "What interest of hers was affected by the treaty? She was despoiled of nothing since Texas was forever lost to her."

Mexico had no case. But the American people did, and they had made it a month earlier, when they elected Polk.

"The great popular election which has just terminated afforded the best opportunity of ascertaining the will of the States and people," Tyler opined, and they had spoken. In contrast to the Whigs' self-flagellation over Frelinghuysen, nativists, and Catholics, Tyler had no doubt that it was Texas that sealed Polk's victory. "The decision of the people and the States and this great and interesting subject, has been decisively manifested. . . . A controlling majority of the people and a large majority of the States have declared in favor of annexation."

Having claimed victory in the name of the people, Tyler demanded that the people's representatives do their bidding.

"The two governments have already agreed, through their respective organs, on the terms of annexation," he said. "I would recommend their adoption by Congress in the form of a joint resolution, or act, to be perfected and made binding on the two countries, when adopted in like manner by the government of Texas."

It was the same proposal he had made during the summer in the wake of the Senate's defeat of the annexation treaty. Now, though, it carried the added weight of an electoral victory by the leading proponent of annexation, Polk, and the prospect of a heavily Democratic Congress coming to power that would in all likelihood make short work of annexation. Opponents were in a bind, but had few options. They could rightly debate that Polk's victory was hardly a ringing endorsement of annexation, but the contention would be derided as the protestations of losers. Even some anti-annexationist newspapers began to fall in line, admitting "that there is a large majority who would be glad to see Texas, in some way or other, united to this country." Within a few weeks, Congress would have before it no fewer than seventeen proposals to bring Texas into the union.

"WE BEGAN TO FEAR THAT WE SHOULD ALL PERISH IN THE SNOW"

After saying their farewells near the pass, the California-bound travelers who were pressing on with their wagons moved westward while Moses Schallenberger, Joseph Foster, and Allen Montgomery turned eastward and headed back down the mountain, accompanied by two scrawny cows "so worn out and poor that they could go no further." The cows would, for a while, provide a secure source of food, although the men were not overly concerned about starving. "We did not care for them to leave us any cattle for food," Schallenberger said, "for . . . there seemed to be plenty of game, and we were all good hunters, well furnished with ammunition, so we had no apprehension that we would not have plenty to eat."

Back at the lakeside camp the next morning, the trio's first order of business was building a cabin. They used axes from the left-behind wagons to cut down trees and employed the underfed and overworked cows to haul the logs to the campsite. Without chink or daub to fill the gaps, they cut notches to make the logs fit together as closely as possible to keep the weather out. The men covered the twelve-by-fourteen–foot cabin with rawhide and pine brush, cut a hole for a door, and added a ten-foot-high log chimney, scrounging around to find stones large enough to use for the jambs and back. There were no windows, resulting in a frequently smoky interior, but on clear days they left the door ajar to let in some light. With plenty of bedding from the wagons, they were able "to make ourselves as comfortable as possible, even if it was for a short time," as they believed it would be.

At first, Schallenberger, Montgomery, and Foster were able to subsist on what they hunted, the game being "exceedingly abundant in the early winter." The knee-deep snow was not much of a hindrance to their mobility.

But within just a few days of their decision to stay, heavy snow began falling, with one storm dropping nearly three feet, almost burying the cabin and scattering to lower elevations any game that might have remained. Still, the three were not much concerned. Temperatures were still fairly mild and they felt certain the snow would soon melt.

Instead, it snowed more. And still more. For a solid week the winds howled and the snow drifted, piling up against the cabin. They went out only to gather firewood. The fireplace kept the small cabin warm, although they now had to close the door and it grew increasingly smoky inside. Unable to get outside—and unlikely to find anything to kill if they did—they slaughtered the two cows and hung the meat up on the north side of the cabin, counting on the frozen climate to keep it fresh.

The meat was safe. The cold would preserve it and there were no animals about to steal it. But they knew it wouldn't last long. And still the snow kept falling. "We began to fear that we should all perish in the snow," Schallenberger remembered.

Then the daily doses of fresh snow caused another problem. "The snow was so light and frosty that it would not bear us up." Even gathering wood for the fire became a problem, although the trees were close enough to the cabin that they could still, with difficulty, bring in enough to keep from freezing to death. The situation was dire, and the men realized they would not be able to survive the winter on the paltry supply of meat from the two cows, and might not even be able to gather wood if the snow continued to fall.

They began rummaging around in the wagons to see if they had materials at hand to build snowshoes, which they had heard about but never seen. They found half-inch-thick wagon bows made of hickory, and strands of rawhide. By bending the bows into an oblong shape, they could string the rawhide across to make a mesh for their feet. The makeshift snowshoes worked reasonably well. "We were now able to walk on the snow to bring in our wood," Schallenberger wrote, "and that was about all there was to do." The shoes expanded their world, but several trips out to look for game yielded no results. Nighttime freezing sometimes created a crust on the snow and they would see a few tracks, coyote or fox, but the tracks never led to a kill, or even a sighting of an animal.

They had eaten nearly half the meat from the slaughtered cows, and it was now about the middle of December. They had lost track of the exact date, but knew they faced several more months alone in the mountains, with their existing food supply dwindling and no prospects of replacing it. They were here to guard the wagons but reasoned that, considering their own difficulties, no one would be around to loot the valuables. "At last, after due consideration, we determined to start for California on foot." They dried the last of the beef from the cattle over the smoky fireplace, giving each man about ten pounds of meat, loaded blankets and ammunition into their packs, strapped on their snowshoes, slung rifles over their shoulders, and left the warmth of their cabin for the perils of the mountain.

The men's meager experience with the snowshoes quickly became apparent. While the jerry-rigged shoes worked well for short jaunts, they were rudely constructed and fastened haphazardly, making it difficult at first to go more than a few steps without tiring themselves. "We fastened them heel to toe," Schallenberger remembered, "and thus had to lift the whole weight of the shoe at every step." The snow that gathered in the shoe weighed them down further. Montgomery and Foster, older and stronger, began to get the hang of it, but young Schallenberger continued to stumble, falling "nearly every fifty steps" with cramps and exhaustion.

Moses knew he was holding the others back, putting their lives at risk needlessly. They would wait for him to catch up, a ghostly sight ahead of him against the snowy mountain. When he did, they would trundle on a bit further, with the two older men pulling ahead again, and they'd repeat the process, as Moses's cramps grew worse and worse. "After each attack I would summon all my will power and press on, trying to keep up with the others," he said.

But it was no use. As darkness approached, they camped near the summit. They cut down a tree for a fire, ate some of the jerky they had brought along in their packs, and tried without much success to get warm and sleep. When morning came, they realized their fire had sunk about fifteen feet into the snow, being ignorant of the mountain man's trick of building a base of green wood below the main fuel to keep the fire from melting the snow underneath. Their fire gone, they had no means of warming up, and had no food to cook in any case. They sat in the freezing snow and pondered what to do. Moses made the case. He begged Foster and Montgomery to let him return to the cabin. There was still some of the cow left, he told them, and they could push on much faster without him and send help back. The men protested, but knew he was right.

"We did not say much at parting," Moses said later. "There was simply a warm clasp of the hand accompanied by the familiar word, 'Good-by,' which we all felt might be the last words we should ever speak to each other."

After more than six months together on the trail, his last two comrades were about to take their leave. Now Schallenberger would be alone, utterly, for God knew how long. He watched Foster and Montgomery until they tromped out of sight, then headed down toward the cabin, consumed by a sense of loneliness like none he had ever experienced in his young life. The overnight cold had frozen their trail, so he was able to dispense with the snowshoes and make better time, which helped revive his spirits. He made it back to the cabin before nightfall, but was so worn out he had to use his hands to lift his leg over the doorsill to get into the cabin. Inside the cabin, he started a fire. Outside, it once again started to snow.

The next morning he strapped his snowshoes on his feet and his gun over his shoulder and ventured out to go hunting. "Plenty of tracks, but no fox," he reported, leaving him "discouraged and sick at heart." After a night of rest, he arose the next morning and took stock. For comfort, he had "plenty of tools, plenty of feather beds, plenty of books, plenty of ammunition— plenty of everything, in short, except food." Along with the mostly useless accoutrements of civilization that were stashed in the wagons—Townsend had brought along a supply of satin and silk to sell in California—he found a few that proved valuable. Foremost among those were some steel traps left behind by Elisha Stevens. He knew there were animals afoot. If he could not take them with his gun, maybe he could trap them.

Using some of the remaining beef for bait, he went out to set the traps. Moses spent an anxious night wondering if his gamble would pay off. He had clipped mostly useless pieces of rawhide and stringy meat off the cows' heads. But those might be morsels he would wish he still had in a few weeks if his trapping effort didn't pay off. At first light, he hurried out to inspect the traps. "To my great delight, I found in one of them a starved coyote," he said.

Moses would never develop much of a taste for coyote, but luckily he began to catch an occasional fox as well, whose "meat, though entirely devoid of fat, was delicious."

Foxes and coyotes kept his body fed; for his mind, he employed Townsend's books. He found volumes of Dickens, Byron, and Scott; to defeat the solitude and silence, he read aloud to himself. His favorite was a collection of Lord Chesterfield's letters to his son on men and manners. As he licked the remains of that day's fox from his fingers, Moses leaned toward the fire for better light and must have appreciated the irony as he delivered his soliloquy to the empty cabin:

> Talk often, but never long: in that case, if you do not please, at least you are sure not to tire your hearers. . . . Most long talkers single out some one unfortunate man in company (commonly him whom they observe to be the most silent, or their next neighbour), to whisper, or at least in a half voice, to convey a continuity of words to. This is excessively ill bred, and in some degree a fraud; conversation-stock being a joint and common property. But on the other hand, if one of these unmerciful talkers lays hold of you, hear him with patience (and at least seeming attention), if he is worth obliging; for nothing will oblige him more than a patient hearing; as nothing would hurt him more than either to leave him in the midst of his discourse, or to discover your impatience under your affliction.

He would build large fires at night so he could stay up late reading, causing him to sleep late "and thus cause the days to seem shorter." As worried as he was for himself—"my life was more miserable than I can describe"—he had the added burden of worrying over his sister and other comrades, whose fate he had no way of learning. Day after day dragged on with a snowy sameness. The foxes and coyotes were still finding their way into his traps so he wasn't starving, but he was constantly fretting about the possibility.

Then, one evening near the end of February, Moses was outside checking traps. Far off in the distance, he saw what he thought looked like a man. Slowly, he began walking toward the vision, and soon enough it became clear that it was a person. His hand went up in a joyous wave and a thrill shot through his body. It had been almost three months since Foster and

Montgomery had disappeared over the pass, since he had seen or talked to another human being. As the man came in clear sight, Moses recognized him as Dennis Martin, a Canadian who had been traveling with the Murphys and who had gone over the mountains with the wagon party.

The men embraced, and Martin assured Moses that everyone was safe, including his sister. Montgomery and Foster had come upon the women and children camped just over the summit, then hurried along to Sutter's. Martin had volunteered to return to the camp and bring the rest of the emigrants into the valley. Elizabeth Townsend, Moses's sister, had begged Martin to proceed on down to the cabin and retrieve her brother, and he had agreed.

It was too late in the day to start back over the mountain, but the next morning Schallenberger and Martin headed back over the pass. The Canadian was well acquainted with snowshoes and showed Moses how to fasten them so the snow would not gather, making their passage much easier. Past the summit they gathered up the remaining women and children from the camp and began the descent into California. A week later they arrived at Sutter's, one day short of a year after Frémont had reached the fort.

"To the Interior of Our Wide-Spread Country"

Two thousand eight hundred miles to the east, while Moses Schallenberger was still reading Chesterfield aloud to himself in the cabin in the Sierra, Asa Whitney sat in his New York apartment, dreaming a dream that would have saved Schallenberger a considerable amount of woe.

A merchant who had made and lost a fortune, along with two wives, Whitney knew a thing or two about traveling. As a man in international trade, he had journeyed to China aboard a leaky ship that took almost three months to get from New York to Macao. That was a marked improvement over just a few decades before, when the trip took as long as six months. But time was money, and Whitney was interested in saving both.

There had to be a better way, and Whitney thought he knew one. Writing as though possessed, he scribbled down a vision of a transcontinental railroad, stretching from New York to California, across the supposed wasteland of the Great Plains, across the Rocky Mountains and on to the Pacific Ocean. It mattered little, or not at all, to Whitney that much of this territory, including the terminus, did not belong to the United States. Caught up in the excitement of Polk's victory and the notion of a nation stretching from sea to sea, Whitney felt certain that America would make happen what it needed to make happen.

With an audience of Congress in mind, he posed the question: were not railroads already in the works that would connect the great eastern cities with the grain producing regions of the Great Lakes? He wrote that railroads would be "producing commercial, political and national rewards and benefits." It would take no stretch of the imagination, Whitney implored, to extend that vision across the Mississippi River "to the interior of our widespread country."

Whitney's vision dovetailed perfectly with that of the newly elected Polk—a continental nation tied together by a transcontinental railroad. No more need for pioneers to risk their lives traversing trackless deserts and snow-blocked mountain passes. No need for slow-moving mule teams to invite attack from hostile Indians down the Santa Fe Trail. No dangerous ocean voyages around the Cape of Good Hope and across the Pacific, or through the jungles of Central America. A speedy, reliable train across the continent, carrying goods and passengers, and an American Pacific coast that would open the world to US trade. Such a venture, Whitney assured Congress, would revolutionize "the entire commerce of the world."

Whitney knew a simple appeal to commerce would not be enough. So he also stressed the political importance of such a railroad, binding east to west, "affording a communication from Washington to the Columbia River in less than eight days." Without the ability to communicate quickly, Oregon might be lost, to independence or a foreign power. That point, he knew, would make an impression on the expansionists in Washington.

Best of all, "being built from the public lands, the road should be free, except so far as sufficient for the necessary expenses of keeping it in operation," Whitney assured the lawmakers. Besides, as far as he could determine, the land was good for little else. As soon as could practicably be done, Congress should order a survey of possible routes.

Whitney's proposal was presented to Congress on January 28, 1845, in the midst of the debate over Texas. Powerful men, including Thomas Hart Benton, took up the cause. Whitney would spend much of the next two decades promoting it. But a multitude of hurdles stood in the way—foremost among them sectional differences—that would keep the project from coming to fruition. It would take two dozen years and a civil war to sort them out.

EPILOGUE

THE SHAPING OF AMERICA

In response to Tyler's renewed call for annexation, no fewer than seventeen resolutions were introduced in the House and Senate, fifteen of those by Democrats. Whigs from James K. Polk's home state of Tennessee introduced one in each chamber.

Abolitionist congressman Joshua Giddings thought "there is no danger of the passage of that measure, even in the House of Representatives, at this session." Giddings estimated there were forty Democrats who would vote against any of the annexation plans. But John Quincy Adams was not so self-assured. As it turned out, the House on January 25 approved the annexation and admission of Texas by a vote of 120–98, with 8 Whigs joining 112 Democrats in favor; 26 Democrats voted no. The measure, sponsored by Tennessee Whig Milton Brown, called for annexation, popular sovereignty on slavery south of the Missouri compromise line, and the possibility of subdividing the state at a later date.

In the Senate, Benton proposed to slow the process by reopening negotiations with Texas and Mexico, partially outlined the border, left the rest of the boundary to the state with the provision that it could be no bigger than any existing state, and left the question of slavery to the citizens of Texas. Then he changed his own plan and offered another proposal, dispensing with almost all of the details and calling simply for annexation and admittance to the union. Benton had heard from his constituents. They wanted Texas.

The constitutional objections to admitting Texas by joint resolution rather than treaty were argued again, but carried little weight. The hypocrisy was obvious, probably even to those making the argument. If Texas could not be admitted under the constitutional provision providing for admission of new states because it was an independent country, then how could anti-annexationists insist that Mexico must be consulted? It was a replay of the Benton-McDuffie debate of June.

By February 19, Adams had thrown in the towel, at least in private. "It is now apparent that it will be consummated, and is written in the Book of Fate," he wrote in his diary.

Benton was the key. In addition to getting direct instructions from the Missouri legislature to support annexation, he was also being lobbied by Andrew Jackson. And besides, Benton wanted Texas. So he found a way to make it happen, with a little help from Robert Walker, who had swayed many with his campaign-season pamphlet on the win-win nature of Texas joining the union.

When the Senate took up the House bill, Walker proposed combining it with Benton's original proposal. What emerged was a resolution that would give the president final authority to choose between two options: immediate annexation or reopened negotiations. This gave just enough Whigs just enough cover, and the combined measure passed by a vote of 27–25, with Benton and every other Democrat solidly in support. Their rationalization apparently was that Polk would handle the implementation, and he was sure to renegotiate Tyler's deal.

They misjudged their men, in both cases.

On February 28, exactly one year after the explosion aboard the *Princeton*, the House accepted the Senate amendment on a vote of 132–76, and Tyler signed the bill March 1. Tyler celebrated along with Polk at a glittering ball attended by three thousand guests. "They cannot say now that I am a President without a party," he joked.

But Tyler did not wait for the new president to take office to begin the process of annexation. On March 3 he dispatched a courier to offer his version of annexation to Texas. Notwithstanding the anti-annexation sentiments of the recently arrived German blue bloods, most Texans were strongly in favor of statehood. On May 19, Texas concluded a treaty with Mexico guaranteeing Texas independence—if it remained a republic rather than joining the United States. Less than a month later, presented with a choice between the treaty with Mexico and annexation to the United States, the Texan Congress chose annexation. But they also provided for a separate convention to consider the question, and put it before the voters. To heighten the irony, the convention met on July 4 and voted to accept the US offer. In October voters overwhelmingly endorsed joining the union, with 95 percent in favor. In a two-week period in the second half of December 1845, both Houses of Congress voted to accept Texas into the union, and Polk signed the final resolution on December 29, making Texas the twenty-eighth state.

The union had moved westward and southward, slavery had been extended, and the stage was now set for a war with Mexico—just as Clay had predicted—that would add even more territory to the union.

———•———

HAVING ACHIEVED THE "great object of his ambition," John Tyler left the White House and lived the quiet life of a Virginia plantation owner, for the most part. But he had an active personal life. Having fathered seven children with his late wife, Letitia, he went on to father eight more with Julia.

In one of the rare instances of public involvement for Tyler after the presidency, he delivered a speech to dedicate a memorial to his old foe, Henry Clay. In the address delivered in Richmond on April 12, 1860—a year to the day before the first shots were fired at Fort Sumter—he praised the "Great Pacificator," but also reminded his listeners of the "bruises and scars" the Kentuckian had "inflicted" on him over the years.

As a farewell to his long career of conflict and obstinacy, Tyler presided over the so-called Peace Convention that met at the Willard Hotel in Washington in the late winter of 1861. The delegates proposed several amendments aimed at preserving both slavery and the union, but they were unacceptable to Republican members of Congress and also faced opposition from hard-line disunionists. After the convention's failure, Tyler threw his lot in with the secessionists and won election to the Confederate Congress. He died on January 18, 1862, before he could take his seat.

———•‹›•———

JOSEPH SMITH HAD dispatched envoys to Texas in the spring of 1844 to investigate the possibility of relocating the saints to the southwest. But it was John C. Frémont's description of the Salt Lake valley that inspired Smith's successor, Brigham Young, to "get our wagons together, form a grand caravan and travel through the country to the Salt Lake, 1000 miles from any civilized settlement."

After Smith's assassination, remaining in Nauvoo became untenable for the saints. Nine men were tried for the murder, but none were convicted. In January 1845 the Nauvoo charter was revoked by the Illinois legislature and nine months later Young agreed to remove to the west. The saints were forced to relocate once again.

The effect of the violence against the Mormons in Illinois bore some resemblance to that of the violence against immigrant Catholics in Philadelphia. Irish Catholic immigrants increasingly chose Boston and New York over Philadelphia as a destination. In these instances, notes the historian of the Philadelphia riots, violence achieved "tangible results," driving the unwanted populations away.

In the dead of winter in February 1846, thousands of Mormons began crossing the frozen Mississippi River, the start of a trek that would eventually lead them to their new Zion in the Great Basin. Disagreements with neighbors and the government—sometimes flaring into violence—would continue to haunt the Mormons, but accommodation would eventually overtake conflict. When the church officially surrendered on polygamy, Utah entered the union in 1896. Today, Mormonism claims fifteen million members and is one of the fastest-growing religions in the world.

———•‹›•———

MORMONISM MOVED WESTWARD with the nation. In contrast, Miller-ism—facing taunts but not violence as the Mormons did—stayed put and waited.

Understandably, the movement quickly began to come apart. Thousands of former adherents returned to their churches and tried to forget they'd ever been a part of Millerism. But others were still trying to understand what had happened. Joshua Himes was dedicated to holding this group together in some fashion, while avoiding the cardinal error of ever again setting a specific date for the return of Christ.

It was not easy. In the democratic ethos of the Second Great Awakening, every man was his own theologian, and the Advent movement quickly splintered. Within a decade there would be as many as twenty-five groups of Adventists. Broadly speaking, though, most fell into one of two categories—the "shut door" and those who opposed the idea of the shut door.

With the backing of William Miller, the shut-door Adventists said that something had happened on October 22, just not what they thought was going to happen. Instead of Christ appearing on Earth, God had simply shut the door to grace. As of that day, all true believers were inside the kingdom of God, and everybody else was on the outside looking in.

It was a handy way to deal with the failure of Christ to return, but Himes wasn't buying it. He argued that nothing had happened on October 22, and while he had to wrestle Miller (intellectually speaking) for several months, eventually the older man came around to Himes's way of thinking, as he had so often done in the past. Miller was not especially interested in carrying on any great movement, and certainly wasn't interested in creating a new sect. Himes wanted to find some way to hold the faithful together, but could not countenance the shut door.

Adventists, as they always had, continued publishing newspapers and tracts. With the dispersal of the movement, these publications sprang up all over and led to a fertile theological debate among the believers and schools of thought. For the most part Miller watched this from the sidelines. Retired to Low Hampton, he corresponded with Himes and other old friends, but by 1848 his health grew worse, he began to lose his eyesight, and the infirmities that had troubled him for years made it impossible for him to travel. He died on December 20, 1849, and was buried in Low Hampton Cemetery beneath a tombstone that quoted the book of Daniel: "At the time appointed the end shall be."

The movement he had founded survived him. In fits and starts, various schools of Adventist thought coalesced into organized churches. Today, more than a dozen denominations can trace their lineage back to the Millerite movement. The largest of these, the Seventh Day Adventists, was founded in 1863, in the midst of Civil War, and now rivals Mormonism as the largest indigenous American denomination, claiming more than seventeen million adherents worldwide.

Joshua Himes chose not to become affiliated with any of the Adventist churches. In 1879 he returned to the Episcopal Church in which he'd been raised, although he corresponded with and offered advice to prominent Adventists, including Ellen White, who had been swept up in the Millerite movement as a child and became a leading figure in the Seventh Day Adventists. Himes died on July 27, 1895, and was buried on a hilltop cemetery as he had requested, because, he said, "he wanted to be on top of a hill when Gabriel blows his trumpet."

DEFEAT OF THE odious gag rule seemed momentous within the confines of Congress. But out in the real world, the even more odious practices of the slave power continued unabated.

In a trial that lasted five days, on December 21, 1844, Delia Webster was convicted of slave stealing. The outcome could hardly have been otherwise, although Webster herself considered the trial fair and praised the prosecutor for his "sedulous care for the safety of the Commonwealth."

The jury recommended a sentence of two years in prison, but took the extraordinary step of writing a letter signed by all twelve jurors, presented to Webster and addressed to Governor William Owsley, imploring him "to interpose his executive power . . . and grant an immediate pardon before the sentence should be pronounced."

Owsley did not do that, but he did enter into a protracted negotiation with the commonwealth's newest prisoner, who did not want to admit guilt by accepting a pardon. At least not right away. She did not suffer while in custody. "I was also furnished with a fine library to which I had free access. Indeed, I had many comforts, and most of all, a faithful, sympathizing, and Christian keeper." Still, a prison is a prison, and eventually a deal was struck, without conditions. Webster was released after less than two months.

She would go on to buy a farm on the Kentucky side of the Ohio River that served as a station on the Underground Railroad. Threatened with violence, she fled to Indiana, where she was once again jailed for abetting the escape of slaves. At one point, her home was burned to the ground. Webster died in 1876. Her accomplice in the 1844 slave stealing case, Calvin Fairbank, would remain in prison for twenty years, befriend John C. Frémont, who lobbied for his freedom, and finally win his release in 1864 in the midst of the Civil War.

Delia Webster's continued commitment to the cause in the absence of any visible progress mirrored that of other antislavery activists.

Abolitionism would never become a majoritarian movement. As was the case with Asa Whitney's dream of a transcontinental railroad, it would take a civil war to realize the dream of freedom.

The Liberty Party's surge of support in the 1844 election proved to be its high-water mark. In 1848 the movement would split, with the abolitionist core remaining in the party while those favoring the less strident position of restricting slavery's spread moved to the newly formed Free Soil Party. The Free Soilers were able to do what the Liberty Party couldn't: attract big-name candidates. Its 1848 ticket included former president Martin Van Buren at the top and Charles Francis Adams—son and grandson of presidents—as the vice presidential choice. One-time Millerite Gerrit Smith would be the Liberty Party presidential nominee that year (and go on to be one of the "secret six" funders of John Brown's raid on Harper's Ferry). The remnants of both movements would become core elements of the new Republican Party, founded in 1854, which eventually would also envelop much of the rump of the American Party, or Know-Nothings, heirs to the nativist impulse that had rocked Philadelphia in 1844.

Other elements of the Benevolent Empire would continue to agitate, in a much less organized form, throughout the nineteenth century. While the reform movement would splinter as American society grew less homogeneous, its effects would continue into the twentieth century and up to the present day. Social activism tinged with religious motivation is perhaps the longest-lasting legacy of the Second Great Awakening—Prohibition, the civil rights movement, and countless other reform crusades owe their existence to the idea—and it continues to shape American politics.

No man embodied that legacy more than Theodore Frelinghuysen. For the rest of his life, Henry Clay's unsuccessful 1844 running mate would remain an outspoken advocate for reform and a leader in multiple Benevolent Empire organizations.

He was president of the American Tract Society until 1848, the American Board of Commissioners for Foreign Missions until 1857, and the American Bible Society until his death in 1862. He labored in various capacities for the American Sunday School Union and the American Temperance Union, whose New Jersey chapter he led for many years. He also served as president of Rutgers University from 1850 until his death.

While the effects of the Benevolent Empire persisted and the urge toward reform became an integral part of American political life, the increasing fractiousness of society—sectionally divided before the Civil War, more culturally divided in the decades after—made it much more difficult to realize Frelinghuysen's dream of a nation molded by Christian principles. Yet, as dedicated as he was to the idea of national salvation, Frelinghuysen never forgot that as a servant of God his first responsibility was personal salvation. After the 1844 election, Frelinghuysen had urged his running mate, Henry Clay, to examine his beliefs and put his trust in Christ. He carried on his mission until literally the final moments of his life.

Just a few hours before he died, Frelinghuysen was visited by the teenage son of a close friend. He placed a Bible from the American Bible Society in the youth's hands and urged him to seek the Lord. But mostly, Frelinghuysen wanted the boy to see the calm acceptance of his passage into the next life. "I want you to see how a Christian can die," he said.

Frelinghuysen passed away on April 12, 1862, the first anniversary of the start of the Civil War, a calamity he and Clay had predicted during the battle over Texas annexation.

HENRY CLAY IS the great "what if" of American political history. Less able as a politician than a policymaker, Clay's considerable gifts were too often buried beneath his own overconfidence in them.

Prominent historians of the period and Clay biographers have frequently written that, had Clay won the election of 1844, American history would have been drastically altered.

A Clay victory would have meant no immediate annexation of Texas. Perhaps, under immense pressure from a Democratic majority in Congress or popular sentiment, Clay would have been forced to negotiate with Mexico, but even then, the outcome likely would have been quite different and possibly peaceful. In either case, war with Mexico would have been averted and the territory that came with it, including California, would have been forfeit. The war brought into focus the broader question of the expansion of slavery into the territories, what Lincoln would call "the only substantial dispute" between North and South. Without the new territory, the dispute would have been moot.

This would not have entirely repressed the irrepressible conflict between North and South, but it certainly would have altered the landscape in which that conflict was adjudicated through the 1850s. There might have been no need for the Compromise of 1850, which allowed California into the union as a free state and established the Fugitive Slave Act. Without the Mexican War there would have been no fight over the Wilmot Proviso, which sought to bar slavery in the newly acquired territory. Without that controversy, the Kansas-Nebraska Act, establishing the principle of popular sovereignty on slavery, likely would not have been enacted, thus, no Bleeding Kansas, no prelude to civil war on the frontier.

Clay was convinced Texas would make a better neighbor to the United States than a part of it. "Texas is destined to be settled by our race, who will carry there, undoubtedly, our laws, our language, and our institutions, and that view of her destiny reconciles me much more to her independence than, if it were to be peopled by another and an unfriendly race," he wrote in late 1843, just as the annexation negotiations were heating up. "We may live as good neighbors, cultivating peace commerce and friendship."

Without the Mexican War, California likely would have taken the same path toward eventual independence from Mexico, particularly after the discovery of gold in 1848, creating just the sort of bookend republics that Clay had envisioned, providing a bulwark against British encroachment on the edges of American empire.

The westering impulse would not have disappeared from the American character. But the government would have done much less to encourage it. Had California, Texas, and Oregon established themselves as true republics, they still would have drawn American settlers, but those settlers would have been less worried about the need for protection from the US government. The great middle of the country, home to the Plains Indians, might well have developed quite differently, even as the railroad sooner or later pushed through (if, indeed, it would have ever pushed through).

Clay believed the country as it existed in 1844 was big enough, and his policies supported that belief. People remember the American System mostly for the idea of "internal improvements"—roads, canals, ports—what today would be called public works. But it was Clay's plan for financing such projects that is often forgotten. Instead of giving away public lands to settlers, Clay wanted to sell land to raise money for his program. Eliminating the possibility of free land for the taking would have slowed westward expansion considerably—not the main purpose in Clay's vision, but certainly a happy byproduct as far as he was concerned.

Defeat in 1844 was by no means the last act for Clay. He returned to the Senate and loudly voiced his opposition to the war with Mexico that he had predicted would follow Texas annexation and in which he lost a son. In his final role as the Great Pacificator, Clay devised the Compromise of 1850, though it was left to the next generation of leaders, particularly Illinois Democrat Stephen A. Douglas, to maneuver it through the Senate. Clay's energies were largely spent. The compromise brought California into the union as a free state, established a harsh fugitive slave act, and brought civil war one step closer. But Clay would not live to see that. He died June 29, 1852.

IN HIS EULOGY for Clay, Abraham Lincoln asked whether the country "could have been quite all it has been, and is, and is to be, without Henry

Clay." Lincoln would never have said such a thing about James K. Polk, but the commendation could apply equally to him. In office, Polk accomplished all that he promised, bringing Texas into the union, settling the Oregon question, acquiring California, establishing an independent Treasury without a national bank, and lowering the tariff. No president save Jefferson added more territory to the union. It was the most remarkable one-term presidency in American history.

Modern historians rarely give Polk the credit he deserves because of his machinations in bringing about the war with Mexico. But without his efforts, the America we know wouldn't exist. It might well stop at the Missouri River, exclude Texas, and have a vastly different legacy of slavery and race relations than we know today. Polk barely got to enjoy the fruits of his labor—he died on June 15, 1849, less than four months after leaving office.

Acting in concert with Polk were others who dreamed big dreams in 1844.

The notion of Manifest Destiny was combined with the idea of a transcontinental railroad and Morse's telegraph to tie the country together east-to-west rather than north-to-south, adding to sectional tensions and strengthening the North economically.

Samuel Colt's firearms technology, eschewed early on by the army, would eventually pay huge—if mixed—dividends, helping win the Mexican War and subdue American Indians across the West. Goodyear's rubber technology took longer to fully exploit, but became a foundation of the modern world.

The two-decade success of overland migration owed much to the decline of the fur trade, which forced former mountain men into the new profession of trail guide. Men like Tom Fitzpatrick, Caleb Greenwood, Joseph Walker, and Kit Carson served their civilian and military parties well, guiding them through rough country, modeling safe behavior among the natives, and effectively passing on knowledge about how to survive in the wild.

Whigs would show the same sort of survival instincts, at least for a while. Just as Democrats grew more comfortable with government intervention in the economy (such as aid to railroads), Whigs eventually became reconciled to expansion, viewing it as just another exercise in moral reform and economic opportunity. Entrepreneurs and missionaries would redeem the American soul by redeeming the West that the Democrats had amorally seized.

In 1849, a Whig president, Zachary Taylor—a hero of the Mexican War who would never have become a hero and thus never have been president if not for Polk's victory in 1844—chose a little-known Whig lawyer to be governor of Oregon. But the man destined to become the most famous former Whig of all turned the job down. Oregon would have to get along without Abraham Lincoln.

THE OREGON IMMIGRANTS of 1844, however, proved a resilient lot. The forlorn Sager orphans came to appreciate life at the Whitman Mission, although it took considerable mothering on the part of Narcissa to bring them around. The firm imposition of discipline, a dose of daily hard work, and a constant refrain of missionary Christianity eventually turned the tide.

CATHERINE, MATILDA, AND ELIZABETH SAGER. *Whitman College*

Frank would run off to the Willamette Valley for a few months to escape the strictures, but returned chastened and ready to fit in. The girls adjusted more quickly, and by the spring of 1845 all had been baptized. "We have as happy a family as the world affords," Narcissa wrote.

Unfortunately for the Sagers, who had already seen more than a lifetime of sorrow in their short time on Earth, the happy times were not to last.

The Cayuse Indians, whose conversion was the intended purpose of the mission at Waiilatpu, had grown increasingly hostile to the Whitmans and the mission enterprise over the years. They were not very receptive to the Protestant evangelical message, and Marcus Whitman spent more time evangelizing on behalf of Oregon settlement than he did saving the souls of the Cayuse. The natives also perceived discrimination—there was a school for the white children at the mission, for example, but none for the Cayuse. The Whitmans were all too ready to provide the growing number of immigrants with supplies as they passed through, but made a show of demanding that the Cayuse work for any stores they claimed from the mission's agricultural output.

When a measles outbreak struck the tribe in the late summer and early fall of 1847, one white girl at the mission died. By October, more than two dozen Cayuse had perished. On what Catherine Sager described as a "cold, foggy" November 29, the Cayuse attacked the mission, killing thirteen people, including both Whitmans and the two Sager boys, John and Frank. The girls, along with fifty other settlers, were taken captive. Six-year-old Louisa died of the measles shortly after being taken hostage. The other four were released about a month later with the rest of the prisoners.

The girls were split up after the massacre, but all stayed in the West. Henrietta Naomi, born on the trail and renamed after her parents, died in California in 1870, the victim of a gunshot that was intended for her husband. Catherine, whose broken leg never entirely healed, settled in Washington, married a Methodist minister, had eight children, lived to age seventy-five, and died in 1910. Both Elizabeth and Matilda also had large families. The last surviving Sager sisters died within three months of each other in 1925.

OF THE CALIFORNIA travelers of 1844, none became more famous than the one who was not an emigrant.

John C. Frémont, with editorial assistance from his wife, Jessie, published the report of his 1843–44 adventure in March 1845, to great acclaim. It instantly became a bible for pioneers bound for California and Oregon. Frémont made more Western explorations, caused a ruckus in California before the Mexican War, typically found himself in legal and military hot water during the war, and was once again bailed out of trouble by his father-in-law. He was elected to the Senate from California as a Democrat and would be the Republican Party's first presidential candidate, losing in 1856 to James Buchanan. Frémont died in 1890.

His widow used her literary talents to guard his legacy and, not incidentally, to earn a living, because her husband had squandered the considerable fortune he had made. She died two days after Christmas in 1902.

Her father, Thomas Hart Benton, grew alienated from his increasingly pro-slavery party and lost his Senate seat in 1851. A year later he was elected to the House, but served only one term. He ran for governor but lost in the same year his son-in-law lost the presidential election, and died two years later.

Benton's conflicted vision of a continental nation became the American legacy. He longed for the West but despised the sectional conflict that was exacerbated by expansion. The two strains were inextricably linked—the conflict over slavery was abetted by the restless American impulse to push ever farther westward, an impulse confirmed by the election of 1844.

———◆———

MOUNTAIN MAN JAMES Clyman, who knew a little something about restlessness, said of the overland emigrants, "I never saw a more discontented community, owing principally to natural disposition. Nearly all, like myself, having been of a roving discontented character before leaving their eastern homes. The long tiresome trip from the States has taught them what they are capable of performing and enduring."

A few years after his safe arrival in California, Moses Schallenberger reflected on his now relatively sedentary existence. "I have nothing worthy of your attention to tell you," he wrote to his brother-in-law and former trail mate, John Townsend. "Times are as dull as the devil here as yet." Even amid the frantic society of the Gold Rush, it certainly must have seemed tranquil after what he'd been through.

Schallenberger became a prosperous fruit and vegetable grower. He and the other overlanders of 1844 and later years proved to be the ultimate antidote to the Millerites, who had sold their farms and possessions because they believed they were leaving this world. The emigrants, in contrast, sold their farms and possessions because they were determined to make their own world better. The living embodiment of the Tyler-Polk-Benton dream of a continental nation, they never cast a vote for Polk but voted with their feet to make his vision a reality. The America they shaped is testament to their success.

Acknowledgments

The digital age has made historical research a less dusty and much faster process than it once was, but it still takes the combined skills of librarians and archivists to organize the material and make it usable by writers.

Those who were especially helpful in providing material for this book were Susan Palmer, curator of the Jenks Memorial Collection of Adventual Materials at Aurora University, and her assistant, Jewel Huggins; Steven M. Bookman and Anne T. Johnson of the Swem Library at the College of William & Mary; Bill Huntington of the Whitman College and Northwest Archives; Nan Mehan and Bill O'Hanlon at Stanford University's Department of Special Collections; and Stephenie Flora at Oregon Pioneers (www.oregonpioneers.com).

The staffs at the Library of Congress's Rare Book and Manuscript Reading Rooms and at the Gainesville branch of the Prince William County Library were always courteous and helpful. The Oregon-California Trails Association also came up with important information at just the right moment.

This book could not have been written without the digitization of materials that has taken place over the past decade, particularly through digital newspaper projects such as the Library of Congress's Chronicling America, the Book of Abraham project at BYU, and the New York State Newspaper Project.

Sincere thanks are due to the editing team at Chicago Review Press— Jerome Pohlen, Devon Freeny, and Kristi Gibson—who made every page better.

Guy Gugliotta offered a wealth of helpful advice, some of which I was even smart enough to take. I can't thank him enough for sharing his wisdom and encouragement.

Thanks to Senator Mike Lee of Utah, for letting me hold a piece of Mormon history in my hands.

It's fair to say *America 1844* would never have been published without the contributions of John M. Adams. And it certainly would not have been without my agent, Jessica Papin.

Thomas Bicknell provided more than one valuable insight that enriched the book.

And Arwen Bicknell provided love, support, and an endless supply of patience, along with her unmatched editing skills. No amount of thanks is sufficient.

NOTES

PROLOGUE: NEW YEAR'S DAY AT THE WHITE HOUSE

"a splendid view of the Potomac". . . Whipple, *Southern Diary*, 166

that "were once no doubt very beautiful . . ." Ibid.

"a poor weeping willow of a creature". . . Crapol, *John Tyler*, 183

"a true Whig". . . Chitwood, *Tyler: Champion*, 217, 387; Seale, *The President's House*, 238; Peterson, *Presidencies*, 252

one of the most audacious examples. . . Crapol, *John Tyler*, 185

"great object of his ambition". . . Ibid., 177

"In my deliberate judgment". . . Wright to James K. Polk, June 2, 1844, in Polk, *Correspondence*, vol. 7, 186

"I can usually keep my face . . ." Silas Wright to Martin Van Buren, January 2, 1844, Van Buren Papers

"Tell Mr. Tyler for me . . ." Garraty, *Silas Wright*, 234–36

1. "THIS GLORIOUS HOPE"

"plain farmer". . . Miller to Truman Hendryx, July 21, 1836, in Knight, *Millennial Fever*, 51

the crowds were so thick . . . Nichol, *Midnight Cry*, February 22, 1844, 241–42

beautiful indeed . . . Whipple, *Southern Diary*, 159

"a great village . . ." Chitwood, *Tyler: Champion*, 389

"Although we never visited a place . . ." Knight, *Millennial Fever*, 161; Bliss, *Memoirs of William Miller*, 253

"show them that an important revolution . . ." Knight, *Millennial Fever*, 160

his first meeting . . . Nichol, *Midnight Cry*, 62

One senator noted . . . Ibid.

"there are very few here . . ." *Brooklyn Eagle*, November 21, 1842

But that never deterred Miller . . . For a detailed explanation of Miller's reasoning, see
    Miller, *Evidence from Scripture,* especially lectures 3, 6, and 19
The New York Herald described . . . *New York Herald,* November 10, 1842
They were there to listen to Miller . . . *New York Herald,* November 13, 1842
Miller described the scene . . . Nichol, *Midnight Cry,* 62
So on the last day . . . Cole, *Van Buren,* 391–92
The ship was the pet project . . . Blackman, "Fatal Cruise of the Princeton"; Peterson,
    Presidencies, 201
"a humbug sort . . . " Fisher, *Philadelphia Perspective,* 159; Merry, *Country of Vast Designs,*
    146; Borneman, *Polk,* 77; Blackman, "Fatal Cruise of the Princeton"; Thulesius,
    Man Who Made, 60–61
"parading with much ostentation . . . " Fisher, *Philadelphia Perspective,* 159; Woodworth,
    Manifest Destinies, 116
"Now, gentlemen . . . " Thulesius, *Man Who Made,* 63
"to fire their souls . . . " Adams, *Memoirs,* vol. 11, 515
"the burning thirst . . . " Ibid., 528
All told, about four hundred guests . . . Blackman, "Fatal Cruise of the Princeton"; Peter-
    son, *Presidencies,* 202; Thulesius, *Man Who Made,* 60
as the ship sailed past Mount Vernon . . . Blackman, "Fatal Cruise of the Princeton"
As the day wore on . . . Ibid.
"disagreeable to her" . . . Patrick Calhoun to John C. Calhoun, February 28, 1844, in
    Calhoun, *Papers,* vol. 17, 807
"The scene upon the deck . . ." *National Intelligencer,* February 29, 1844; DeRose, *Con-
    gressman Lincoln,* 29; Benton, *Thirty Years' View,* vol. 2, 568
in his own hand . . . Chitwood, *Tyler: Champion,* 350
"will have, I fear . . . " Isaac Van Zandt to Anson Jones, February 29, 1844, in Crapol,
    John Tyler, 210
The fault lay in Stockton's design . . . Woodworth, *Manifest Destinies,* 115
"The lousy Stockton" . . . Thulesius, *Man Who Made,* 60–61
"The dreadful catastrophe . . . " Knight, *Millennial Fever,* 161; Bliss, *Memoirs of William
    Miller,* 253
Miller's deist tendencies . . . Bliss, *Memoirs of William Miller* 49–50; Rowe, *God's Strange
    Work,* 50
"At the commencement of the battle . . . " Bliss, *Memoirs of William Miller,* 53
Within two years . . . Rowe, *God's Strange Work,* 105; Knight, *Millennial Fever,* 36
"this intimate world . . . " Rowe, *God's Strange Work,* 102–3
"The more I presented it . . . " Miller, *Apology and Defense,* 16
He continued to talk . . . Rowe, *God's Strange Work,* 1–2; Land, *Adventism,* 5
Miller began traveling . . . Knight, *Millennial Fever,* 59, 61; Rowe, *God's Strange Work,*
    132
"We hope ministers or churches . . . " Knight, *Millennial Fever,* 61
"this, Father Miller's recovery . . . " *Utica Daily Gazette,* July 3, 1843
"sixteen acres of rye . . . " *Brooklyn Eagle,* March 16, 1843

"strange deluded sect" . . . *Times and Seasons*, March 1, 1843, 114–16

"personally an infidel . . ." Warner, "Changing Image," 6

"This Miller does not appear . . ." Knight, *Millennial Fever*, 63; Rowe, *God's Strange Work*, 132

"it was vain to reason with him . . ." Finney, *Autobiography*, 370–71

"the Lord will not come . . ." *Times and Seasons*, March 1, 1843, 113

"a remarkably active and zealous man" . . . *Liberator*, February 10, 1843, 23

"organizational modernity" . . . Barkun, *Crucible*, 128

"We have advocates . . ." Nichol, *Midnight Cry*, 62

"providence permitting" . . . *New York Tribune*, March 12, 1844

With Miller on his way home . . . Lundeberg, *Samuel Colt's*, 40

On March 14 . . . Bliss, *Memoirs of William Miller*, 254; Howe, *What Hath God Wrought*, 290–91; Barkun, *Crucible*, 132

Miller was at peace . . . Rowe, "Millerites: A Shadow Portrait," in Numbers and Butler, *Disappointed*, 7–11; Howe, *What Hath God Wrought*, 291; Nichol, *Midnight Cry*, 63

"solemn as eternity" . . . *Brooklyn Eagle*, July 24, 1843

A twelve-year-old boy . . . Jay, *Autobiography*, 18

"Do you think, supposing it to be true . . ." Angelina Grimke Weld to Theodore Weld, January 30, 1843, in Graybill, "The Abolitionist-Millerite Connection," in Numbers and Butler, *Disappointed*, 145

believed the Millerite case "to be conclusive . . ." Buttles Diaries, January 5, 1843, and March 1, 1843

"we shall probably hear no more . . ." *Oneida Whig*, April 2, 1844

"still looking for the Dear Savior . . ." Knight, *Millennial Fever*, 162

"It has been our sincere and solemn conviction . . ." *Advent Herald*, April 10, 1844

"I take the responsibility upon myself . . ." Smith, *Essential Joseph Smith*, 231

2. A PROPHET FOR PRESIDENT

"What will be your rule of action" . . . *Times and Seasons*, October 1, 1843, 344

"I can enter into no engagements . . ." Clay to Joseph Smith, November 15, 1843, in Roberts, *History of the Church*, vol. 6, 376

"The case does not come . . ." John C. Calhoun to Joseph Smith, December 2, 1843, in Calhoun, *Papers*, vol. 17, 583

"If the General Government has no power . . ." Roberts, *History of the Church*, vol. 6, 158; *Warsaw Signal*, June 5, 1844

"The power of Congress to interfere . . ." Adams, *Memoirs*, vol. 12, 5

"all honorable means . . . *to secure his election"* . . . Garr, *Presidential Candidate*, 38

"If you attempt to accomplish this" . . . Roberts, *History of the Church*, vol. 6, 188

"Our interests, our property, our lives . . ." *Times and Seasons*, February 15, 1844, 441

"a malarial riverbottom swamp" . . . Stegner, *Gathering of Zion*, 23; Remini, *Joseph Smith*, 140–41; *Missouri Republican*, April 25, 1844

"What can I do" . . . Bushman, *Rough Stone Rolling,* 392

In meetings with the Illinois delegation . . . Ibid., 394–97

"a few artless villains" . . . *Times and Seasons,* May 15, 1844, 535; Stegner, *Gathering of Zion,* 24

He began with a manifesto . . . Garr, *Presidential Candidate,* 46

"We have had democratic presidents . . ." *Times and Seasons,* May 15, 1844, 533

"Petition your state legislature . . ." Ibid., 531–32

"Give every man his constitutional freedom . . ." Ibid., 532; not too many years later President James Buchanan would use his unfettered authority to act in the territories to suppress what he saw as a rebellion by the Mormons

"In the millenarian mood of the early years" . . . Bushman, *Rough Stone Rolling,* 513; Bowman, *Mormon People,* 87–88

"have a government of our own" . . . Bushman, *Rough Stone Rolling,* 519; Arrington, *Brigham Young,* 109

"the union spread from the east to the west sea . . ." *Times and Seasons,* May 15, 1844, 532

"prevents that arch fiend . . ." De Bruhl, *Sword of San Jacinto,* 302; Crapol, *John Tyler,* 198

Upshur had reason to believe . . . Peterson, *Presidencies,* 198–99; De Bruhl, *Sword of San Jacinto,* 302

"the only man in the country . . ." Peterson, *Presidencies,* 203–04; George McDuffie to Calhoun, March 1 and March 5, 1844, in Calhoun, *Papers,* vol. 17, 809, 815; Robert Barnwell Rhett to Calhoun, March 5, 1844, in Calhoun, *Papers,* vol. 17, 816

"whether it would meet with your approbation . . ." Theophilus Fisk to Polk, March 9, 1844, in Polk, *Correspondence,* vol. 7, 82

"there are many others . . ." Theophilus Fisk to Polk, March 13, 1844, in Polk, *Correspondence,* vol. 7, 89; Polk to Fisk, March 20, 1844, in Polk, *Correspondence,* vol. 7, 91–92

The most celebrated defense . . . Robert Walker, *Letter,* 11; Silbey, *Storm,* 34; Merk, *History,* 289

"Gentlemen of the South . . ." Miller, *Arguing About Slavery,* 365

"the standing supremacy . . ." Ford, *Campaign,* 34; Freehling, *Road to Disunion,* 351

"life-and-death struggle . . ." Miller, *Arguing About Slavery,* 373–74; Adams, *Memoirs,* vol. 11, 455; 468; *House Journal,* February 28, 1844, 498

"far too lethargic upon . . ." Upshur to Calhoun, August 14, 1843, in Merk, *Slavery and Annexation,* 20

"would be a transfer of our political power . . ." Joshua R. Giddings to J. A. Giddings, April 28, 1844, in Holt, *Rise and Fall,* 169; Freehling, *Road to Disunion,* 411

"The voice of the country" . . . Calhoun to W. S. Murphy, April 13, 1844, in Bartlett, *Calhoun,* 310; treaty provisions are in Merk, *Slavery and Annexation,* 271–75

"walked no more with us" . . . Knight, *Millennial Fever,* 163, 171

"I confess my error . . ." Bliss, *Memoirs of William Miller,* 256

Starkweather, on the other hand . . . Knight, *Millennial Fever,* 174–75; Butler, "Making of a New Order" in Numbers and Butler, *Disappointed,* 192

"*No two were of one mind*"... Knight, *Millennial Fever*, 176
As early as February 1844... Ibid., 190–91
He planned a tour of the west... Bliss, *Memoirs of William Miller*, 264
"*there is oratory enough in the Church*..." Bushman, *Rough Stone Rolling*, 515; Garr,
    Presidential Candidate, 51; *Times and Seasons*, April 15, 1844, 504–6, May 15,
    1844, 528–33; June 1, 1844, 544–48
Non-Mormon newspapers also took notice... *New York Tribune*, January 27, 1844; *Warsaw Signal*, February 21, 1844
"*I am in my cauling and duing my duty*"... Young, *Manuscript History*, 164; Arrington,
    Brigham Young, 110–11; Garr, *Presidential Candidate*, 56; *The Radical*, April 6,
    1844; *Sunbury American and Shamokin Journal*, March 30, 1844
"*live to put his foot upon the neck*..." *Times and Seasons*, June 1, 1844, 552; Garr, *Presidential Candidate*, 52; Poll, *Joseph Smith*, 19–20; *Nauvoo Neighbor*, June 5, 1844

3. "ANNEXATION AND WAR... ARE IDENTICAL"

"*clever gentleman*..." Remini, *Henry Clay*, 631–32
"*I consider the Union a great political partnership*"... Henry Clay to Stephen H. Miller,
    July 1, 1844, in Clay, *Private Correspondence*, 491
"*intelligence which has greatly surprised me*"... Clay to John J. Crittenden, February 15,
    1844, in Crapol, *John Tyler*, 203
"*entertained no hopes*"... Henry Clay to James Clay, March 17, 1844, in Clay, *Private Correspondence*, 486; Henry Clay to William C. Preston, March 20, 1844, in
    Remini, *Henry Clay*, 636
Clay would waver on his determination... Clay to John J. Crittenden, March 24, 1844,
    in Remini, *Henry Clay*, 637
He feared the Millerites might be right... Peterson, *Triumvirate*, 358–59
"*a miserable political humbug*..." Ibid., 359
Beginning to weary of all the activity... Remini, *Henry Clay*, 637
voters had largely rejected the Whigs... Holt, *Rise and Fall*, 165; *New York Tribune*, July
    2, 1844
As 1844 had approached... Merry, *Country of Vast Designs*, 56; Adams, *Memoirs*, vol.
    11, 446; Peterson, *Triumvirate*, 335–36; Klein, *President James Buchanan*, 158;
    Peterson, *Presidencies*, 211
"*had, during a longer period*..." Zieber, *Life of General Lewis Cass*, 132
Personalities aside... Silbey, *Storm*, 59; Holt, *Rise and Fall*, 167
A Harper's Weekly cartoon early... "The Presidental Sweepstakes of 1844," HarpWeek,
    http://loc.harpweek.com/LCPoliticalCartoons/IndexDisplayCartoonMedium
    .asp?UniqueID=44&Year=1844
"*If we cannot beat Van Buren*"... Willie P. Mangum to Paul Cameron, February 10,
    1844, in Holt, *Rise and Fall*, 165
"*Let me implore you*..." R. B. Rhett to Calhoun, December 2, 1843, in Bartlett, *Calhoun*, 305

The chairman of the Foreign Relations Committee . . . Butler and Wolff, *US Senate Election*, 47–48

"expressed in the most awkward, inelegant, and bungling manner" . . . Fisher, *Philadelphia Perspective*, 164; Schlesinger, *Political Parties*, 550; Bartlett, *Calhoun*, 312–14; Adams, *Memoirs*, vol. 12, 36

"drive off every Northern man . . ." Remini, *Andrew Jackson*, vol. 3, 496; Freehling, *Road to Disunion*, 415; Haley, *Sam Houston*, 279; Polk to Cave Johnson, May 13, 1844, in Polk, *Correspondence*, vol. 7, 134

"The Texian question . . ." Cave Johnson to Polk, April 15, 1844, in Polk, *Correspondence*, vol. 7, 103

An unpledged delegate . . . *Washington Globe*, April 27, 1844; Garraty, *Silas Wright*, 247

"long-winded, complex and typically cautious argument" . . . Silbey, *Storm*, 63

"insure beyond the probability of a doubt . . ." Peterson, *Presidencies*, 222–23; Cole, *Van Buren*, 395; Niven, *Van Buren: Romantic Age*, 532

"I have shed tears of regret" . . . Remini, *Andrew Jackson*, vol. 3, 498

"I conceive that no motive for the acquisition of foreign territory . . ." *National Intelligencer*, April 27, 1844

"the exemplar and chief of sordid politicians . . ." *New York Tribune*, May 31, 1844

"militia of Kentucky . . . *alone"* . . . *Annals of Congress*, 11th Cong., 2nd sess., February 22, 1810, 579; *National Intelligencer*, April 27, 1844

"I have no hesitation in declaring . . ." Chase et al. to Polk, in Polk, *Correspondence*, vol. 7, 99–100; Polk to Chase et al., in Polk, *Correspondence*, vol. 7 105–6

Concurrent with the final pre-convention maneuverings . . . Lundeberg, *Samuel Colt's*, 40; Niven, *Van Buren: Romantic Age*, 524; Land, *Adventism*, 21

In truth, the youthful and arrogant . . . Hosley, *Colt*, 19; Thulesius, *Man Who Made*, 62

Colt's secretiveness about his "submarine battery". . . Lundeberg, *Samuel Colt's*, 17

"if adopted for the service of our Government . . ." Colt to Tyler, June 19, 1841, in Lundeberg, *Samuel Colt's*, 18

Southard persuaded Congress . . . Lundeberg, *Samuel Colt's*, 17, 19–20

"the whole plans and secrets of my inventions" . . . Ibid., 21

"excite the jealousy . . ." Colt to Southard, January 2, 1842, in Lundeberg, *Samuel Colt's*, 21

The city was abuzz . . . *National Intelligencer*, April 15, 1844; Lundeberg, *Samuel Colt's*, 40, 42; Hosley, *Colt*, 22

On April 13, the day of the test . . . Lundeberg, *Samuel Colt's*, 42; *National Intelligencer*, April 15, 1844

"Ah, what a pity, it is a failure" . . . *National Intelligencer*, April 15, 1844; Hosley, *Colt*, 22

"views in reference to the claims . . ." William Wilkins to Robert Hare, April 29, 1844, in *Colt's Submarine Battery*, House doc., 11

"galvanic process employed . . ." Robert Hare to William Wilkins, May 1, 1844, in *Colt's Submarine Battery*, House doc., 12–13

"The method now generally used . . ." Joseph Henry to William Wilkins, May 3, 1844, in *Colt's Submarine Battery*, House doc., 16

Colt never claimed originality . . . Lundeberg, *Samuel Colt's*, 36, 47, 52

4. "WHO THE DEVIL IS POLK?"

"that this convention . . ." New York Tribune, May 3, 1844

The motion was greeted . . . Ibid.

"weather beaten" and "hoarse" . . . Adams, *Memoirs*, vol. 12, 20; CQ Press, *National Party Conventions*, 29

In about a hundred words . . . CQ Press, *National Party Conventions*, 30; Howe, *Political Culture*, 143

Clay disavowed any interest . . . Remini, *Henry Clay*, 630

Frelinghuysen led on the first ballot . . . New York Tribune, May 3, 1844

"representative of a culturally transforming Protestant Whiggery . . ." Eells, *Forgotten Saint*, 55, 60, 71–80; Holt, *Rise and Fall*, 188; there are eight entries in the Library of Congress online catalog for authors born in the 1830s and 1840s named in honor of Frelinghuysen

"conceived in frustration and self-delusion" . . . Aileen S. Kraditor, "The Liberty and Free Soil Parties" in Schlesinger, *Political Parties*, 741

The party's dismal showing . . . R. Johnson, *The Liberty Party*, 34; A. Johnson, *Dictionary of American Biography*, vol. 2, 292

"with a strong hand" . . . Vermont Phoenix, September 22, 1843

"While the pretended friends of the slave . . ." Rowe, *God's Strange Work*, 185

Democrats would claim victory . . . Stahr, *Seward*, 94

"A set of citizens . . ." Feldberg, *Philadelphia Riots*, 66, 80

"Come down here . . ." Ibid., 80–81

three thousand people . . . Ibid., 82–84

"Keep the damned natives out . . ." Ibid., 84

"Men with their wives . . ." Perry, *Full and Complete Account*, 32–33

In short order . . . Feldberg, *Philadelphia Riots*, 86–90

"Let every man come armed to defend himself" . . . Ibid., 92–93

By Tuesday afternoon . . . Perry, *Full and Complete Account*, 12–13; Feldberg, *Philadelphia Riots*, 108

"little fellows scarce able to carry a musket . . ." Ibid., 95; Fisher, *Philadelphia Perspective*, 167–68

Several small groups . . . Feldberg, *Philadelphia Riots*, 96–99

"No Popery Here" . . . Ibid., 99; *New York Tribune*, May 10, 1844

When the steeple toppled . . . "Philadelphia Catholic Riots," *Catholic Magazine*, 379–81; Feldberg, *Philadelphia Riots*, 101

Tasting success against the "rabble" . . . Feldberg, *Turbulent Era*, 36

"Nothing was done . . ." Feldberg, *Philadelphia Riots*, 105–6; Fisher, *Philadelphia Perspective*, 165, 168; Perry, *Full and Complete Account*, 39

Six people were known dead, all nativists . . . Feldberg, *Philadelphia Riots*, 109; "Philadelphia Catholic Riots," *Catholic Magazine*, 381; Fisher, *Philadelphia Perspective*, 167–68

"quite a serious riot" . . . New York Tribune, April 5, 1844; Adams, *Memoirs*, vol. 12, 24; Gleeson, *Irish*, 96; Fisher, *Philadelphia Perspective*, 177

"Vans opponents . . ." Cave Johnson to Polk, May 3, 1844, in Polk, *Correspondence*, vol. 7, 116

"deep regret" . . . Merry, *Country of Vast Designs*, 55; Borneman, *Polk*, 89

The strategy carried certain risks . . . Merry, *Country of Vast Designs*, 57

"General Jackson says . . ." Polk to Cave Johnson, May 13, 1844, in Polk, *Correspondence*, vol. 7, 134–35

"now encountering the very identical difficulties . . ." Cave Johnson to Sarah Polk, January 14, 1844, in Borneman, *Polk*, 372

A cartoon in Harper's Weekly . . . "Not a Drum Was Heard Nor a Funeral Note," HarpWeek, http://loc.harpweek.com/LCPoliticalCartoons/IndexDisplayCartoonMedium .asp?UniqueID=27&Year=1844; Cave Johnson to Polk, May 8, 1844, in Polk, *Correspondence*, vol. 7, 126

"discontent, division, despondency . . ." Ford, *Campaign*, 16

The Democrats convened . . . *New York Tribune*, May 29, 1844

"room was not crowded . . ." Peterson, *Presidencies*, 224–25; Chitwood, *Tyler: Champion*, 376; *New York Tribune*, May 29, 1844

debate on the two-thirds rule . . . Borneman, *Polk*, 99–100; Cave Johnson to Polk, May 27, 1844, in Polk, *Correspondence*, vol. 7, 157; Niven, *Van Buren*, 534

On Tuesday the convention backed the two-thirds rule . . . *New York Tribune*, May 30, 1844; Niven, *Van Buren: Romantic Age*, 535

To win the nomination . . . Borneman, *Polk*, 100; *New York Tribune*, May 30, 1844; Stewart was not active in politics, but his grandson was future Irish nationalist leader Charles Stewart Parnell

His totals sank . . . *New York Tribune*, May 30, 1844; Borneman, *Polk*, 101

But Van Buren's backers . . . Garraty, *Silas Wright*, 259

"the damned rotten corrupt venal Cass cliques" . . . *New York Tribune*, May 30, 1844; Merry, *Country of Vast Designs*, 89; Borneman, *Polk*, 102; Cole, *Van Buren*, 397

"Never before or since . . ." Sellers, *James K. Polk*, vol. 2, 94; Borneman, *Polk*, 102–4

On the first ballot of Wednesday . . . *New York Tribune*, May 31, 1844

"When the announcement was made . . ." Ibid.

"Certainly the man beaten twice . . ." *New York Tribune*, June 1, 1844; *Nashville Republican Banner*, June 7, 1844

A Harper's Weekly cartoon . . . "Polk in His Extremity," HarpWeek, http://loc .harpweek.com/LCPoliticalCartoons/IndexDisplayCartoonMedium.asp ?UniqueID=32&Year=1844

"Polk is a fourth-rate partisan politician . . ." Fisher, *Philadelphia Perspective*, 169–70

"safe and right" . . . Stahr, *Seward*, 96

"Are our Democratic friends serious . . ." Henry Clay to Willie P. Mangum, June 7, 1844, in Holt, *Rise and Fall*, 173

"the great mass of the people . . ." Borneman, *Polk*, 108, 111; Theophilus Fisk to Polk, May 31, 1844, in Polk, *Correspondence*, vol. 7, 171; William M. Gwin to Polk, June 8, 1844, in Polk, *Correspondence*, vol. 7, 217; *Brooklyn Eagle*, August 5, 1844

The telegraph was new . . . *New York Tribune*, May 31, 1844

The first ballot of the morning . . . *New York Tribune,* June 1, 1844

"the domestic institutions of the several states" . . . CQ Press, *National Party Conventions,* 30

Samuel F. B. Morse, already well known as a painter . . . Silverman, *Lightning Man,* 221; Coe, *Telegraph,* 33

Before the news of Polk's nomination . . . Silverman, *Lightning Man,* 234; Burlingame et al., *Scribner's,* 653

"simple & plain" . . . Whipple, *Southern Diary,* 168; McCullough, *Greater Journey,* 151; Burlingame et al., *Scribner's,* 654

To enhance the drama of the moment . . . Coe, *Telegraph,* 32

"It is his work . . ." Samuel F. B. Morse to Sidney Morse, May 31, 1844, Morse Papers

"The conventions at Baltimore . . ." Ibid.

Vail sent regular updates . . . Silverman, *Lightning Man,* 237; *New York Tribune,* June 8, 1844

"The enthusiasm of the crowd . . ." Samuel F. B. Morse to Sidney Morse, May 31, 1844, Morse Papers; *New York Tribune,* May 27, 1844; Burlingame et al., *Scribner's,* 655

"Illinois goes for Polk . . ." Silverman, *Lightning Man,* 237–38

"Even the most inveterate opposers . . ." Samuel F. B. Morse to Sidney Morse, May 31, 1844, Morse Papers

"All this is calculated . . ." *New York Tribune,* June 8 and May 2, 1844; also see, for example, Hugill, *Global Communications;* John, *Spreading the News*

"a heaven-sent deliverance from the tyranny of distance" . . . Howe, *What Hath God Wrought,* 563

"We should so live and labor in our time . . ." Samuel F. B. Morse to Sidney Morse, May 31, 1844, Morse Papers; *Christian Work and the Evangelist,* 650

"to monopolize intelligence . . ." Remini, *Henry Clay,* 643–44; Silverman, *Lightning Man,* 250

"It is conceded on all sides . . ." *Jeffersonian Republican,* May 2, 1844

"one of the largest meetings ever held by our citizens" . . . DeRose, *Congressman Lincoln,* 31

"yes, I had a fight with Jackson . . ." Roberts, *Newer World,* 121; Kennedy, *Profiles in Courage,* 81–82

Tyler wanted the treaty . . . Merk, *Slavery and Annexation,* 72

He started by demanding . . . Merk, *History,* 281–83

Benton's motion . . . *Senate Executive Journal,* May 13, 1844, 276–77

"no communication whatever . . ." Merk, *Slavery and Annexation,* 73

"since the commencement of the negotiations . . ." *Senate Executive Journal,* May 15, 1844, 279

"In consequence of the declaration . . ." Ibid.

"if negotiation fails . . ." Haley, *Sam Houston,* 280

The decision to defend Texas . . . Crapol, *John Tyler,* 217

"the most successful negotiation . . ." Adams, *Memoirs,* vol. 12, 78

Standing to his full height . . . Gugliotta, *Freedom's Cap,* 54–55 describes the Senate chamber

"I—the first denouncer of the treaty of 1819 . . ." Congressional Globe, Senate, 28th Cong., 1st sess., May 16, 18, 20, 1844, 476

"Would we take 2,000 miles . . ." Merk, Slavery and Annexation, 79

There were other speeches . . . Merk, History, 287; Congressional Globe, Senate, 28th Cong., 1st sess., June 15, 1844, 720–22

"He gives a bad reason for doing a good thing" . . . Congressional Globe, House of Representatives, 28th Cong., 1st sess., May 21, 1844, 699

Andrew Jackson was convinced . . . Merk, Slavery and Annexation, 74; Borneman, Polk, 116

It wasn't even close . . . Freehling, Road to Disunion, 431

"last card for a popular whirlwind . . ." Adams, Memoirs, vol. 12, 22; Senate Executive Journal, June 12, 1844, 419

"Some hundreds went a few years ago . . ." Congressional Globe, Senate, 28th Cong., 1st sess., June 3, 1844, 637

"All obey the same impulse" . . . Benton, Selections, 3, 5

5. THE MISSIONARY AND THE PUBLICIST

On the day of the Texas annexation vote . . . Jessie Benton Frémont to Adelaide Talbot, June 15, 1844, in J. B. Frémont, Letters, 23; Denton, Passion and Principle, 97–98

"second lieutenants cannot indulge in secretaries" . . . Herr, Jessie Benton Frémont, 83, 87; Goetzmann, Army Exploration, 86; Denton, Passion and Principle, 86; Menard, Sight Unseen, 29; J. C. Frémont, Exploring Expedition, 276–77

"to connect the reconnaissance of 1842 . . ." J. C. Frémont, Exploring Expedition, 123; Goetzmann, Exploration and Empire, 244

Two months later . . . Denton, Passion and Principle, 87–89; Preuss, Exploring with Frémont, 81; Goetzmann, Army Exploration, 86–87; Slack, Noble Obsession, 32

He had arranged . . . John C. Frémont to Stephen Watts Kearney, ca. May 8, 1843, in Jackson and Spence, Expeditions, 343; Thomas Hart Benton to John C. Frémont, March 20, 1843, in Jackson and Spence, Expeditions, 164–65; Chaffin, Pathfinder, 148; Denton, Passion and Principle, 88–89

"the young explorer who held his diploma from Nature . . ." Benton, Thirty Years' View, vol. 2, 580

"We could count on each other . . ." Herr, Jessie Benton Frémont, 91

"I had been too much a part of the whole plan . . ." Denton, Passion and Principle, 90–91

"It was in the blessed day before telegraphs" . . . Ibid., 91

"rejected contemptuously by the Senate" . . . Herr, Jessie Benton Frémont, 91

"wild flax three and a half feet high" . . . Goetzmann, Army Exploration, 89; J. C. Frémont, Exploring Expedition, 23, 31; Preuss, Exploring with Frémont, 83–84; Lavender, Bent's Fort, 241; Chaffin, Pathfinder, 158

Frémont sent Lucien Maxwell toward Taos . . . Lavender, Bent's Fort, 240–41

Kit Carson, a mountain man extraordinaire . . . Denton, Passion and Principle, 93; Lavender, Bent's Fort, 242

None of Frémont's original party knew the route . . . Chaffin, *Pathfinder*, 162

"for his mercy in placing the Rocky Mountains there" . . . Unruh, *Plains Across*, 44; J. C. Frémont, *Exploring Expedition*, 60; Webb, *Adventures*, 108; Preuss, *Exploring with Frémont*, 86; for the first history of the Santa Fe Trail, see Gregg, *Commerce of the Prairies*

"I am doubtful if the followers of Balboa . . ." J. C. Frémont, *Exploring Expedition*, 151

"had been seen only by trappers . . ." J. C. Frémont, *Exploring Expedition*, 132; Goetzmann, *Army Exploration*, 91

Frémont outfitted Horace Day's rubber boat . . . Slack, *Noble Obsession*, 32; Roberts, *A Newer World*, 37

Born in 1800 . . . Slack, *Noble Obsession*, 15, 21–24

India Rubber Company . . . Korman, *Goodyear Story*, 24

"Forget your valve . . ." Slack, *Noble Obsession*, 28

By the late 1820s . . . Ibid., 32

Years of torment . . . Ibid., 44–45

With an assist from a fellow inventor . . . Ibid., 79–80; Korman, *Goodyear Story*, 56

"the instrument in the hands of his Maker" . . . Slack, *Noble Obsession*, 97

"We used to laugh and think . . ." Korman, *Goodyear Story*, 62

"Goodyear's industrial world had shrunk . . ." Slack, *Noble Obsession*, 94–95, 98; Korman, *Goodyear Story*, 36

Later, Goodyear's patent would be . . . Remini, *Daniel Webster*, 731; Korman, *Goodyear Story*, 137

After a year of working with sulfur . . . Slack, *Noble Obsession*, 110–11

And still, by the summer of 1842 . . . Ibid., 128–34

Hancock got his British patent . . . Ibid., 137–38; Korman, *Goodyear Story*, 93

"The history of inventions . . ." Slack, *Noble Obsession*, 139

"miserable rubber boat" . . . Roberts, *A Newer World*, 130; Preuss, *Exploring with Frémont*, 88; Chaffin, *Pathfinder*, 168–70

"Mr. Preuss and myself . . ." J. C. Frémont, *Exploring Expedition*, 159; Preuss, *Exploring with Frémont*, 85, 89

Luckily for Frémont's wife, Jessie . . . Denton, *Passion and Principle*, 95; J. B. Frémont to Adelaide Talbot, September 16, 1843, in J. B. Frémont, *Letters*, 13

"this side trip to the Salt Lake . . ." Preuss, *Exploring with Frémont*, 88; Unruh, *Plains Across*, 202

"A military post, and a civilized settlement . . ." J. C. Frémont, *Exploring Expedition*, 160

On September 19 and 20 . . . Ibid., 162; Preuss, *Exploring with Frémont*, 90

"fine-looking large family of emigrants . . ." J. C. Frémont, *Exploring Expedition*, 182–83; John C. Frémont to J. J. Abert, November 24, 1843, in Jackson and Spence, *Expeditions*, 354

By 1844, McLoughlin had provided . . . Unruh, *Plains Across*, 31, 357–59; Dary, *Oregon Trail*, 49–50; Preuss, *Exploring with Frémont*, 97

He wouldn't make it by Christmas . . . J. B. Frémont to J. F. H. Claiborne, October 30, 1843, in J. B. Frémont, *Letters*, 14; Preuss, *Exploring with Frémont*, 90 *"many details of the Summer's campaign"*. . . J. B. Frémont to Adelaide Talbot, December 3, 1843, in J. B. Frémont, *Letters*, 15

"We were roused, on Christmas morning . . ."J. C. Frémont, *Exploring Expedition*, 210

"our new year's eve was rather a gloomy one . . ." Ibid., 213, 219

"somewhat rough-looking mountain" . . . Ibid., 221; Roberts, *A Newer World*, 131; Preuss, *Exploring with Frémont*, 83, 104; Watson, "Frémont's Second Expedition," 3

"satisfied me that he would be here in February" . . . J. B. Frémont to Adelaide Talbot, February 1, 1844, in J. B. Frémont, *Letters*, 17

Still heading west . . . Roberts, *A Newer World*, 133; Preuss, *Exploring with Frémont*, 113; Watson, "Frémont's Second Expedition," 4

"The meat train did not arrive this evening . . ."J. C. Frémont, *Exploring Expedition*, 234; Watson, "Frémont's Second Expedition," 5; Chaffin, *Pathfinder*, 215–16

"On the 19th . . ." J. C. Frémont, *Exploring Expedition*, 235

"hill side sprinkled with grass enough for the night" . . . J. C. Frémont, *Exploring Expedition*, 240; Preuss, *Exploring with Frémont*, 116–17

"surpassingly beautiful country". . . Roberts, *A Newer World*, 134; J. C. Frémont, *Exploring Expedition*, 244–45

John Augustus Sutter was a Swiss émigré . . . Malone, *Dictionary of American Biography*, vol. 18, 224–25

John Bidwell, one of the leaders . . . Owens, *Gold Rush Saints*, 91–92

"he cannot be here until the middle of April". . . J. B. Frémont to Adelaide Talbot, March 3 and March 24, 1844, in J. B. Frémont, *Letters*, 18, 20

"he will not be here until the middle of May" . . . J. B. Frémont to Adelaide Talbot, April 21, 1844, in J. B. Frémont, *Letters*, 21

On April 24 . . . J. C. Frémont, *Exploring Expedition*, 261–63; Roberts, *A Newer World*, 135–36; Frémont eventually discovered the bodies of the two men who had been riding with Fuentes; the women had apparently been taken captive; see J. C. Frémont, *Exploring Expedition*, 265

"at a little spring of bad water". . . J. C. Frémont, *Exploring Expedition*, 280

"look for their being here the first of July" . . . J. B. Frémont to Adelaide Talbot, June 15, 1844, in J. B. Frémont, *Letters*, 23

"The starvation and fatigue they had endured . . ." *New York Tribune*, June 21, 1844

"repeated discharges from the guns". . . Lavender, *Bent's Fort*, 247; Preuss, *Exploring with Frémont*, 138; J. C. Frémont, *Exploring Expedition*, 288

"thin as a shadow". . . Herr, *Jessie Benton Frémont*, 99–100

6. To Oregon and California

Seventeen-year-old Moses Schallenberger . . . Schallenberger Narrative, 1–2, Schallenberger Papers

"would find themselves under more sympathetic conditions . . ." Ibid., 3

Everyone who encamped at Council Bluffs . . . Unruh, *Plains Across*, 119 *simple farm wagons* . . . Stewart, *California Trail*, 110–11

"150 lbs. of flour . . ." Boon's Lick Times, September 14, 1844

"ignorant, deluded men" . . . Unruh, *Plains Across*, 42

But the cows had other ideas . . . Stewart, *Opening*, 51

"Greenwood is nearly blind" . . . Hammer, *Emigrating Company*, 48

"In camp today because it is raining" . . . Ibid., 77

"a river about the size of the Wabash at Terre Haute" . . . Ibid., 78

The emigrants couldn't cross the next major river . . . Ibid., 80–81; Stewart, *Opening*, 53;
   Carleton, *Prairie Logbooks*, 95; later in the summer, a company of dragoons under
   Major Clifton Wharton would put on a show of force along the Platte and parley
   with the Pawnee in an attempt to impose a peace; see Carleton, *Prairie Logbooks*

"those that are doing wrong willfully" . . . Hammer, *Emigrating Company*, 82; Rumer,
   Wagon Trains, 82–83

"so that it might not be noticed by the savages . . ." Hammer, *Emigrating Company*, 87–88

"reckless bravery born of frontier life" . . . Stewart, *Opening*, 51

"we come in sight of the chimnies" . . . Hammer, *Emigrating Company*, 89; Rumer, *Wagon
   Trains*, 53; Mattes, *Great Platte River Road*, 361, 382; Clyman, *Journal*, 97

"an abundance of meat from younger buffaloes . . ." Stewart, *Opening*, 54

"one of the restless ones . . ." Sager, *Across the Plains*, 5–6; Sager, Sager, and Sager, *Whitman Massacre*, 10–11

Cornelius Gilliam, a veteran of the Black Hawk and Seminole wars . . . Dary, *Oregon
   Trail*, 111–12; Rumer, *Wagon Trains*, 75

"bright spring morning" . . . Sager, *Across the Plains*, 5–6

"The first encampments . . ." Ibid., 5, 37

The early road was rough . . . Rumer, *Wagon Trains*, 70, 85; Parrish, *Oregon Trail Diary*,
   20; Sager, *Across the Plains*, 6

Like those who had left from Council Bluffs . . . Sager, *Across the Plains*, 6; Clyman, *Journal*, 76; Rumer, *Wagon Trains*, 259

"It rained on them incessantly . . ." Boon's Lick Times, September 14, 1844

"The passenger pigeons were flying in flocks southward" . . . Lowe, *John Minto*, 23

From the Black Vermillion . . . Dary, *Oregon Trail*, 114; Rumer, *Wagon Trains*, 89; Parrish, *Oregon Trail Diary*, 27–28

Eventually the torrential rains gave way . . . Dary, *Oregon Trail*, 91–94; Clyman, *Journal*,
   90–94, 108; Sager, Sager, and Sager, *Whitman Massacre*, 13; Parrish, *Oregon Trail
   Diary*, 30, 35

"several musical instruments . . ." Sager, *Across the Plains*, 6

On July 18 . . . Ibid., 7; Sager, Sager, and Sager, *Whitman Massacre*, 13–14; Rumer,
   Wagon Trains, 101; Clyman, *Journal*, 99; Parrish, *Oregon Trail Diary*, 35; Thompson, *Shallow Grave*, 21

"My dear child . . ." Sager, *Across the Plains*, 7; Sager, Sager, and Sager, *Whitman Massacre*, 14

Sugar could cost $1.50 a pound . . . Unruh, *Plains Across*, 251; *Boon's Lick Times*, Septem-
   ber 14, 1844; Clyman, *Journal*, 99; Dary, *Oregon Trail*, 99

"We had a beautiful camp on the bank of the Laramie . . ." Lowe, *John Minto,* 32; Clyman, *Journal,* 82

For many, Fort Laramie afforded the first real chance . . . Stewart, *Opening,* 54; Hammer, *Emigrating Company,* 117

There was, naturally . . . Unruh, *Plains Across,* 185, 250

Along the Sweetwater . . . Stewart, *Opening,* 55–57

On July 16 . . . Hammer, *Emigrating Company,* 118; Meldahl, *Hard Road West,* 97

"near a small spring in the side of the rock" . . . Hammer, *Emigrating Company,* 120

"in sight of the everlasting snows on the Rock mountains" . . . Ibid., 121

"Here is about as good road as any that we have yet traveled on" . . . Ibid., 122; Clyman, *Journal,* 109

Emerging from South Pass . . . Meldahl, *Hard Road West,* 137

Days after reaching South Pass . . . Dary, *Oregon Trail,* 102; Parrish, *Oregon Trail Diary,* 55; Hammer, *Emigrating Company,* 123

Some emigrants followed the road less traveled . . . Meldahl, *Hard Road West,* 143; Stewart, *Opening,* 60

They started out at daylight . . . Kelly, *Old Greenwood,* 56–57; Clyman, *Journal,* 110

Unfortunately, after slaking their thirsts . . . Kelly, *Old Greenwood,* 56–57; Stewart, *Opening,* 61–62

The California-bound party left the Green River . . . Stewart, *Opening,* 63; Meldahl, *Hard Road West,* 164

Meanwhile, in the Oregon-bound group . . . Thompson, *Shallow Grave,* 23

"Though feeble" . . . Sager, *Across the Plains,* 7

"The sick man . . ." Rumer, *Wagon Trains,* 103; Lowe, *John Minto,* 34; Sager, *Across the Plains,* 7; Clyman, *Journal,* 110; Parrish, *Oregon Trail Diary,* 52

Henry Sager, age thirty-eight . . . Rumer, *Wagon Trains,* 163

Prince Carl of Solms-Braunfels . . . Prince Carl, *Voyage,* 2

Inspired by tales . . .Geue and Geue, *New Land,* 3

As is often the case . . . Ibid., 3–4

"The weather was beautiful". . . Prince Carl, *Voyage,* 16–24

"Unbelievable heat . . ." Ibid., 27

"low coast line with dunes" . . . Ibid.

He also appreciated the difficulty . . . Geue and Geue, *New Land,* 7; Prince Carl, *Voyage,* 1

"The so-called American nation". . . Prince Carl, *Voyage,* 206–8

"All were pleased with my arrival in this country" . . . Geue and Geue, *New Land,* 23, 37

7. SUMMER OF DISCONTENT

"settled mostly by emigrants . . ." *Messages and Papers,* vol. 5, 2177; Cave Johnson to Polk, May 25, 1844, in Polk, *Correspondence,* vol. 7, 154

Along with the message . . . Merk, *Slavery and Annexation,* 83–84 *"violent and rancorous"*... *Congressional Globe*, Senate, 28th Cong., 1st sess., June 15, 1844, 451–52; former Democratic congressman David Crockett of Tennessee died at the Alamo; Adams, *Memoirs*, vol. 12, 56

"I am utterly at a loss..." Adams, *Memoirs*, vol. 12, 589

"The treaty was made..." *Congressional Globe*, Senate, 28th Cong., 1st sess., June 15, 1844, 608; Merk, *Slavery and Annexation*, 93; Adams, *Memoirs*, vol. 12, 56

"the oldest advocate for the recovery of Texas"... *Congressional Globe*, Senate, 28th Cong., 1st sess., June 15, 1844, 610

"annexed the United States to Texas..." Ibid., 498

"I do not see any good that can arise from it"... Cave Johnson to Polk, June 10, 1844, in Polk, *Correspondence*, vol. 7, 228; J. George Harris to Polk, June 25, 1844, in Polk, *Correspondence*, vol. 7, 282; Polk to Andrew J. Donelson, June 26, 1844, in Polk, *Correspondence*, vol. 7, 286–87; Polk to Andrew Jackson, July 22, 1844, in Polk, *Correspondence*, vol. 7, 380; Polk to George M. Dallas, August 29, 1844, in Polk, *Correspondence*, vol. 7, 478; *Brooklyn Eagle*, August 26, 1844; Adams, *Memoirs*, vol. 12, 57

On June 26, the couple married... Chitwood, *Tyler: Champion*, 400; Adams, *Memoirs*, vol. 12, 67; Peterson, *Presidencies*, 236–37, 240

"Papa was the only handsome man..." Julia Gardiner Tyler to her mother, August 16, 1845, and July 1844, in Chitwood, *Tyler: Champion*, 401, 405

"most disagreeable duty"... Peterson, *Presidencies*, 237; Chitwood, *Tyler: Champion*, 378

"as brethren and equals"... Peterson, *Presidencies*, 238; Chitwood, *Tyler: Champion*, 381; Robert J. Walker to Polk, July 10, 1844, in Polk, *Correspondence*, vol. 7, 337; Polk to Andrew Jackson, July 23, 1844, in Polk, *Correspondence*, vol. 7, 388; Jackson to Polk, July 26, 1844, in Polk, *Correspondence*, vol. 7, 401; and Polk to Jackson, August 3, 1844, in Polk, *Correspondence*, vol. 7, 430

"Support the cause of Polk..." Peterson, *Presidencies*, 238–39; Chitwood, *Tyler: Champion*, 380; Borneman, *Polk*, 118–19

"one delusion worse than Millerism..." Warner, "Changing Image," 7

"To My Friends throughout the Union"... Peterson, *Presidencies*, 239–40

"The convention was addressed..." Garr, *Presidential Candidate*, 64–65

"A large number of rowdies"... Ibid., 65

"Sometimes the Mormons are all killed..." Garr, *Presidential Candidate*, 67; Ronald Walker, "Six Days in August"

"not a spontaneous, impulsive act..." Oaks and Hill, *Carthage Conspiracy*, 6

"determined upon driving Mormons out of the State..." Bushman, *Rough Stone Rolling*, 508

They started by demanding... Roberts, *History of the Church*, vol. 6, 356; *Warsaw Signal*, May 15, 1844

Turning to the county courts... Roberts, *History of the Church*, vol. 6, 356; *Warsaw Signal*, May 29, 1844; Oaks and Hill, *Carthage Conspiracy*, 14 *"sought a reformation in the church"* . . . Bushman, *Rough Stone Rolling*, 539; Oaks and Hill, *Carthage Conspiracy*, 14

"calculated to destroy the peace of the city" . . . Roberts, *History of the Church*, vol. 6, 438, 442

Debate resumed on Monday . . . Oaks and Hill, *Carthage Conspiracy*, 15

"to exterminate, utterly exterminate . . ." *Warsaw Signal*, June 19, 1844; Roberts, *History of the Church*, vol. 6, 454

The clear declaration . . . Roberts, *History of the Church*, vol. 6, 521, 538, 541

"we had better go back and die like men" . . . Oaks and Hill, *Carthage Conspiracy*, 17

They were first held . . . Roberts, *History of the Church*, vol. 6, 570

In court that day . . . Roberts, *History of the Church*, vol. 6, 567–69; Oaks and Hill, *Carthage Conspiracy*, 18

"There is no danger of any extermination order" . . . Roberts, *History of the Church*, vol. 6, 605; Oaks and Hill, *Carthage Conspiracy*, 20; Remini, *Joseph Smith*, 172

At about four in the afternoon . . . Remini, *Joseph Smith*, 173–74; Oaks and Hill, *Carthage Conspiracy*, 21

"if conducted with discretion and prudence" . . . Holt, *Rise and Fall*, 191

"less convenient, less cheap, or less expeditious" . . . Basler, *Collected Works*, vol. 1, 338

"asserted my opinions . . ." Stahr, *Seward*, 98

Following the May riots . . . Feldberg, *Philadelphia Riots*, 135

"efforts of a portion of the community . . ." Ibid., 136

"In the present excited state of popular feeling" . . . McMichael letter, June 28, 1844, Philadelphia Riots Collection; Feldberg, *Philadelphia Riots*, 142–48

As it turned out, the parade . . . Feldberg, *Philadelphia Riots*, 142, 148–49; *Pennsylvania Freeman*, July 18, 1844; Perry, *Tremendous Riots*, 3

"Information has been conveyed to me . . ." McMichael letter, July 6, 1844, Philadelphia Riots Collection

Nativists responded by organizing . . . Feldberg, *Philadelphia Riots*, 152

"I have . . . been into the Church . . ." Perry, *Tremendous Riots*, 3–4; Feldberg, *Philadelphia Riots*, 153

His demonstration did not settle the crowd . . . *Pennsylvania Freeman*, July 18, 1844; Feldberg, *Philadelphia Riots*, 154

On Saturday, Philadelphia would not be so lucky . . . Feldberg, *Philadelphia Riots*, 157–58

But Cadwalader went a step further . . . Ibid., 158–59

Sight of the cannon . . . Ibid., 157–59

Simultaneously with the order to aim . . . Ibid., 160; Perry, *Tremendous Riots*, 8; Fisher, *Philadelphia Perspective*, 172

That seemed to be the end of it . . . Feldberg, *Philadelphia Riots*, 161, 164; Perry, *Tremendous Riots*, 8

After some back-and-forth . . . Feldberg, *Philadelphia Riots*, 164

About half of them did . . . Feldberg, *Philadelphia Riots*, 165; Perry, *Tremendous Riots*, 9; Fisher, *Philadelphia Perspective*, 173

Things were quickly getting out of hand . . . Feldberg, *Philadelphia Riots*, 167; Perry, *Tremendous Riots*, 10

Instead of scaring away the assault . . . Feldberg, *Philadelphia Riots*, 167–68

Then Cadwalader arrived . . . Feldberg, *Philadelphia Riots*, 170–73; Perry, *Tremendous Riots*, 13

Many of the party members fled . . . Feldberg, *Philadelphia Riots*, 174–75; Perry, *Tremendous Riots*, 13

Cadwalader eventually sent for cavalry help . . . Feldberg, *Philadelphia Riots*, 175–77

Within days, two thousand soldiers . . . *Pennsylvania Freeman*, July 18, 1844; *New York Tribune*, July 9, 1844; *Sunbury American and Shamokin Journal*, July 13, 1844; Richard Rush to Polk, July 19, 1844, in Polk, *Correspondence*, vol. 7, 371

Into the vacuum stepped Sidney Rigdon . . . Ronald Walker, "Six Days in August"

With a 575-mile head start . . . Ibid.

"Well, well! Brother Pratt" . . . Arrington, *Brigham Young*, 113; Ronald Walker, "Six Days in August"

"second-class vision" . . . Arrington, *Brigham Young*, 113

On Tuesday the sixth . . . Arrington, *Brigham Young*, 113; Ronald Walker, "Six Days in August"

Ten members of the Quorum . . . Arrington, *Brigham Young*, 113–14; Ronald Walker, "Six Days in August"

"a spokesman for Joseph Smith" . . . Arrington, *Brigham Young*, 113–14

"but one thing I must know . . ." Ibid., 114

On the eighth . . . Ibid.

"I will manage this voting . . ." Ronald Walker, "Six Days in August"; Arrington, *Brigham Young*, 114–15

"You cannot appoint a prophet" . . . Arrington, *Brigham Young*, 115–16

"In your acceptance . . ." Aaron V. Brown to Polk, May 30, 1844, in Polk, *Correspondence*, vol. 7, 166

"that if the nomination made by the convention . . ." Polk to Henry Hubbard et al., June 12, 1844, in Polk, *Correspondence*, vol. 7, 241

"making revenue the object . . ." Andrew J. Donelson to Polk, June 14, 1844, in Polk, *Correspondence*, vol. 7, 251; Robert J. Walker to Polk, May 30, 1844, in Polk, *Correspondence*, vol. 7 168; Polk to John K. Kane, June 19, 1844, in Polk, *Correspondence*, vol. 7 267

"very well written . . ." *Congressional Globe*, Senate, 28th Cong., 1st sess., May 30, 1844, 631

machinations of the Calhoun "clique" . . . Wright to Polk, June 2, 1844, in Polk, *Correspondence*, vol. 7, 186.

"Clays letter has had no influence on Southern whigs" . . . Cave Johnson to Polk, May 3, 1844, in Polk, *Correspondence*, vol. 7, 116; Holt, *Rise and Fall*, 177–79

"notorious Sabbath-breaker . . ." Remini, *Henry Clay*, 648; Howe, *Political Culture*, 124; Adams, *Memoirs*, vol. 12, 46

At the same time . . . Borneman, *Polk*, 121–22

"not a member of any Christian Church" . . . Remini, *Henry Clay*, 649–50; Theodore Frelinghuysen to Henry Clay, May 11, 1844, in Clay, *Private Correspondence*, 488

"much too mixed up with these Bible societies" . . . Eells, *Forgotten Saint*, 39, 43

"countenancing the slanders . . ." Northern Galaxy, November 13, 1844

"the sentiments & conduct of the intolerant Whigs" . . . Remini, *Henry Clay*, 654; Sellers, "Election of 1844," 365

Liberty Party candidate James G. Birney . . . R. Johnson, *Liberty Party*, 42

"No man has labored so hard . . ." New York Tribune, October 10, 1844; R. Johnson, *Liberty Party*, 43–45

"The Native Americans are falling . . ." Adams, *Memoirs*, vol. 12, 67

"Personally I could have no objection . . ." Woodworth, *Manifest Destinies*, 133; Merry, *Country of Vast Designs*, 109

Having tried to assuage both sides . . . Woodworth, *Manifest Destinies*, 133–35; Remini, *Henry Clay*, 660

"things look blue" . . . Stahr, *Seward*, 97; Remini, *Henry Clay*, 660

Whigs won control of the Louisiana state legislature . . . Holt, *Rise and Fall*, 181

"It will be most unfortunate . . ." Polk to Andrew Jackson, August 3, 1844, in Polk, *Correspondence*, vol. 7, 431

A man of duty . . . Jenkins, *Life of Silas Wright*, 167; Merry, *Country of Vast Designs*, 100; *Brooklyn Eagle*, September 7, 1844; Niven, *Van Buren: Romantic Age*, 545; Nicholas Carroll to Willie P. Mangum, September 8, 1844, in Holt, *Rise and Fall*, 174

"in the speedy coming of our Saviour" . . . Boston Post, June 1, 1844, in Bliss, *Memoirs of William Miller*, 263

"was listened to with unusual interest" . . . Land, *Adventism*, 15

They moved southwest across Ohio . . . Bliss, *Memoirs of William Miller*, 264

"Is your name Miller" . . . Ibid., 264–67

At a camp meeting in Exeter . . . Nichol, *Midnight Cry*, 81; Knight, *Millennial Fever*, 188–89

"When that meeting closed . . ." Nix, "Oh, When Shall I See Jesus?"

"Dear Sir" . . . Boon's Lick Times, November 9, 1844

8. THE GREAT DISAPPOINTMENT

"I am once more at home . . ." Bliss, *Memoirs of William Miller*, 268

"I found on my arrival here . . ." Ibid., 268–69

"I see a glory in the seventh month . . ." Nichol, *Midnight Cry*, 87

"this thing has gone over the country like lightning" . . . Ibid.; Rowe, *Thunder and Trumpets*, 135

"We are shut up to this faith . . ." Nichol, *Midnight Cry*, 88

George Storrs was to Snow . . . Knight, *Millennial Fever*, 193–99; Land, *Adventism*, 27; Rowe, *Thunder and Trumpets*, 121

"The evangelical movement supplied Whiggery . . ." Howe, *Political Culture*, 153

The religious ferment of the day . . . Bowler, *Theories of Human Evolution*, 43–45; Tweed, *American Encounter*, 2

"I have never taught a neglect . . ." Miller, *Apology and Defense*, 28

But with heaven at hand . . . Land, *Adventism*, 16, 29; Rowe, *Thunder and Trumpets*, 137

Many struggled with the logical dilemma . . . Knight, *Millennial Fever*, 206–7; "Henry B. Bear's Advent Experiences" in Numbers and Butler, *Disappointed*, 216; Bliss, *Memoirs of William Miller*, 277

"Those who sincerely love Jesus . . ." White, *Life Sketches*, 56; *New York Tribune*, October 21, 1844

"In the evening, a rabble came up . . ." Nix, "Oh, When Shall I See Jesus?"

October 22 dawned a bright, clear day . . . Land, *Adventism*, 29; Rowe, *Thunder and Trumpets*, 137–38

"We held meeting all day . . ." Sally Nichols to "The Family," December 21, 1844, in Rowe, *God's Strange Work*, 191

"The 22nd of October passed . . ." Arthur, "After the Great Disappointment," 5

"deplorable fantasy of the brain" . . . Knight, *Millennial Fever*, 220; *Sunbury American and Shamokin Journal*, November 30, 1844

"My mind is perfectly calm" . . . Bliss, *Memoirs of William Miller*, 277; Knight, *Millennial Fever*, 219

After Oregon-bound Henry Sager died . . . Sager, *Across the Plains*, 7–8

"The nights and mornings were very cold" . . . Ibid., 8

"suffered intensely" . . . Ibid.

She "was taken delirious" . . . Ibid.; Thompson, *Shallow Grave*, 31

As she passed in and out of consciousness . . . Sager, Sager, and Sager, *Whitman Massacre*, 107; Sager, *Across the Plains*, 8

On September 22 . . . Parrish, *Oregon Trail Diary*, 63; Rebecca Parrish survived the accident and lived until 1909

"without water or grass . . ." Parrish, *Oregon Trail Diary*, 63; Clyman, *Journal*, 119

"Oh, Henry, if you only knew how we have suffered" . . . Sager, *Across the Plains*, 8

"The tent was set up . . ." Ibid.

The trail turned northward . . . Ibid., 9

They still had the tent . . . Thompson, *Shallow Grave*, 35–36

"the first potatoes we had eaten . . ." Sager, *Across the Plains*, 9

Narcissa became pregnant . . . Jeffrey, *Converting*, 143

"very little more trouble than one" . . . Ibid., 170–71

"if he had a hundred strings tied to him . . ." Ibid., 185–86

The Whitmans were always welcoming . . . Unruh, *Plains Across*, 361; Thompson, *Shallow Grave*, 37

"very sick, with doubts of its recovery" . . . Sager, *Across the Plains*, 9

"For weeks this place . . ." Ibid., 9–11; Thompson, *Shallow Grave*, 39

"Poor boys . . ." Sager, *Across the Plains*, 10–11

"that a missionary's duty was to do good . . ." Ibid., 11; Chitwood, *Tyler: Champion*, 335

"If you are going to have the girls" . . . Jeffrey, *Converting*, 187; Sager, *Across the Plains*, 11–12

"Our faithful friend . . ." Sager, *Across the Plains*, 12

"in the hands of an old filthy woman . . ." Thompson, *Shallow Grave*, 42; Sager, *Across the Plains*, 8

After the parting of the ways . . . Meldahl, *Hard Road West*, 179, 185

The Humboldt, or Mary's River . . . Ibid., 208; Stewart, *Opening*, 64; Frémont would name the river the Humboldt the next year, in honor of Alexander von Humboldt, a Prussian geographer and explorer

"grasshoppers, rats, roots, and grass seed" . . . Kelly, *Old Greenwood*, 61

"knowledge of their guides entirely ceased" . . . Schallenberger Narrative, 3, Schallenberger Papers

"the cattle were let out to grass . . ." Quigley, *Irish Race*, 200–201

"forage and trees" . . . Schallenberger Narrative, 4, Schallenberger Papers

Three of the older men . . . Stewart, *Opening*, 65–66

"conduct on the march . . ." Ibid.

To cross the Forty-Mile Desert . . . Schallenberger Narrative, 4, Schallenberger Papers; Stewart, *Opening*, 66

Having found the river and what appeared to be . . . Stewart, *California Trail*, 69

As late October bore down on the party . . . Stewart, *Opening*, 68

Truckee's directions . . . Stewart, *Opening*, 68–69; Schallenberger Narrative, 6, Schallenberger Papers; the fork of the river is today the site of the town of Truckee

It was the middle of November . . . Stewart, *Opening*, 69; Bryant, *What I Saw*, 230

"thought it would be impossible . . ." Schallenberger Narrative, 5, Schallenberger Papers

"There seemed little danger to me . . ." Stewart, *Opening*, 70

It was a brave, loyal, and possibly foolhardy move . . . Schallenberger Narrative, 5, Schallenberger Papers

Slogging through two feet of snow . . . Stewart, *Opening*, 68–69; Stewart, *California Trail*, 72

They stayed a week . . . Stewart, *California Trail*, 73; Schallenberger Narrative, 6, Schallenberger Papers

The men who were headed to Sutter's Fort . . . Stewart, *California Trail*, 73–74

All assumed they would quickly gather a rescue party . . . Stewart, *California Trail*, 74; Stewart, *Opening*, 80

9. "THE SEVEREST STRUGGLE EVER WITNESSED"

Voting for president . . . Sellers, "Election of 1844," 323

John Slidell, a New York native . . . Gleeson, *Irish,"* 99

After the debacle . . . Sellers, "Election of 1844," 362; Howe, *Political Culture*, 176

"play hide & seek with the Abolitionists". . . Cave Johnson to Polk, April 15, 1844, in Polk, *Correspondence*, vol. 7, 103

"Mr. C. M. Clay's letter . . ." Remini, *Henry Clay*, 661–62

"I am decidedly opposed . . ." Sellers, "Election of 1844," 362; Cave Johnson to Polk, May 31, 1844, in Polk, *Correspondence*, vol. 7, 172; Johnson specifically warned Polk against responding to any letters from Joseph Smith, upon the advice of members of Congress from Illinois

"Clay . . . has at last determined . . ." William Taylor to Polk, October 17, 1844, in Polk, *Correspondence*, vol. 8, 201

Just as had happened in July . . . R. Johnson, *Liberty Party*, 39–40

"Imprisoned, ironed and manacled . . ." Runyon, *Delia Webster*, 40, 43

"The great desire of their hearts . . ." Ibid., 44

"For the elevation of the great embodiment . . ." Ibid., 41

While Clay was creating more confusion . . . Sellers, "Election of 1844," 366

Here, Clay's muddling of the issue . . . Schurz, *Life of Henry Clay*, 265; Prendergast, *Catholic Voter*, 39; Holt, *Rise and Fall*, 188; Gleeson, *Irish*, 99

"to unite in putting down the Catholics . . ." George M. Dallas to Polk, October 8, 1844, in Polk, *Correspondence*, vol. 8, 164; John Catron to Polk, June 8, 1844, in Polk, *Correspondence*, vol. 7, 215

"they did not think it worth while . . ." *Sunbury American and Shamokin Journal*, September 21, 1844; Silas Wright to Polk, October 31, 1844, in Polk, *Correspondence*, vol. 8, 251

"They are literally bargaining right and left" . . . George M. Dallas to Polk, October 16, 1844, in Polk, *Correspondence*, vol. 8, 194; Dallas to Polk, November 1, 1844, in Polk, *Correspondence*, vol. 8, 253; Cave Johnson to Polk, November 2, 1844, in Polk, *Correspondence*, vol. 8, 257

"magnificent beyond any description" . . . John McKeon to Polk, November 2, 1844, in Polk, *Correspondence*, vol. 8, 259; Borneman, *Polk*, 127

"not undertake to give you an opinion . . ." Stahr, *Seward*, 98; Goodwin, *Team of Rivals*, 13

Last-minute efforts in Pennsylvania . . . Sellers, "Election of 1844," 366

"glorious victory" . . . James Buchanan to Polk, November 4, 1844, in Polk *Correspondence*, vol. 8, 263

"brethren all concluded to vote for Polk and Dallas" . . . Stout, *On the Mormon Frontier*, 8

"the severest struggle ever witnessed in this city" . . . Fernando Wood to Polk, November 5, 1844, in Polk, *Correspondence*, vol. 8, 274; Garraty, *Silas Wright*, 325; Holt, *Rise and Fall*, 203

Early returns from the city . . . Sellers, "Election of 1844," 370–71

"I feel as though our country . . ." Samuel Medary to Polk, November 10, 1844, in Polk, *Correspondence*, vol. 8, 301; Sellers, "Election of 1844," 367

"I have thought for three or four days . . ." Millard Fillmore to Henry Clay, November 11, 1844, in Clay, *Private Correspondence*, 497–98

"The result of this election . . ." Philip Hone to Clay, November 28, 1844, in Remini, *Henry Clay*, 665

"My Country! Oh, my Country . . ." Webb, *Adventures*, 118

"gave us one vote only . . ." Stahr, *Seward*, 99

"Abolitionists and foreign Catholics" . . . Millard Fillmore to Clay, November 11, 1844, in Clay, *Private Correspondence,* 497–98

"partial associates of Native Americans . . ." Adams, *Memoirs,* vol. 12, 110

"I thought his election highly probable . . ." Daniel Webster to Edward Everett, December 15, 1844, in Remini, *Daniel Webster,* 596

"But, my dear sir . . ." Theodore Frelinghuysen to Clay, November 9, 1844, in Clay, *Private Correspondence,* 496

"gave notice that I should . . ." Adams, *Memoirs,* vol. 12, 115

As good as his word . . . *Congressional Globe,* Senate, 28th Cong., 2nd sess., December 3, 1844, 7

"Perseverance has crowned . . ." Miller, *Arguing About Slavery,* 477

"Blessed, forever blessed, be the name of God" . . . Adams, *Memoirs,* vol. 12, 115–16

"I am fearful that this election will cause difficulty" . . . Charles Bent to Manuel Alvarez, January 24, 1845, in Lavender, *Bent's Fort,* 254

"After eight years of feeble and ineffectual efforts . . ." *Congressional Globe,* Senate, 28th Cong., 2nd sess., December 3, 1844, 4

"The great popular election which has just terminated . . ." Ibid., 4–5

"The two governments have already agreed . . ." Ibid., 5

"that there is a large majority . . ." *New York Evening Post,* January 23, 1845, in Silbey, *Storm,* 81

"so worn out and poor that they could go no further" . . . Stewart, *Opening,* 70–71

"to make ourselves as comfortable as possible . . ." Ibid., 71

"exceedingly abundant in the early winter" . . . Schallenberger Narrative, 7, Schallenberger Papers

Instead, it snowed more . . . Ibid.; Stewart, *Opening,* 71–72

"We began to fear that we should all perish in the snow" . . . Stewart, *Opening,* 72

"The snow was so light and frosty . . ." Ibid.

"At last, after due consideration . . ." Ibid.

"We fastened them heel to toe" . . . Schallenberger Narrative, 7, Schallenberger Papers; Stewart, *Opening,* 73

"After each attack . . ." Schallenberger Narrative, 7, Schallenberger Papers

But it was no use . . . Stewart, *Opening,* 73–74; Schallenberger Narrative, 7, Schallenberger Papers

"We did not say much at parting" . . . Ibid.

After more than six months together . . . Stewart, *Opening,* 74–75

"Plenty of tracks, but no fox" . . . Schallenberger Narrative, 7–8, Schallenberger Papers; Stewart, *Opening,* 75

"To my great delight . . ." Stewart, *Opening,* 75

Foxes and coyotes . . . Schallenberger Narrative, 8, Schallenberger Papers; Chesterfield, *Letters to His Son,* 83

"and thus cause the days to seem shorter" . . . Schallenberger Narrative, 8, Schallenberger Papers

Then, one evening near the end of February . . . Stewart, *Opening*, 77–78; Schallenberger Narrative, 8, Schallenberger Papers

"producing commercial, political and national rewards and benefits" . . . Whitney, *National Railroad*, 1

"the entire commerce of the world" . . . Ibid., 2

"affording a communication . . .*"* Ibid., 3–4

"being built from the public lands . . .*"* Ibid., 4

Epilogue: The Shaping of America

In response to Tyler's renewed call for annexation . . . Merk, *Slavery and Annexation*, 121

"there is no danger of the passage of that measure . . .*"* Silbey, *Storm*, 86–87

In the Senate, Benton . . . Merk, *Slavery and Annexation*, 122–23

"It is now apparent . . .*"* Adams, *Memoirs*, vol. 12, 133, 171

When the Senate took up the House bill . . . Silbey, *Storm*, 87

"They cannot say now . . .*"* Crapol, *John Tyler*, 221

"bruises and scars" . . . Chitwood, *Tyler: Champion*, 424–25

"get our wagons together . . .*"* J. C. Frémont, *Memoirs*, 415

"tangible results" . . . Feldberg, *Turbulent Era*, 37

With the backing of William Miller . . . Knight, *Millennial Fever*, 236

"At the time appointed the end shall be" . . . Bliss, *Memoirs of William Miller*, 383

"he wanted to be on top of a hill . . .*"* Knight, *Millennial Fever*, 293

"sedulous care for the safety of the Commonwealth" . . . Webster, *Kentucky Jurisprudence*, 55

"to interpose his executive power . . .*"* Runyon, *Delia Webster*, 53

"I was also furnished with a fine library . . .*"* Webster, *Kentucky Jurisprudence*, 78–79

He was president of . . . Eells, *Forgotten Saint*, 73–78

"I want you to see how a Christian can die" . . . Ibid., 94

Prominent historians of the period . . . See especially Howe, *Political Culture*, 137; Remini, *Henry Clay*, 668; Kornblith, "Rethinking the Coming of the Civil War," 84–86

"Texas is destined to be settled by our race . . .*"* Henry Clay to John J. Crittenden, December 5, 1843, in Kornblith, "Rethinking the Coming of the Civil War," 86

The two-decade success of overland migration . . . Unruh, *Plains Across*, 244

Just as Democrats grew more comfortable . . . Abraham Lincoln to John M. Clayton, September 27, 1849, in Lincoln Papers

"We have as happy a family as the world affords" . . . Jeffrey, *Converting*, 197

"cold, foggy" November 29 . . . Sager, *Across the Plains*, 36

"I never saw a more discontented community . . .*"* Clyman, *Journal*, 134

"I have nothing worthy of your attention to tell you" . . . Moses Schallenberger to John Townsend, October 12, 1850, Schallenberger Papers

BIBLIOGRAPHY

Books and Periodicals

Adams, John Quincy. *Memoirs of John Quincy Adams.* Vols. 11 and 12. Edited by Charles Francis Adams. Freeport, NY: Books for Libraries Press, 1969.

Arrington, Leonard J. *Brigham Young: American Moses.* Urbana: University of Illinois Press, 1986.

Arthur, David T. "After the Great Disappointment: To Albany and Beyond." *Adventist Heritage,* January 1974.

Bain, David Howard. *Empire Express.* New York: Penguin, 1999.

Barkun, Michael. *Crucible of the Millennium: Burned-Over District of New York in the 1840s.* Syracuse University Press, 1986.

Bartlett, Irving H. *John C. Calhoun: A Biography.* New York: W. W. Norton and Company, 1994.

Basler, Roy P., ed. *Collected Works of Abraham Lincoln.* New Brunswick, NJ: Rutgers University Press, 1953.

Benton, Thomas Hart. *Selections of Editorial Articles from the St. Louis Enquirer, On the Subject of Oregon and Texas, and Originally Published in That Paper in the Years 1818–19.* St. Louis, Missourian Office, 1844.

———. *Thirty Years' View.* New York: D. Appleton and Company, 1854–56.

Blackman, Ann. "Fatal Cruise of the Princeton." *Navy History,* 2005. www.military .com/NewContent/0,13190,NH_0905_Cruise-P1,00.html.

Bliss, Sylvester. *Memoirs of William Miller.* Boston: Joshua V. Himes, 1853.

Borneman, Walter. *1812: The War That Forged a Nation.* New York: Harper Perennial, 2005.

———. *Polk: The Man Who Transformed the Presidency and America.* New York: Random House, 2008.

Bowler, Peter J. *Theories of Human Evolution: A Century of Debate, 1844–1944.* Baltimore: Johns Hopkins University Press, 1986.

Bowman, Matthew. *The Mormon People: The Making of an American Faith*. New York: Random House, 2012.

Bryant, Edwin. *What I Saw in California*. Lincoln: University of Nebraska Press, 1985.

Bull, Malcom, and Keith Lockhart. *Seeking a Sanctuary: Seventh-Day Adventism and the American Dream*. 2nd ed. Bloomington: Indiana University Press, 2007.

Burlingame, Edward Livermore, et al., eds. *Scribner's Magazine*. Vol. 11. New York: Charles Scribner's Sons, 1892.

Bushman, Richard. *Joseph Smith: Rough Stone Rolling*. New York: Knopf, 2005.

Butler, Anne M., and Wendy Wolff. *United States Senate Election, Expulsion and Censure Cases, 1793–1990*. Washington: Government Printing Office, 1995.

Calhoun, John C. *Papers of John C. Calhoun*. Columbia: University of South Carolina, 1987.

Carleton, J. Henry. *The Prairie Logbooks: Dragoon Campaigns to the Pawnee Villages in 1844 and to the Rocky Mountains in 1845*. Lincoln: University of Nebraska Press, 1983.

Catholic Magazine. "The Philadelphia Catholic Riots." June 1844.

Chaffin, Tom. *Pathfinder: John Charles Frémont and the Course of American Empire*. New York: Hill and Wang, 2002.

Chesterfield, Earl of (Philip Dormer Stanhope). *Letters to His Son on the Art of Becoming a Man of the World and a Gentleman, 1746–47*. Stockbridge, MA: Hard Press, 2006.

Chitwood, Oliver Perry. *John Tyler: Champion of the Old South*. Newtown, CT: American Political Biography Press, 1990.

Christian Work and the Evangelist. Vol. 78. January 7, 1905.

Clay, Henry. *Private Correspondence of Henry Clay*. Edited by Calvin Colton. New York: Books for Libraries Press, 1971; orig. publ. 1855.

Clyman, James. *Journal of a Mountain Man*. Edited by Linda M. Hasselstrom. Boise, ID: Tamarack Books, 1998.

Coe, Lewis. *The Telegraph: A History of Morse's Invention and its Predecessors in the United States*. Jefferson, NC: McFarland & Co., 2003.

Cole, Donald B. *Martin Van Buren and the American Political System*. Princeton, NJ: Princeton University Press, 1984.

Colt's Submarine Battery. 28th Cong., 2nd sess., n.d., House doc. no. 127.

CQ Press. *National Party Conventions 1831–1992*. Washington, DC: CQ Press, 1995.

Crapol, Edward P. *John Tyler: The Accidental President*. Chapel Hill: University of North Carolina Press, 2006.

Dary, David. *The Oregon Trail: An American Saga*. New York: Knopf, distributed by Random House, 2004.

De Bruhl, Marshall. *Sword of San Jacinto: A Life of Sam Houston*. New York: Random House, 1993.

Denton, Sally. *Passion and Principle: John and Jessie Frémont, the Couple Whose Power, Politics, and Love Shaped Nineteenth-Century America*. New York: Bloomsbury USA, 2007.

DeRose, Chris. *Congressman Lincoln: The Making of America's Greatest President.* New York: Simon & Schuster, 2013.

Eells, Robert J. *Forgotten Saint: The Life of Theodore Frelinghuysen.* Lanham, MD: University Press of America, 1987.

Feldberg, Michael. *The Philadelphia Riots of 1844: A Social History.* PhD dissertation, University of Rochester, 1970.

———. *The Turbulent Era: Riot and Disorder in Jacksonian America.* Oxford: Oxford University Press, 1980.

Finney, Charles Grandison. *Autobiography.* Charleston, SC: Nabu Press, 2011.

Fisher, Sidney George. *A Philadelphia Perspective: The Diary of Sidney George Fisher Covering the Years 1834–1871.* Edited by Nicholas B. Wainwright. Philadelphia: Historical Society of Pennsylvania, 1967.

Ford, Worthington Chauncey. *The Campaign of 1844.* Reprinted from the Proceedings of the American Antiquarian Society, October 1909. Worcester, MA: Davis Press, 1909.

Freehling, William W. *The Road to Disunion: Secessionists at Bay.* New York: Oxford University Press, 1991.

Frémont, Jessie Benton. *Letters of Jessie Benton Frémont.* Edited by Pamela Herr and Mary Lee Spence. Urbana: University of Illinois Press, 1993.

Frémont, John Charles. *The Exploring Expedition to the Rocky Mountains, Oregon and California.* Washington, DC: Gales and Seaton, Printers, 1845.

———. *Memoirs of My Life and Times.* New York: Cooper Square Press, 2001.

Garr, Arnold K. *Joseph Smith: Presidential Candidate.* Orem, UT: Millennial Press, 2007.

Garraty, John A. *Silas Wright.* New York: Columbia University Press, 1949.

Geue, Chester William, and Ethel Hander Geue. *A New Land Beckoned: German Immigration to Texas, 1844–1847.* Waco, TX: Library Binding Co., 1966.

Gleeson, David T. *The Irish in the South, 1815–1877.* Chapel Hill: University of North Carolina Press, 2001.

Goetzmann, William H. *Army Exploration in the American West: 1803–1863.* New Haven, CT: Yale University Press, 1959.

———. *Exploration and Empire: The Explorer and the Scientist in the Winning of the American West.* New York: Knopf, 1966.

Goodwin, Doris Kearns. *Team of Rivals: The Political Genius of Abraham Lincoln.* New York: Simon & Schuster, 2005.

Gregg, Josiah. *Commerce of the Prairies.* Torrington, WY: Narrative Press, 2001. Originally published in 1844.

Gugliotta, Guy. *Freedom's Cap: The United States Capitol and the Coming of the Civil War.* New York: Hill and Wang, 2012.

Haley, James L. *Sam Houston.* Norman: University of Oklahoma Press, 2002.

Hall, Claude H. *Abel Parker Upshur, Conservative Virginian.* Madison: State Historical Society of Wisconsin, 1964.

Hammer, Jacob. *This Emigrating Company: The 1844 Oregon Trail Journal of Jacob Hammer.* Editorial commentary by Thomas A. Rumer. Spokane, WA: A. H. Clark Co., 1990.

Herr, Pamela. *Jessie Benton Frémont.* Norman: University of Oklahoma Press, 1988.

Holt, Michael F. *The Rise and Fall of the American Whig Party.* New York: Oxford University Press, 1999.

Hosley, William. *Colt: The Making of an American Legend.* Amherst: University of Massachusetts Press, 1996.

Howe, Daniel Walker. *The Political Culture of the American Whigs.* Chicago: University of Chicago Press, 1984.

————. *What Hath God Wrought: The Transformation of America, 1815–1848.* New York: Oxford University Press, 1999.

Hugill, Peter J. *Global Communications Since 1844: Geopolitics and Technology.* Baltimore: Johns Hopkins University Press, 1999.

Jackson, Donald, and Mary Lee Spence, eds. *The Expeditions of John Charles Frémont.* Urbana: University of Illinois Press, 1970.

Jay, Allen. *Autobiography of Allen Jay.* Richmond, IN: Friend United Press, 2010; orig. publ. 1910.

Jeffrey, Julie Roy. *Converting the West: A Biography of Narcissa Whitman.* Norman: University of Oklahoma Press, 1994.

Jenkins, John S. *The Life of Silas Wright.* Auburn, NY: Alden & Markham, 1847.

John, Richard R. *Spreading the News: The American Postal System from Franklin to Morse.* Cambridge, MA: Harvard University Press, 1995.

Johnson, Allen, ed. *Dictionary of American Biography.* Vol. 2. New York: Charles Scribner's Sons, 1929.

Johnson, Reinhard O. *The Liberty Party, 1840–1848: Antislavery Third-Party Politics in the United States.* Baton Rouge: Louisiana State University Press, 2009.

Kelly, Charles. *Old Greenwood: The Story of Caleb Greenwood, Trapper, Pathfinder and Early Pioneer of the West.* Reno, NV: Jack Bacon and Co., 2005.

Kennedy, John F. *Profiles in Courage.* New York: Harper Perennial Modern Classics, 2006.

Klein, Philip S. *President James Buchanan: A Biography.* Newtown, CT: American Political Biography Press, 1995.

Knight, George R. *Millennial Fever and the End of the World: A Study of Millerite Adventism.* Boise, ID: Pacific Press Publishing Association, 1993.

Korman, Richard. *The Goodyear Story: An Inventor's Obsession and the Struggle for a Rubber Monopoly.* San Francisco: Encounter Books, 2002.

Kornblith, Gary J. "Rethinking the Coming of the Civil War: A Counterfactual Exercise," *Journal of American History,* June 2003.

Krug, Howard. "October Morn: Adventism's Day of Insight." *Adventist Review,* October 24, 2002.

Land, Gary, ed. *Adventism in America: A History.* Grand Rapids, MI: William B. Eerdmans Publishing Co., 1986.

Lavender, David. *Bent's Fort*. Garden City, NJ: Doubleday, 1954.

Lowe, Beverly Elizabeth. *John Minto: Man of Courage, 1822–1915*. Salem, OR: Kingston Price and Company, 1980.

Lundeberg, Philip K. *Samuel Colt's Submarine Battery: The Secret and the Enigma*. Washington, DC: Smithsonian Institution Press, 1974.

Malone, Dumas, ed. *Dictionary of American Biography*. Vol. 18. New York: Charles Scribner's Sons, 1936.

Mattes, Merrill J. *The Great Platte River Road: The Covered Wagon Mainline via Fort Kearny to Fort Laramie*. Rev. ed. Lincoln: University of Nebraska Press, 1987.

Mayer, Henry. *All On Fire: William Lloyd Garrison and the Abolition of Slavery*. New York: St. Martin's Press, 1998.

McCullough, David. *The Greater Journey: Americans in Paris*. New York: Simon & Schuster, 2011.

Meldahl, Keith Heyer. *Hard Road West: History and Geology Along the Gold Rush Trail*. Chicago: University of Chicago Press, 2007.

Menard, Andrew. *Sight Unseen: How Frémont's First Expedition Changed the American Landscape*. Lincoln: University of Nebraska Press, 2012.

Merk, Frederick. *History of the Westward Movement*. New York: Knopf, 1978.

———. *Manifest Destiny and Mission in American History: A Reinterpretation*. New York: Knopf, 1963.

———. *Slavery and the Annexation of Texas*. New York: Knopf, 1972.

Merry, Robert W. *A Country of Vast Designs: James K. Polk, the Mexican War, and the Conquest of the American Continent*. New York: Simon & Schuster, 2009.

Messages and Papers of the Presidents. Vol. 5. New York: Bureau of National Literature, 1897.

Miller, William. *Apology and Defense*. Boston: Joshua V. Himes, 1845.

———. *Evidence from Scripture and History of the Second Coming of Christ, About the Year 1843*. Boston: Joshua V. Himes, 1842.

Miller, William Lee. *Arguing about Slavery: John Quincy Adams and the Great Battle in the United States Congress*. New York: Vintage, 1998.

Nagle, Paul C. *John Quincy Adams: A Public Life, a Private Life*. New York: Knopf, 1997.

Nichol, Francis D. *The Midnight Cry: A Defense of the Character and Conduct of William Miller and the Millerites, Who Mistakenly Believed That the Second Coming of Christ Would Take Place in the Year 1844*. Washington, DC: Review and Herald Publishing Association, 1945.

Niven, John. *Martin Van Buren: The Romantic Age of American Politics*. New York: Oxford University Press, 1983.

Nix, James R. "Oh, When Shall I See Jesus?" *Adventist Review*, October 28, 2004.

Numbers, Ronald L., and Jonathan M. Butler, eds. *The Disappointed: Millerism and Millenarianism in the Nineteenth Century*. Knoxville: University of Tennessee Press, 1993.

Oaks, Dallin H., and Marvin S. Hill. *Carthage Conspiracy: The Trial of the Accused Assassins of Joseph Smith*. Urbana: University of Illinois Press, 1979.

Owens, Kenneth N. *Gold Rush Saints: California Mormons and the Great Rush for Riches*. Norman: University of Oklahoma Press, 2004.

Parrish, Edward Evans. *The Oregon Trail Diary of Edward Evans Parrish in 1844*. Edited by Bert Webber. Medford, OR: Webb Research Group, 1988.

Perry, John B. *A Full and Complete Account of the Late Awful Riots in Philadelphia*. New York: Nafis & Cornish, 1844.

————. *Tremendous Riots in Southwark*. New York: Nafis & Cornish, 1844.

Peterson, Merrill D. *The Great Triumvirate: Webster, Clay and Calhoun*. New York: Oxford University Press, 1987.

Peterson, Norma Lois. *The Presidencies of William Henry Harrison and John Tyler*. Lawrence: University Press of Kansas, 1989.

Polk, James K. *Correspondence of James K. Polk*. Vols. 7 and 8. Edited by Herbert Weaver. Nashville, TN: Vanderbilt University, 1969–2009.

Poll, Richard D. "Joseph Smith and the Presidency, 1844." *Dialogue, a Journal of Mormon Thought* 3, no. 3 (1968).

Prendergast, William B. *The Catholic Voter in American Politics: The Passing of the Democratic Monolith*. Washington, DC: Georgetown University Press, 1999.

Preuss, Charles. *Exploring with Frémont: The Private Diaries of Charles Preuss*. Translated and edited by Erwin G. and Elisabeth K. Gudde. Norman: University of Oklahoma Press, 1958.

Prince Carl of Solms-Braunfels. *Voyage to North America 1844–45: Prince Carl of Solms's Texas Diary of People, Places and Events*. Translated by Wolfram M. Von-Maszewski. Denton: German-Texas Heritage Society and the University of North Texas Press, 2000.

Quigley, Hugh. *The Irish Race in California and on the Pacific Coast*. San Francisco: A. Roman & Co., 1878.

Remini, Robert V. *Andrew Jackson and the Course of American Democracy: 1833–1845*. Baltimore: Johns Hopkins University Press, 1997.

————. *Daniel Webster: The Man and His Time*. New York: W. W. Norton & Company, 1997.

————. *Henry Clay: Statesman for the Union*. New York: W. W. Norton & Company, 1991.

————. *Joseph Smith*. New York: Penguin, 2002.

Roberts, B. H. *History of the Church of Jesus Christ of Latter-Day Saints*. Salt Lake City: Deseret News, 1902.

Roberts, David. *A Newer World: Kit Carson, John C. Frémont, and the Claiming of the American West*. New York: Touchstone, 2000.

Rowe, David L. *God's Strange Work: William Miller and the End of the World*. Grand Rapids, MI: William B. Eerdmans Publishing Co., 2008

————. *Thunder and Trumpets: Millerites and Dissenting Religion in Upstate New York 1800–1850*. Scholars Press, 1985.

Rumer, Thomas A. *The Wagon Trains of '44: A Comparative View of the Individual Caravans in the Emigration of 1844 to Oregon*. Spokane, WA: A. H. Clark Co., 1990.

Runyon, Randolph Paul. *Delia Webster and the Underground Railroad*. Lexington: University of Kentucky Press, 1999.

Sager, Catherine. *Across the Plains in 1844*. Fairfield, WA: Ye Galleon Press, 1989. Orig. publ. in *Pioneer Days of Oregon History*, vol. 2, by S. A. Clarke (Portland: J. K. Gill, 1905).

Sager, Catherine, Elizabeth Sager, and Matilda Sager. *The Whitman Massacre of 1847*. Fairfield, WA: Ye Galleon Press, 1986.

Schlesinger, Arthur M., Jr. *The Age of Jackson*. Boston: Little, Brown and Co., 1945.

Schlesinger, Arthur M., Jr., ed. *History of U.S. Political Parties, Volume I, 1789–1860: From Factions to Parties*. New York: Chelsea House Publishers, 1973.

Schurz, Carl. *Life of Henry Clay*. New York: Houghton Mifflin, 1887.

Seale, William. *The President's House: A History*. Vol. 1. Washington, DC: White House Historical Association, 1986.

Sellers, Charles. "Election of 1844," in *History of American Presidential Elections, 1789–2008*, vol. 1. Edited by Gil Troy, Arthur M. Schlesinger, Jr., and Fred L. Israel. New York: Facts on File, 2012.

———. *James K. Polk*. Princeton, NJ: Princeton University Press, 1957.

Sides, Hampton. *Blood and Thunder: An Epic of the American West*. New York: Doubleday, 2006.

Silbey, Joel H. *Storm over Texas*. New York: Oxford University Press, 2007.

Silverman, Kenneth. *Lightning Man: The Accursed Life of Samuel F. B. Morse*. New York: Da Capo Press, 2004.

Slack, Charles. *Noble Obsession: Charles Goodyear, Thomas Hancock, and the Race to Unlock the Greatest Industrial Secret of the 19th Century*. New York: Hyperion, 2003.

Smith, Joseph. *The Essential Joseph Smith*. Salt Lake City: Signature Books, 1995.

———. *General Smith's Views of the Power and Policy of the Government of the United States*. Pittsburgh: J. E. Page, 1844.

Stahr, Walter. *Seward: Lincoln's Indispensable Man*. New York: Simon & Schuster, 2012.

Stegner, Wallace. *The Gathering of Zion*. Lincoln: University of Nebraska Press, 1992.

Stewart, George R. *The California Trail: An Epic with Many Heroes*. New York: McGraw-Hill, 1962.

———, ed. *The Opening of the California Trail: The Story of the Stevens Party From the Reminiscences of Moses Schallenberger*. Berkeley: University of California Press, 1953.

Stout, Hosea. *On the Mormon Frontier: The Diary of Hosea Stout, 1844–1889*. Vol. 1. Edited by Juanita Brooks. Salt Lake City: University of Utah Press/Utah State Historical Society, 1964.

Thompson, Erwin N. *Shallow Grave at Waiilatpu: The Sagers' West*. Portland: Oregon Historical Society, 1973.

Thulesius, Olav. *The Man Who Made the Monitor: A Biography of John Ericsson, Naval Engineer*. Jefferson, NC: McFarland & Company, 2007.

Tweed, Thomas A. *The American Encounter With Buddhism 1844–1912*. Bloomington: Indiana University Press, 1992.

Unruh, John D., Jr. *The Plains Across: The Overland Emigrants and the Trans-Mississippi West, 1840–1860.* Urbana: University of Illinois Press, 1993.

Walker, Robert. *Letter of Mr. Walker of Mississippi Relative to the Annexation of Texas.* Washington, DC: Printed at the Globe Office, 1844.

Walker, Ronald W. "Six Days in August: Brigham Young and the Succession Crisis of 1844." In *A Firm Foundation: Church Organization and Administration,* edited by David J. Whittaker and Arnold K. Garr. Provo, UT: Religious Studies Center, Brigham Young University; Salt Lake City: Deseret Book, 2011, 161–96. Available at https://rsc.byu.edu/archived/firm-foundation/8-six-days-august-brigham-young-and-succession-crisis-1844.

Warner, Madeline. "The Changing Image of the Millerites in the Western Massachusetts Press." *Advent Heritage,* Summer 1965.

Watson, Jeanne H. "Frémont's Second Expedition." *Overland Journal,* Fall 1994.

Webb, James Josiah. *Adventures in the Santa Fe Trade 1844–1847.* Lincoln: University of Nebraska Press, 1995.

Webster, Delia. *Kentucky Jurisprudence.* Ithaca: Cornell University Library, 1845.

Whipple, Henry Benjamin. *Bishop Whipple's Southern Diary, 1843–44.* New York: Da Capo Press, 1968.

White, Ellen G. *Life Sketches of Ellen G. White.* Mountain View, CA: Pacific Press Publishing Association, 1915.

Whitney, Asa. *National Railroad Connecting the Atlantic and Pacific.* 28th Cong., 2nd sess., January 28, 1845, House doc. no. 72.

Woodworth, Steven E. *Manifest Destinies: America's Westward Expansion and the Road to Civil War.* New York: Knopf, 2010.

Young, Brigham. *Manuscript History of Brigham Young.* Edited by Jay Watson. Salt Lake City: Smith Secretarial Service, 1968.

Zieber, G. B., & Co. *Life of General Lewis Cass: Comprising an Account of His Military Service In the North-west During the War With Great Britain, His Diplomatic Career And Civil History. To Which Is Appended, a Sketch of the Public And Private History of Major-General W. O. Butler, of the Volunteer Service of the United States.* Philadelphia: G. B. Zieber & Co., 1848.

NEWSPAPERS, MANUSCRIPTS, AND ELECTRONIC RESOURCES

Advent Herald

Boon's Lick Times

Brooklyn Eagle

Jeffersonian Republican (Stroudsburg, PA)

Liberator

Midnight Cry

Missouri Republican

Nashville Republican Banner

National Intelligencer

Nauvoo Neighbor

New York Herald

New York Tribune

Northern Galaxy (Middlebury, VT)

Oneida Whig

Pennsylvania Freeman

The Radical (Bowling Green, MO)

Sunbury American and Shamokin Journal   *Vermont Phoenix*
Times and Seasons   *Warsaw Signal*
Utica Daily Gazette   *Washington Globe*

Abraham Lincoln Papers, Library of Congress
Joel Buttles Diaries, Ohio Historical Society
Martin Van Buren Papers, Library of Congress
Moses Schallenberger Papers, Stanford University
Papers of Samuel Finley Breese Morse, Library of Congress

Adventist Review, www.adventistreview.org
Dialogue: A Journal of Mormon Thought, www.dialoguejournal.com
HarpWeek: American Political Prints, 1766–1876, http://loc.harpweek.com
Philadelphia Riots Collection, Villanova University, http://digital.library.villanova
.edu/Item/vudl:255898

INDEX